SSSP

Springer
Series in
Social
Psychology

SSSP

Linda Silka

Intuitive Judgments
of Change

Springer-Verlag New York Berlin Heidelberg
London Paris Tokyo

Linda Silka
Department of Psychology
University of Lowell
Lowell, Massachusetts 01854
USA

With 1 Illustration

Library of Congress Cataloging-in-Publication Data
Silka, Linda.
  Intuitive judgments of change.
  (Springer series in social psychology)
  Bibliography: p.
  Includes indexes.
  1. Social change – Psychological aspects.
2. Personality change. 3. Judgment. 4. Social
surveys. 5. Intuition (Psychology) I. Title.
II. Series.
HM101.S54   1988   303.4   88-16006

Typeset by Publishers Service, Bozeman, Montana.
Printed and bound by R.R. Donnelley and Sons, Harrisonburg, Virginia.
Printed in the United States of America.

9 8 7 6 5 4 3 2 1

ISBN 0-387-96763-X Springer-Verlag New York Berlin Heidelberg
ISBN 3-540-96763-X Springer-Verlag Berlin Heidelberg New York

Dedicated to Laurence D. Smith

Preface

Years ago while reading popular accounts of contemporary life such as the book *Future Shock*, I was struck by how often people claim that things have changed. Even cursory attention to the content of newspapers, magazines, popular books, and everyday conversations revealed the great variety of intuitive judgments of change that enliven social discourse. Those claims about change—whether in regard to the self, others, or the social environment—seemed to be made with boldness and alacrity, but only rarely was the basis for the claims apparent. Turning to the literature in psychology and sociology to learn more, I found two relevant bodies of work—the first on social perception and the second on social change—but little research that attempted to bring the two together. What is reported here is a program of research that is intended to lay groundwork for the study of intuitive change judgments and to show why the empirical investigation of impressions of change represents a promising direction for research.

The treatment of change judgments presented here is organized along the following lines. In the first three chapters, the topic of change judgments is introduced (Chapter 1), previous research on change and on social perception is discussed (Chapter 2), and a framework for the study of change judgments is developed (Chapter 3). Each of the subsequent chapters treats a particular topic in the domain of change judgments, beginning with an analysis of the problems involved and then reporting a sample of empirical research emerging from the analysis. In Chapter 4, consideration is given to how people's readiness to see change can be reconciled with the large body of research suggesting that social perception is strongly stability-oriented. Chapter 5 examines the informational tasks faced by the perceiver in making change judgments and investigates how knowledge about the present and past shapes particular change judgments. Chapter 6 considers the fact that perceivers' interest in change is often prompted by some event viewed by them as likely to have caused a change; two common consequences of this fact—namely, that perceivers will be looking for change and yet that they will not have commensurable baseline data—are investigated in the chapter. Chapter 7 focuses on issues central to judgments of person change, addressing such topics as the ambiguity of evidence for change and stability and the question of whether perceivers ever see change as truly deep-seated. Judgments of social change are the focus of Chapter 8, in which the informational analysis developed in the book is applied to such phenomena as the nostalgic fallacy. The ninth and final chapter presents a systematic integration of the ideas set forth in earlier chapters and also indicates directions for future research in this emerging area.

Many people have helped shape the thinking that went into this volume. Foremost among them are the social psychologists that served as my teachers and role models during my graduate school years at the University of Kansas: Dan Batson, Hobb Crockett, Chuck Kiesler, Sara Kiesler, Mike Pallak, Suzanne Pallak, Mike Storms, Larry Wrightsman, and especially my dissertation adviser, Jack Brehm. The insights of these individuals into the research enterprise and the level of critical thought they sought to engender in students greatly enriched my understanding of social psychology. The ways in which the present work fails to reflect the high standards they set remain my responsibility alone.

I would like to thank Springer-Verlag for encouraging me to attempt a book-length treatment of this research area and for supporting the writing endeavor once under way. The help of the many colleagues who commented on various drafts of this manuscript is gratefully acknowledged, with special thanks to Linda Malloy, Kevin McCaul, and Bill Scott for their insightful comments. I also wish to thank the students who served so conscientiously as research assistants and collaborators on the projects reported here: Linda Albright, John Borrelli, Maureen Garry, Barbara Gruber, Cindy Shupe, Laura Stella, and Kathy Wrobel. The generosity of the University of Lowell in supporting my research through the provision of release time, seed monies, and summer support is gratefully acknowledged. I would also like to acknowledge the National Science Foundation for grant support of certain of the studies reported here. During the sabbatical year that yielded the first draft of this manuscript, the Psychology Department of the University of Maine was most helpful in making office space and facilities available to me. I would like to thank the Research Group at the University of Lowell—Bob Kunzendorf, Charlotte Mandell, Anne Mulvey, and Ron Pickett—for their support, ideas, and encouragement throughout the project. My gratitude also goes to Bill Bukowski, Joel Gold, Betsy Hoza, Bill Stone, and Al Stubbs of the University of Maine for their support and comraderie during the sabbatical year. The encouragement and tolerance throughout the project of my parents and family is greatly appreciated, as is the kindness and supportive good humor of Mary, Tom, and Lillian.

Finally, my greatest debt of gratitude is to Larry Smith. He not only served as a sounding board for many of the ideas contained in the book, but he also patiently read various drafts of the manuscript and provided invaluable criticism and suggestions for ways to transform inexact or inelegant wordings. His enormous skill at writing remains a distant goal but a constant inspiration. Without his support through the highs and lows of finishing a book, this project could not have been brought to fruition.

Linda Silka

Contents

Preface vii

1. The Ubiquity of Intuitive Change Judgments 1

2. Change and its Perception: Prior Research 17

3. A Framework for the Study of Change Judgments 35

4. Stability Reassessed: Finding Opportunities for Change Judgments .. 57

5. Judging Change with Informal Data 79

6. Looking for Change 99

7. Judgments of Person Change: A Closer Look 121

8. Judgments of Social Change: A Closer Look 143

9. Past and Future Directions for the Study of Change Judgments 169

References 185

Author Index 201

Subject Index... 209

Chapter 1

The Ubiquity of Intuitive Change Judgments

The humorist and social commentator James Thurber once wrote that we have changed so much that new fairy tales are needed to reflect the modern age. In his pointed revision of "Little Red Riding Hood," the little protagonist no longer cowers in the corner and depends on her wits when confronted by the wolf; instead, Little Red Riding Hood now solves her problem by pulling out a gun and dispatching the beast. And there is a new moral to the story: it's not so easy to fool little girls nowadays as it used to be.

Things have changed and people have changed, or so we have come to believe. Change is a subject of great interest in the everyday course of events. People talk about the dramatic changes they see in various aspects of culture and society. Political commentators ponder whether society is more violent now than it once was. Parents wonder if the experience of childhood has changed from what it was like when they were young. And speculation on change is not limited to society at large. Much of the talk about change involves speculation about change in individuals, both in those who are personal friends and in those known only through the media.

At the level of personal acquaintances, we may worry about the declining powers of our aging parents. In addition, personal relationships of many sorts are bound up with differing perceptions of change that the partners hold—perceptions of how much change has occurred over time in the other, in the self, and in the shared relationship.

At the level of public life, people wonder whether particular political leaders or social figures have changed. In the political arena people also look for change at a broader level. Beliefs about change often dominate discussions of politically sensitive social programs, with decisions about their continued funding or even eventual abandonment being influenced by intuitive judgments of whether things have changed since the program's inception.

Such judgments have made themselves felt in many areas of social life and are common to many areas of social experience. It comes as little surprise then that people's intuitive conclusions about change have from time to time provoked intense speculation and commentary concerning the motivation underlying intuitive views of change: Why do people so willingly believe that change has resulted from social programs even in cases where the programs are demonstrably ineffective? Why do people so readily perceive change in themselves and others after even ineffective therapeutic interventions? Why does the average citizen in the street so readily regard the family as being in decline or America as once again "standing tall"? Why do people so confidently assert that social problems—whether they concern education, child abuse, divorce, drug abuse—are undergoing dramatic shifts? Commentary about everyday change conclusions has often been marked by a concern with the problematic nature of these judgments—they have been assumed to be a largely capricious and unreliable form of judgment having a limited basis in fact—hence the widely felt need among professionals to measure change and avoid relying simply on what laypersons have to say about change. Change is often regarded as something that is frequently misconstrued in the service of personal motives and about which myths are readily believed.

This intense interest in what people believe about change notwithstanding, there has been little attempt to account for everyday change judgments in anything other than the most descriptive of terms. Unlike many other areas of judgment—for which detailed accounts of the underlying judgment processes have now been provided— the analysis of everyday change judgments has remained the province of speculation, with change impressions still being regarded as having a largely self-evident character, one that can be understood without reference to an empirical base. Yet a moment's reflection will show that this class of judgments is anything but self-evident: at a minimum, such judgments would appear to involve the comparison of events from different points in time and thus the storage and retrieval of relevant information from the past. The intent of this monograph is to outline and analyze the rich set of questions raised by the phenomenon of intuitive change judgments and to frame the issues in a way that permits their systematic investigation by empirical means, and to report the results of studies that bear, in at least a preliminary way, on these issues.

Hearing people make reference to change is so much a part of our lives that we no longer give judgments of change special notice or attend to their richness and variety. This initial chapter will serve first, to highlight the fact that change judgments are not limited to a single area but are common to many areas, and, second, to show that an understanding of change judgments will be useful for many areas of social science, not the least of which are some important areas of psychology. Although there have been few systematic studies of the prevalence of impressions of change, we can readily discover the diversity of topics for which there is an intuitive interest in change simply by perusing a variety of everyday sources—books, newspapers, magazines, and the like. Examples of change judgments taken from such sources not only indicate the diversity of change judgments but also suggest that certain questions about change judgments are common to all change judgments regardless of differences in context or content. Beneath the diversity there is a common core of issues in need of exploration and interpretation. In sum, this chapter will be used to reawaken an awareness of and interest in change judgments as a class of judgments, and will be used to raise questions that will guide both the subsequent examination of existing literature and the later development of a theoretical approach to the study of change judgments. Before the base of specific examples is presented, a working definition of change judgments will be provided, along with some accompanying explanation of the differences between change judgments and related judgments.

Some Definitional Issues

Change judgments are assertions that have as their content some statement or conclusion about change. In such assertions something is said to be different from the way it once was in one or more of its characteristics or in its frequency of occurrence. Intuitive change judgments can be made about a wide array of events or entities, and the perceiver might use any of a family of related change terms to label the change. Thus, change could be referred to by saying that someone or something has improved, declined, grown, deteriorated, or become different in some other way. These change ascriptions could be made in reference to individuals, aggregates of individuals, or to larger social trends. A friend might be described as having changed, an important relationship of some years could be described as having faltered, one's own political views might be perceived as having undergone a shift, family life in America could be referred to as having deteriorated, or people could speak of the world as having changed such that life is no longer safe in the ways it once was. In each case, the focus of the judgment is on a difference that is perceived between things as they were in the past and things as they now stand.

All change judgments have the common element of referring to a change; the particulars that are asserted to have changed can vary enormously. When Watergate co-conspirator Charles Colson described himself as having become a different person after being "born again" (Colson, 1976), he was making a change assertion. When Mazur (1977) reported that "over the past twenty years, many commentators have claimed that there is a growing distrust of science in the United States" (p. 123), he was reporting on change judgments. And speaking of the college freshman experience, Sifford (1984) said: "You can't go home again. It's Thanksgiving vacation and time to visit home, family, and friends. But it's not like the good old days, and yes, Thomas Wolfe was right. Things at home have changed, or perhaps you have changed" (p. 90). Here reference is made not only to inferences of change, but also to the difficulties of deciding *what* has changed. Despite differences in area, such statements share the common feature of making an assertion that something is different than it used to be.

Change judgments—which have as their content a conclusion about differences—are not to be confused with changed judgments—which are judgments that have changed over time. As an example of the latter, consider the case of someone who once believed in capital punishment but now opposes the death penalty. The judgment has changed but the content of the judgment itself is not about change. From previous work (Bem & McConnell, 1970; Goethals & Reckman, 1973; Ross, McFarland, & Fletcher, 1981), it is clear that changed judgments can exist without an accompanying perception of change: someone might change an attitude without realizing it. On the other hand, a person might perceive his or her attitudes to have changed without any change having actually taken place. Although change of beliefs and perception of change will sometimes be linked, the underlying processes of changing beliefs and those of believing change to have occurred cannot be assumed to be the same.

The brief working definition of change judgments outlined here omits reference to certain issues that will receive detailed treatment in later chapters. For example, the working definition does not prejudge the quality or veridicality of intuitive change judgments that are made. Later chapters will provide information germane to this question of veridicality. The definition also remains neutral on the question of exactly what people intend by their use of the term "change." For example, when applied to persons, is the term "change" reserved for deep-seated shifts in individuals' personalities or is it used primarily to describe superficial variation? Finally, the definition also does not draw distinctions in use of the term across different areas: later we shall find that some such distinctions might usefully be made.

In the remainder of this introductory chapter, intuitive judgments of change drawn from everyday sources will be used to illustrate the extent to which change judgments have become a part of American life—indeed have become a frequent interpretation offered of social events. At one level these are merely examples intended to stimulate interest; at another level they point to important issues. By bringing together many examples in this way that are normally treated separately, questions emerge about how it is that people come to these conclusions. On what basis do people confidently assert that people and events have changed? An inviting point of departure for our examination of change judgments is the richly varied group of judgments that concern social change.

The Times They Are 'Achangin': Perceptions of Social Change

Perhaps the prototypic change judgment is that having to do with social change. Many change judgments are exactly of this sort: they involve comments about widespread social change and changing social trends. Such judgments take a variety of forms and can be about many different kinds of social change. People readily make claims that dramatic changes have taken place in attitudes and values across the decades (cf. comments by Lasch, 1978; Reich, 1971; Toffler, 1971; Yankelovich, 1981). The 1960s are said to have been radically different from the 1950s, and the 70s from the 80s. Liberalism is said to have given way to conservatism. What used to be tolerated or encouraged in sexual behavior is now actively discouraged. The kind of harmony that was once commonplace in the 1950s family life is now said to be rare. There is no shortage of headlines and titles that implicitly refer to such perceptions of change: "We are leaving the 'me' decade behind" (Boston Globe, 1982, p. 47), "ROTC marches back to college campuses" (Longcope, 1982, p. 79).

Perceptions of social change pervade the explanations offered for decisions, elections, and outcomes. Of Reagan's election, it is said that "Americans, reacting against the cultural and political liberalism of the 1960s, are turning back toward more traditional roles, institutions, and ideologies, seeking a restoration of the good old days before rising divorce rates, working women, the 'me' generation, and the cult of intimacy" (Keniston, 1981, p. 7). In introducing and justifying a new season's television programing, one television executive remarked, "Our new schedule reflects something important that's happening in the country right now. There's an evolving mood based on a renewal of traditional values: home and family, courage and honesty, respect for authority and teamwork" (Schwartz, 1981, p. 31).

This willingness to make social change inferences of a political sort is even reflected in interpretations given to the behavior of public officials. In a lengthy article on Robert Dole, then Senator from Kansas and majority leader of the Senate, *The New York Times* reported on views among Dole's friends of how much Dole had changed with the political times (Clark, 1982). Former Senator McGovern was one such person: "'When I first got to know Bob Dole,' says McGovern, 'he was tough and mean.' That was back in the early 1970's, when Robert J. Dole was a most ascerbic Republican Party chairman and Senator McGovern was a most liberal Democratic candidate for President. Today, the two men count each other as friends. 'He has changed,' says McGovern – not only on the personal and psychological levels he adds, 'but in his approach to government'" (p. 65). Linking the political with the interpretation of individuals, Vice President Bush has been described as having changed. "What has happened is that Bush has changed in his four-and-a-half years in the White House serving President Reagan. He has changed, as have many people in the country. He has become more conservative . . . . but he has difficulty saying he has changed" (Healy, 1985, p. 19).

Many familiar intuitive change judgments are about social problems such as child abuse, crime, and teen pregnancy; often such change statements are implicitly statistical in nature, as the following examples suggest: " . . . crime against children seems to be on the increase, both in terms of number and viciousness" (Pashdag, 1981, p. 42), "The problems of teen-age suicide, violent crimes in school-related incidents, teenage pregnancies, and drug abuse have reached epidemic proportions in our society" (Van Niel, 1987, p. 11), and "In the time it takes to read this article, more than 150 teen-agers will try to commit suicide . . . . No generation in American history has been more self-destructive" (Thomas, 1987, p. 63).

Social change is sometimes perceived in deep-seated cultural characteristics – something as fundamental as the perceived level of helpfulness in society, for example. Reports of failures to help in the city, on the subway, and so forth, make their way into newspaper stories and give rise to comments about how much less helpful people are these days than in the past. The conclusion that people have become less helpful figured in interpretations given to the behavior of bystanders in the Kitty Genovese case; in their work on bystander intervention, Latane and Darley (1970) referred to such change perceptions when they wrote of "the general feeling that present-day society is fragmented, that compassion is disappearing, that old moralities are crumbling" (p. 1). In a more recent and widely reported "Baby Doe" case, in which the parents of a multiply-handicapped newborn infant chose to allow their child to die, the decision of this single set of parents was treated as a sign of how deeply changed society as a whole had become: "How callous and indifferent to human life our society has become" (Editorials on File, 1982).

Change judgments can be heard about fundamental change in the institutions of society such as that of the family. For example, in 1981 a television station in the Boston area produced a series of programs in which Boston families were interviewed about what they saw happening to the American family ("The Changing Family," 1981). Among the recurrent change assertions were claims that there has been a great increase in the "throwaway child" and that commitment to families has disappeared. Such changes are believed to have happened quickly and dramatically: "Dear Readers, here is another letter that reflects the disintegration of American family life. I would not have received such a letter even five years ago" (Landers, 1982, p. 22).

Signs of how much we have changed are even seen in our reactions to heroes and in the disappearance of hero worship. The claim is made that something has happened to heroes—that people who once would been heroes no longer behave like heroes ("Cowboys don't shoot straight like they used to," in the words of a recent country-western song) and that as a society we have lost our ability to believe in heroes with the kind of innocence that was once typical in the past. In a recent article entitled "Trying to Coach in an Age of Fallen Diamond Heroes," one writer noted that "life was relatively simple for the young baseball fanatic 15 to 20 years ago. . . . Today the magical and majestic image . . . has been stripped, the innocence of the illusion shattered" (Pisarik, 1987, p. 20). Concomitant with the perception of the loss of heroes is the more general impression of a loss of innocence. This perception of lost innocence is often heard in statements about society having become increasingly complex and daily life having changed toward less simplicity and less security. Times supposedly were simpler and more innocent in the past: "We now live in a cynical age" (Boston Globe, 5/23/82, p. 22). Times were once innocent for children and young people. As one mother put it describing the experience of growing up in the 1950s, "I remember my teenage years as a giddy, happy, and frivolous time. I know the world was more secure back then . . . " (Boston Globe, 1982, p. 15).

Many intuitive social change judgments carry the theme of how much better things were in the past. For example, in an article titled, "When Stars Were Brighter," McGrory bemoans the decline in the movie industry and the absence of the kind of outstanding acting that was once commonplace (McCrory, 1982). Comments about the Boston art scene in the 50s reflect a similar theme: "Somehow those seemed heroic days . . . . Did the Boston art scene 30 years ago possess a heroism, a grandeur, a sense of mission lacking today?" (Boston Globe, 1984, p. 93).

Social change judgments do not always refer to changes in the country as a whole or even the culture in its entirety. Social change judgments sometimes refer to small groups; they can be about perceived changes in a scientific field, a small organization, a local community. In academic departments one often hears change comments about declines in the quality of incoming students: "Students don't work as hard as they used to." "Whatever happened to the quality of students we used to get?" or "Graduate students aren't bright and hardworking like they were when we were in school."

From the examples included in this section we can see the wide variety of areas in which people conclude that things today are different than things used to be. That people so readily make these judgments raises questions about how they come to see change. How do people know and decide that graduate students were once more hardworking than they are at present? How do people decide that life used to be simpler? What leads observers to conclude that people were once more helpful? In other words, on what basis are these judgments made and how do they come to be made with such confidence? In general terms, what do perceivers know about the past that makes things in the present look different by comparison? When people go about making informal change comparisons in different areas, how are the heterogeneous items of information for different periods used as a basis for comparison? And of the nearly limitless aspects of past events and experiences, which features are highlighted in our representations of the past and which are underreported or poorly conveyed in everyday information sources?* Finally, to what extent are these problematic inferences or are these inferences made in ways that make them systematic and predictable?

Judgments of social change are so common in contemporary culture and so salient a part of public awareness that they have perhaps become the most intuitively familiar type of change judgment. There is, however, another type of change judgment that is, at least in terms of frequency of occurrence, just as much a part of the currency of social exchange — mainly, judgments of change in individuals. Change judgments about individuals can regularly be observed where there is concern with the individual, for example, with growth and maturation in childhood, with deterioration and decline of mental and physical powers in late adulthood, and even with personality change throughout the lifespan. To show how varied and commonplace such judgments are, the following sections present a series of examples of person change judgments. In addition to conveying a sense of the familiarity of these judgments, the examples also suggest some of the ways in which questions about the nature of intuitive change judgments are intertwined with certain important issues about intuitive views of persons. By their very nature, intuitive change judgments in these areas raise questions about the kind of change people see in others: Is it deep change? Is perceived change in persons limited to specific ages or to some other relatively narrow set of circumstances? Given that much of the change we see in individuals would seem to concern amorphous personal qualities, how do people draw conclusions about how those ill-defined qualities have changed? In what ways do prior views regarding the ability of the individual to change influence the judgments that are made?

The Intuitive Perception of Change in Childhood

Adults have an inveterate habit of making change judgments about children. This is apparent in its most obvious form in the enormous interest parents display in monitoring changes in their children and in comparing those changes with what

---

*"Representations" is intended here to include all forms in which the past is recorded, whether mental or physical, individual or social. Included are written records, personal memories, data banks, folklore, etc.

experts regard as typical; a lucrative market has been created for books and articles discussing childhood change. Although such intuitive judgments about childhood change often center on age-related changes, change judgments also focus on changes resulting from specific—often unexpected—life events. Children are sometimes perceived to have changed markedly after a divorce or similar crisis. Children may be perceived to have been permanently changed by traumatic life events, such as childhood sexual abuse, the death of a parent, or the experience of a serious illness. The pages of advice columns are filled with such concerns. Preoccupation with childhood change is shown is other ways. Divorced parents and parents who have to be away from their children for extended periods of time often describe their anguish at not being around to see the changes their children go through. For example, the explorer Dodge Morgan's concerns while sailing solo around the world exemplify this pervasive expectation of and concern with change: "Antarctica, with its icebergs and gale winds two of every three days, seemed less a worry for Morgan than the separation from his children. 'They'll be different when I get back . . . . They'll have changed'" (Thomas, 1987, p. 12).

This fascination with childhood change is also apparent when a more active approach is taken to bringing about change. In the lives of American children certain life events are introduced with the sole aim of bringing about change. Parents and teachers deliberately attempt to engineer changes based on assumptions about how best to foster change in childhood; even in cases where knowledge of how to induce change is felt to be wanting, change is of enough concern that more knowledgeable individuals are sought out for advice on how to bring it about. In the belief that change in childhood is possible, children are sent out to have change-inducing experiences—such as the Outward Bound experience—and parents join organizations like Tough Love and adopt new methods of discipline as a way to create change. Then the evidence is intuitively considered: Were the strategies effective? Has the child changed? Is the child different now? Somehow a conclusion is reached that the strategies either worked or did not, that the child's present behavior does or does not show evidence of change.

The interest in change perception also appears in the emphasis on change as a diagnostic sign. Parents are commonly advised to pay careful attention when they observe changes in their children because those changes may reflect an underlying shift in the child's emotional health and well-being. It is said that a teenager who has changed from being adolescently miserable to being depressed could be suicidal, or that a child whose behavior has undergone a dramatic change may have developed a drug-abuse problem. The credence implicitly placed in everyday change impressions by those who give such advice rests not only on the seemingly unproblematic assumption that parents are actively involved in looking for change and in making change judgments but also on the (questionable) assumption that such judgments are generally made with some degree of validity.

Perceptions of childhood change become all the more intriguing when considered in light of the possibility that the nature of childhood is itself perceived to have changed. Examples of judgments about changes in the nature of childhood are readily found:

> The diminished emphasis on fantasy and play and imaginative activities in early childhood education and the increased focus on early academic-skill acquisition have helped to change childhood from a play-centered time of life to one more closely resembling the style of adulthood: purposeful, success-centered, competitive. (Winn, 1983, p. 18)

In the book *The Child and Other Cultural Inventions* (Kessel & Siegel, 1983), it has been persuasively argued that the very notion of what constitutes childhood — indeed, what constitutes the nature of the child — is itself culturally and historically delimited and has undergone change across time (see also Aries, 1962); thus, the most basic of assumptions about childhood are shaped by shifting cultural beliefs and expectations. While Kessel and others have focused on the implications of the social constructionist analysis for the issue of whether an objective account of childhood can ever be achieved, their analysis of the power of social construction may have particular cogency as a framework for an area they have not focused on: the nature of perceptions of individual change in children and childhood. The application of this perspective to intuitive conceptions of childhood change has broad implications, particularly in light of the fact that perceiving change in the nature of childhood may influence and shape the perception of change in individual children. Kagan (1984) and Gergen (1977, 1980), among others, have begun to explore the implications of cultural relativism and social construction for such concepts as developmental change and stability; a similar analysis at the level of intuitive perceptions of change and stability may prove equally enlightening.

In sum, many aspects of childhood behavior and childhood experience evoke intuitive judgments of change. The examples and issues introduced above give rise to an inviting set of questions about the nature and process of seeing change in children. How is information used to arrive at a conclusion that a child has been changed by some experience or event? How do people decide that childhood itself has changed and changed dramatically? Do intuitive assessments such as these differ systematically from assessments of change that would be likely to be made by developmentalists? When laypersons encountering psychological assessments of childhood change are confronted with discrepancies between their intuitive judgments and the formal assessments, can we expect them to place greater reliance on the former? Do social and cultural conventions about what changes to expect in children play an important role in determining the changes that are perceived? Do such conventions ever preempt the role of behavioral observations in making judgments of change? How can a general understanding of change judgments shed light on the particular change judgments that occur in this area?

Intuitive Perceptions of Individual Change in Adulthood

Are we "still stable after all these years" as life-span developmentalists Costa and McCrae (1980) contend, or does each of us undergo significant change in adulthood? This surprisingly elusive issue has been at the forefront of much research and controversy in the area of adult development, yet the answer to the puzzle of stability and change in adulthood remains very much at issue. In seeking a more informed understanding of the actual level of change among adults, investigators have placed the emphasis on finding means for the formal measurement of that change. How those same changes are perceived by laypersons at an intuitive level is an equally intriguing issue. Ultimately we may find that people undergo little real change in adulthood despite whatever kinds of diversifying experiences they may have; yet to the extent that they are perceived as changing, such intuitive convictions, however inaccurate, are likely to a critical determinant of how perceivers behave with respect to one another. Given that intuitive perceivers are very unlikely to have access to the relevant systematic data on person change before deciding whether change has occurred, it is clearly of interest to explore the nature of the change conclusions that they draw on their own. Perhaps people rarely see change in adults; perhaps they infer change with more frequency than would be warranted on the basis of objective measures.

It is readily apparent that people do, as a matter of course, find informal evidence of change in others in adulthood. Comments referring to adults as having changed — often as having changed in ways that perceivers have come to expect — appear wherever there are opportunities for people to voice their opinions about others, for example, in magazine articles, in advice columns, and in books. In parallel with the age-related thrust in the life-span literature, intuitive change comments often contain specific age-related content, as when a person's leadership qualities or intellectual acumen are called into question on the basis of advancing age alone. Comments about change also focus on changes brought about by predictable life-course events, such as getting married, having children, or getting divorced (e.g., Jaffe & Viertel, 1979). Intuitive concerns with adult change reliably emerge in certain specific contexts. Reunions provide one conspicuous example: "We are at this reunion really to see how our old classmates have changed and also to see — reflected back in their eyes — how much we have changed" (Goodman, 1979, p. 4; see also Lamb & Reeder, 1986). Change judgments also arise in the workplace: "She changed the minute she was promoted" (Scott, 1984, p. 5).

People seem to worry about the changes they expect to occur in themselves as a result of undergoing certain events — getting married, having children, encountering success — perhaps as a consequence of having perceived change in others under similar circumstances. Concern about success-induced change has been a topic of speculations about professional athletes. Commenting on the basketball star Larry Bird, one sports writer has written:

> I have long suspected that Bird must occasionally, at least, work at maintaining his rural image, simply because he would never want to convey the wrong image back home. In his mind, the worst thing that could happen to him during the off season would be for someone to come up and say, "Larry, you've changed." (Ryan, 1987, p. 90)

This concern with change was powerful enough to carry over into the coverage of Bird's would-be teammate Reggie Lewis. The headline announcing Lewis' selection by the Boston Celtics in the college draft read: "Lewis' No. 1 Priority: Stay The

Same Person" (MacMullan, 1987, p. 81). Impressions and expectations for change seem to be important to them and thus influential in their lives regardless of their veridicality. The significance and emotion attached to expectations for change is also highlighted in reactions to situations where age-related change expectations are strong. During the 1980 presidential campaign, for example, responses to the fact that President Reagan was well beyond retirement age often hinged on strongly held convictions about inevitable changes and deterioration people were believed to undergo at such advanced ages. Not only did concerns with change become an issue throughout the campaign but they remained a point of contention at various problem points during the presidency itself: what is the capacity of a person at that age to change, what is the likelihood of change occurring or taking place? In the wake of the Irangate scandal, Edmund Muskie, a member of the Tower Commission, asked the question "Can Reagan change? Can an old dog change his style?" (Feinsilber, 1987, p. 60).

The literature on formal life-span change assessment is replete with examples of the difficulties involved in the assessment of such change (see Chapter 2). The existence of these difficulties raises intriguing questions about how perceivers overcome or fail to overcome these problems in making intuitive judgments of change across the life span. What kinds of informal data do people rely on when they are making change judgments about others? How do people judge change when the available information is incomplete or time-limited, i.e., when the information does not cover the full range of events or times? What happens when the available information concerns cohorts rather than particular individuals in the past? How is it that people are able to informally assess change in cases where formal considerations would severely limit the possibility of coming to any conclusions about change? Are naive judgments held with sufficient conviction that they shape the response to, or even override, formal data that might provide a different picture of change?

Intuitive Judgments of Personality Change

Just as some psychologists have focused on life-span issues in their attempt to understand individual behavior, others have focused their attention on personality—on those deep-seated, stable characteristics that determine an individual's behavior across time and across situations. For psychologists, "personality" has often been regarded as synonymous with that which is unchanging and stable. Yet everyday perceivers appear to have a concept of personality change—a concept that would be regarded as practically oxymoronic by many personality psychologists—and laypeople use the concept to capture the fact that people are sometimes seen as having changed in deep ways, perhaps as a consequence of the profoundly change-producing life experiences now a part of life in a rapidly changing world. Several examples from literature and everyday life highlight questions about the conditions under which perceivers make these judgments about deep-seated change.

In *The Razor's Edge* (1943), Somerset Maugham's novel of World War I, the plot centers on the personality change that takes places in a young fighter pilot after the death of his best friend and fellow pilot in the war. Throughout the book the pilot's friends and family struggle to understand why he changed: "The war did something to Larry. He didn't come back the same person that he went. It's not only that he's older. Something happened that changed his personality" (p. 32). And, "He gives me such an odd impression sometimes; he gives me the impression of a sleep walker who suddenly wakened in a strange place and can't think where he is. He was so normal before the war . . . . What can have happened to change him so much?" (p. 54).

Such talk of dramatic change is by no means limited to the realm of fiction. Like Maugham's characters, people in everyday life sometimes perceive deep-seated change in those around them. They are concerned with the question of how and why others change particularly when the changes have altered or disrupted relationships. This concern with change in those with whom we are involved can be found in people of all age groups. A young teenager writes, "My boyfriend is changing in ways I don't understand . . . I feel so alone" (Boston Globe Magazine, 1982, p. 5). A man in his thirties writes: "I didn't want this divorce. I want my wife back. I want her back the way she was and it's impossible. She's changed so much, it can't ever be" (Goodman, 1979, p. 187). In a letter to an advice columnist, a husband describes how surgery has changed his wife of many years: "Since the operation she has had a complete personality change. She used to be very warm and affectionate, but now she is belligerent, hostile and disagreeable" (Landers, 1981, p. 8). A woman in another letter comments on the changes she sees in her spouse after retirement: "I have been married to a man who has changed completely since he retired 10 months ago" (Landers, 1983, p. 19).

These intuitive perceptions of deep-seated change can take many forms, including those involving radical religious and political change. In their account of cults, Conway and Siegelman (1979) provide many examples of intuitive beliefs that drastic changes can result from involvement in cults. To capture the radical and sudden nature of these personality changes, the authors vividly refer to these cases as instances of "snapping," and they argue that over the last decade there has been an epidemic of cases of snapping. Similarly, deep-seated change is often perceived in presumed cases of brainwashing, which is widely believed to have the power to radically change individuals. From the case of Patty Hearst to the cases of hostages held in Iran and Lebanon, the hold that the concept of brainwashing has on the popular imagination is evident. Although such phenomena as cult conversion, snapping, and brainwashing may represent extreme cases, they nonetheless demonstrate the fascination with, and belief in the possibility of, marked personality change on the part of social perceivers.

Less dramatic but more common are cases of perceived changes in the basic value systems of others, changes that are often believed to result from political events and social movements. The editors of *Ms.* magazine, for its tenth anniversary edition (1982), solicited information from its readers about changes they saw in others and in themselves over the previous decade of changes in women's experience. According to the editors, hundreds of responses were received about the changes readers saw. In a typical response one reader wrote: "My father has been a very conservative man for most of his life. He used to believe that a woman's place was strictly in the home and that the man was in control .... A few years ago I started to notice a change slowly coming over him" (p. 35). In a book devoted to the exploration of personal change associated with shifting role expectations (Goodman, 1979), many people described what they perceived as deep changes in themselves and others as a result of transformations in male and female roles. One interviewee wrote: "I am completely different. I've been through metamorphosis. I feel like Kafka's George Samsa. I feel as if one morning I woke up to find myself completely different. Maybe not as a beetle, like George Samsa, but so changed that everyone would notice and react. I am just not the same person I was three months ago. I look back and cannot believe that I was her. My life has changed totally and forever" (Goodman, 1979, p. 69).

Conclusions about personal change sometimes extend to judgments that dramatic change has taken place as is indicated by the aforementioned examples. The conditions under which such judgments arise and the various forms such judgments take will be issues of considerable interest. Whether laypeople regularly find evidence of deep change and whether they see change of a dramatic sort as predictable (or even inevitable) under some circumstances are questions that have implications for how people judge the nature of persons and the degree of stability in personality.

Intuitive Change Judgments in Program Evaluation and Clinical Psychology

While the several areas noted thus far give some indication of the pervasiveness with which intuitive change judgments occur, an examination of other areas not only reinforces the sense of pervasiveness but illustrates as well the important role that views of change judgments and of their reliability can play in those areas where the process of change is important. In the area of clinical psychology, intuitive judgments about therapeutic change are a recognized part of the therapeutic process for both client and therapist; in the field of program evaluation, intuitive impressions of program-induced change often co-exist with formal outcome information about a program's success. In different ways these two areas exemplify how assumptions about change impressions can be important—a further reason for attempting to understand the dynamics underlying intuitive judgments of change.

Consider the view of intuitive change judgments common to the area of program evaluation. Campbell's (1969) classic article, "Reforms as Experiments," was intended to interest psychologists in program evaluation as a technique for formally assessing program change. Campbell sought to illustrate the need for formal program evaluation in part by demonstrating the problems inherent in intuitive judgments of the changes believed to be brought about by programs and by changes in laws. Perhaps the most compelling of the examples used by Campbell was that of the egregious errors in intuitive change judgments made by Connecticut officials after the adoption of tougher laws against speeding. Then-governor Ribicoff purported that his program had been highly successful in bringing about a decline in the accident rate. Yet, as Campbell so vividly illustrated, no real change could be said to have occurred when fatalities were analyzed through more systematic techniques that took into account prior variability in the year-to-year accident rates.

The evaluation field has gone well beyond such initial demonstrations of the importance of formal evaluation, yet the underlying diagnosis of the need for avoiding dependence on informal impressions of change has remained largely the same. Much work has been founded on the premise that intuitive change judgments are unreliable and therefore must be replaced by more systematic and more thorough data collection procedures.

Just as program evaluators have been concerned with the intrusion of personal impressions, intuitive impressions have been a concern in the clinical area (Bergin & Lambert, 1978). Yet here informal impressions—when made by the clinicians themselves—have also sometimes served as a sort of informal data base in disputes about the effectiveness of different therapies. Goldfried has framed the issue as follows:

> There exist certain "timeless truths" consisting of observations of how people change. Although it is clear that a systematic and more objective study of the therapeutic change process is needed in order to advance our body of knowledge, it would be a grievous error to ignore what has been unsystematically observed by so many. (1980, p. 996)

What has been unsystematically observed by so many, to use Goldfried's phrase, is change in individuals as a result of therapy, and these intuitive judgments of therapeutic change have played a part in the lively controversy about the effectiveness of therapeutic interventions.

Regardless of differences in the therapies involved, the controversy about therapeutic effectiveness has typically focused on disputes about the implications of the research data (Strupp, 1982). That is, critics of a given school of therapy often base their case on systematic data that are taken to show that the therapy is less effective at bringing about significant change than proponents assume to be the case (Eysenck, 1952; Harvey & Parks, 1982; VandenBos, 1986). This in turn has led proponents to question the adequacy of the data, often arguing on the basis of their experience with the system's effectiveness that the data themselves must surely be flawed (Bergin & Lambert, 1978; Kazdin, 1982). Intuitive judgments of change are often the implicit counterpoints to the systematic data. Reliance on intuitive judgments of change has clearly occurred here: the belief that change that has somehow been missed by systematic approaches can be intuitively observed has lain at the center of the objections to the data and has added force to these objections.

This is not to suggest that intuitive change judgments are universally accepted as valid data for assessing therapies. On the contrary, whereas some, like Goldfried, see an important place for such judgments, others largely dismiss the usefulness and verdicality of intuitive assessments (see Kazdin, 1982; VandenBos, 1986; Zilbergeld, 1983). Many have argued that change cannot be adequately assessed without the aid of systematic techniques. But neither position has focused on the issue of what can be known generally about change judgments that might elucidate the nature of change judgments in clinical settings. Such a direction, although not entirely absent, has remained an infrequent focus of interest (e.g., Minz, Auerback, Luborsky, & Johnson, 1973; Stiles, Shapiro, & Elliot, 1986), and only rarely has it been integrated into discussions about differences in interpretations of the effectiveness of therapy.

In both of these areas—program evaluation and clinical psychology—views of change judgments and of their reliability have played intriguing roles in ongoing debates in areas where issues of change and its occurrence are central. What is true of these two is true of many others: informal impressions of change may play a central role in controversies and disagreement over the nature and extent of change, as well as its causes and consequences, be it change in the political realm or change in the person realm.

Looking Ahead: The Systematic Study of Intuitive Change Judgments

Throughout this chapter we have worked at the level of specific examples. Those examples point to a common class of judgments. All of these examples have in common the process of individuals looking at events or people and deciding that something is now different than it was in the past. Collectively the examples provide a groundwork for raising questions about how people go about concluding that there are differences over time. Across the different content areas, the same basic questions emerge: In the process of making intuitive change judgments, what kinds of information are used? In what way is information used in arriving at the judgments? What role do prior beliefs about the nature and likelihood of change play when impressions of change are formed? Do change judgments occur under predictable circumstances? Do these judgments represent systematic interpretations of available information or are they largely capricious conclusions that fail to represent the amount of personal and social change that has taken place?

In the next two chapters we will explore the present status of research relevant to this important class of social judgments. To begin with, the research on change will be examined and will be shown to have been oriented toward professionalizing change assessment rather than toward investigating the intuitive impressions of change formed by laypersons. We shall see that although the knowledge base regarding the problem of change assessment is substantial, much less is known about the processes by which people arrive at their personal conclusions about change. The upshot will be that a richly interesting but barely tapped set of problems about individual judgments of change remains to be explored. In Chapter 3 a programmatic approach will be outlined for the study of change judgments. The approach to be sketched there draws on previous research on social judgment in general and employs the insights from past work on the formal assessment of change. The aim is to develop a means of investigating the general processes underlying change judgments that can then be applied to the specific problems of change judgment discussed in subsequent chapters.

Chapter 2

Change and Its Perception: Prior Research

Just as everyday social perceivers show a marked interest in change, so too do researchers in the social sciences. The pervasiveness of this professional interest in change can be seen in any number of ways. It is apparent, for example, in the range of topics that have been targets of change research. From television viewing habits to sexual practices, from political views to leisure activities, from the problem of child abuse to the problems of old age, few aspects of personal and social life have been untouched by attempts on the part of researchers to study change. Researchers have sought to assemble information capable of providing answers to the questions of change: Are certain practices becoming more common or less? In certain areas are things improving or deteriorating? Is life becoming better or worse? The breadth of the interest in change is also apparent in the wide variety of entities that have been examined for changes of various kinds. Change across the life span in the individual has been a focus of interest, but so has change across decades in large aggregates of individuals and societies as wholes. The investigation of change has sometimes been directed at the study of change in small groups but it has also involved the investigation of change in large-scale organizations.

The extent of professional interest in change is seen in other ways. It is indicated by the number of disciplines currently devoted in whole or part to the issue of change and its assessment. For example, a concern with social change and with providing a sounder basis for its measurement has been a central theme in the social indicators movement; concerns with change have been central to the program evaluation movement and the attempts there to evaluate the effectiveness of programs in bringing about change; concerns with person change have been important to life span developmental psychology and the focus there on measuring whether person change takes place across the life span. The level of interest in change is further evidenced by the appearance of large numbers of monographs and journals that address the issue of change. Across the various disciplines the extensive efforts that have been directed to the development and refinement of methodologies for the purpose of measuring change (e.g., time series analysis) is yet another indication of the level of interest in change.

The pervasiveness of interest in change probably needs no further illustration. Expanding the knowledge base about change has been and continues to be an important goal for research. The particular areas of change that concern individual investigators have differed greatly, but transcending these differences has been a common focus on the challenge of measuring and documenting change. Indeed, in each area attempts to expand the knowledge base of change have been similar, reflecting the same core question of how best to measure change: How should one measure change in the prevalence of various social problems? How should one measure change due to the effects of a social program? How does one measure change in an individual? After therapy? Across the life span?

This detailed study of change has rarely included the study of how social perceivers arrive at their intuitive judgments of those same changes, probably for the very reason that the formal measurement emerged as a concern in the first place. Intuitive views of change have simply been assumed to be of questionable reliability, thus giving rise to the need to systematically assess change. Intuitive impressions have been treated as if their inadequacies had been established and need no further examination. Yet there is much of interest to be learned about how judgments of change are made, aside from any issue about their accuracy. And, as will become apparent in this chapter, little is known of their degree of veracity, much less of the process by which these judgments are made.

In this chapter we examine the direction of previous work that has influenced current understanding of change and change judgments. The first section looks at the literature's focus on change assessment and derives some lessons for the study of change judgments from that work. The outgrowth of much of that work will be shown to be an emerging understanding of the difficulties that change poses both as a concept and as something to be measured. The second section describes the literature's emphasis on the impact of change on perceivers and its consequent failure to encompass the study of the perceivers' impressions of those changes. The final section will point to the absence of work on change perception by those whose professed area of study is social perception. The study of social perception will be shown to have centered on accounting for stability in judgments, with the result that relatively few of the many studies on social perception have considered how people arrive at their intuitive impressions of change. At one level then these three aspects of the literature will together indicate why existing work has so rarely focused on change judgments; at another level the review of previous work will point to important questions for the study of intuitive change judgments and will reveal just how deeply intertwined questions about the perception of change are with many of the concerns that lie at the heart of attempts to understand change.

Measuring Change

The widespread interest that we humans show in change places us in a paradoxical position. Change strikes us as worthy of attention, for both its promising and its threatening qualities, yet change is almost unique in our social world in the degree to which it is refractory to being accurately gauged. To understand the bearing of this point on the context in which intuitive change judgments are made, we need to look at what has been done to measure change and the difficulties that have arisen in the process. As it turns out, there is an interesting story to told here – the professionalizing process that began by assuming that there are insurmountable weaknesses in intuitive judgments has gradually brought us to a more precise understanding of the fact that all change assessments, intuitive or professional, are fraught with difficulties. That is, the movement originally intended to provide accurate measurements of change has wound up instead yielding an increasingly clear understanding of the limitations on our abilities to know whether change has occurred.

To see this, it must first be noted that the professionalizing emphasis in the study of change has stimulated a remarkable array of projects designed to reliably measure change, including many aspects of social change. For example, there have been efforts to measure changes in sexual behavior, in gender roles (Baruch, Barnett, & Rivers, 1983; Gurin, 1985; Kimmel, 1987), in the family (Caplow, Bahr, Chadwick, Hill, & Williamson, 1983), in the amount of violence in television and movies (Gerbner, 1972), and in the content of books and periodicals (Malamuth & Spinner, 1980). In education, the assessment of changes in institutions, practices, and outcomes has been a perennial focus of concern (Boyer, 1987; Ferriss, 1969; Wirtz, 1977). There have been attempts to measure changes in the prevalence of various social problems; in the levels of racism in society (Kinder & Rhodebeck, 1982; Smith & Dempsey, 1983), and in rates of family violence (Straus, Gelles, & Steinmetz, 1980), teen pregnancies (Chilman, 1979), and crime (Block & Block, 1984). Attempts have been made to measure changes in public opinion, for example, in attitudes toward inequality (Kluegel & Smith, 1986), shifting conservatism of political beliefs (Mueller, 1983), and beliefs about national priorities and foreign policy assumptions (Hero, 1973; Page & Shapiro, 1982).

Just as there have been many attempts to measure social change, there have been numerous attempts to measure various kinds of change at the individual level. We have seen, for example, that there has been great interest among clinicians in assessing change due to a range of therapeutic interventions (Bergin & Lambert, 1978; Mahoney, 1980; Strupp, 1982; see also Kazdin, 1982; Smith & Glass, 1977). Similarly, in developmental psychology there has been great interest in finding ways to measure change in childhood as well as change across the life span (Baltes, Reese, & Nesselroade, 1977). Among those who study personality issues, attempts have been made to assess the extent to which there is longitudinal change in values, interests, traits, and the like (Costa & McCrae, 1980; Moss & Susman, 1980).

Across all of these areas, a central aim has been to develop a base of reliable information about individual and social change, with the ultimate aim of generating comprehensive theories of the causes and consequences of individual and social change. On the face on it these efforts have been successful. Attempts at systematic measurement have yielded valuable new documentation of the kinds and amounts of change that are taking place in modern life. This enriched information base has made itself felt in a variety of ways in the recent literature on change. In studies of social change, it has guided the development of more sophisticated models of the general processes or social change (e.g., Boudan, 1983; Zollschan & Hirsch, 1976). It has provided a basis for the detailed analysis of the specific forces and processes that account for the social changes taking place in American life (e.g., Caplow, Bahr, Chadwick, Hill, & Williamson, 1983). In developmental areas, the base of information on change has informed the search for factors governing those changes (e.g., Munnichs & Munnichs, 1985; Nesselroade & Eye, 1984). Similarly, various models of thera-peutic change have been proposed in light of findings about which areas of function-ing show change and about the conditions under which that change occurs (e.g., Mahoney, 1982).

Although the sort of reliance on the facts of change that is reflected in the fore-going examples suggests that formal change assessment has proceeded without difficulty, this is far from the case. At the same time that researchers have sought to exploit the findings on change in various ways, they have also become increasingly aware of the complex difficulties that arise in assessing change and of the resulting limitations on the usefulness of the data. The character of these methodological problems and the difficulties they pose for change conclusions have received con-siderable scrutiny and commentary (e.g., Harris, 1963; Nesselroade & Reese, 1973). Here, two extended examples will be used to illustrate how difficult the whole enterprise of obtaining a true picture of change can be. The first example, involving the assessment of changes in rates of child abuse, illustrates the kind of difficulties that analysts have faced in attempting to draw conclusions about change when the comparison information cannot be assumed to have been uniformly collected over time. The second example, drawn from longitudinal developmental research, illus-trates the kinds of subtle and conceptually linked methodological issues that still remain even when problems of the first sort have been eliminated. These two representative cases—one drawn from the area of social change and one drawn from the area of person change—will serve not only to illustrate the methodological problems in the formal assessment of change but also to raise parallel methodo-logical issues relevant to informal change judgments. Because informal change judgments are made under methodologically adverse circumstances, it will be important to ask how the problems of judging change are surmounted and even how intuitive change judgments can be made at all in light of pervasive methodological difficulties.

Methodological Issues in Evaluating Change in Rates of Child Abuse

Attempts to assess change necessarily involve comparisons of the present with the past, yet often initial interest in change in an area has come much too late for researchers to have control over the data. Instead, they have had to rely on whatever information happened to have been collected about the problem in the past. The area of child abuse is like many others in this respect. Here interest in the question of change and whether this problem was once less common than it is today has of necessity involved attempts to make comparisons between whatever information exists from earlier times and that derived from more formal measures of current rates of abuse. As many have discovered, the figures that are available for different periods are problematic for direct comparison. Often it is only long after the earlier baseline period has been over that interest has been directed to the development of an information base suitable for making across-time comparisons. Thus, what is available in the way of information comes in different forms, from different sources, and from highly different conditions of measurement, with the result that it has become increasingly apparent that egregious errors can occur when the available numbers are taken at face value.

In their attempts to determine the degree to which past and present figures can be compared, investigators of change in this area have identified a growing list of potentially confounding factors that make change evidence difficult to interpret. Over the comparison period the methods of reporting child abuse have not always remained constant (Helfer & Kempe, 1987). Laws requiring that suspected cases of abuse be reported have not remained the same (American Humane Association, 1970; Bybee, 1979; Gelles & Straus; 1979). The legal definition of abuse has broadened in most states in recent years (Gelles & Straus, 1979; Nelson, 1984). The number of police and child welfare workers available for receiving and investigating reports of suspected abuse has varied considerably over time (Gelles & Straus, 1979). The very technology available for maintaining records on abuse and for identifying suspected cases of abuse has undergone transformation (Baxter, 1985; Demos, 1986). Public attitudes may not have stayed the same regarding the appropriateness of reporting cases of suspected abuse as compared to respecting the privacy of families (Gelles, 1978; Radbill, 1980). The visibility of the problem of child abuse has not remained the same (Bybee, 1979; Nelson, 1984; Pleck, 1987); indeed, the "discovery" of abuse as a social problem may even have been recent (Nelson, 1984; Pfoll, 1977). The cultural definition of what constitutes abuse seems to have undergone subtle shifts over time (Gelles, 1987; Nelson, 1984; Radbill, 1980). As Gelles and Straus (1979) have noted: "At the heart of the problem is the fact that the term 'child abuse' is intended to draw attention to acts which are believed to deviate from appropriate standards of behavior for caretakers. Such standards vary over time, across cultures, and between social and cultural strata" (p. 19).

Problems such as those listed above have cast considerable doubt on the validity of comparing figures about abuse that happen to be available for different periods. Although rates of child abuse may appear to have increased, it is difficult to know whether this apparent increase represents a genuine change or whether it is a spurious effect resulting from differences across time in the collection of relevant information. Furthermore, there is no clear way of calculating the exact impact of these factors on the past figures because there is little access at present to definitive information about the effects of these cultural factors at past points in time. It is thus not possible to apply a known correction factor to bring information from different periods into a form that would allow comparison.

The problems in comparing past and present facts on child abuse are by no means unique; such problems are typical of those encountered in the many cases where retrospective change analysis is the only means available for change comparison and where data cannot be assumed to have been uniformly collected over time. O'Brien

(1985) has written at length about the difficulties in comparing crime and victimization data from different points in time. In the area of local crime assessment, O'Brien has pointed to problems in interpreting changes in crime rates in the absence of uniform data-collection procedures (see also Archer & Gartner, 1984). Problems are encountered as a result of such factors as abrupt changes in city administrations that are accompanied by shifts in resources allocated for police staffing; such changes can render available statistics incommensurable across comparison periods, heightening the difficulty of drawing conclusions about change (McCleary, Nienstedt, & Erven, 1982; Wilson, 1978). Researchers concerned with assessing change in the incidence of rape have commented on the methodological difficulties in interpreting information about change in rates of rape (Bowker, 1978; Chappell, 1976; Gager & Schurr, 1976; Hindelang & Davis, 1977); for example, because rape is a highly underreported crime, factors at different time periods may separately influence reporting rates and incidence rates (Feldman-Summers & Ashworth, 1981). Thus, a decrease in reported rapes may represent a real change or merely a less favorable political climate for reporting instances of sexual assault.

As the above examples suggest, later comparisons are often made difficult by the fact that shifts in reported incidence can occur as problems receive more publicity. This problem of shifts in the visibility of problems has plagued assessments of change in a number of areas. Those investigating rates of child abductions have described the almost intractable problems that are posed in evaluating change in this now highly visible problem by means of comparing current rates with reported rates in the past when the problem was much less publicized (Schneider, 1987). Trying to assess the degree to which there have been changes in corporate and governmental corruption, researchers have found that periodic shifts in visibility are problematic (Geis & Stotland, 1980; Wickman & Dailey, 1982). Attempts to draw conclusions about changes in rates of spouse abuse have prompted analysis of the difficulties that are encountered in trying to make comparisons across different periods where visibility differs (e.g., Straus et al., 1980).

Nor are the difficulties that have arisen in using available information for change assessment by any means limited to change in social problems. Those who have attempted to assess changes in such routine activities as reading habits, leisure activities, educational activities, patterns of family interactions, and the like, have commented on a variety of similar difficulties (e.g., Caplow et al., 1983). Thus, attempts to interpret changes in national aptitude scores (e.g., SAT scores) have been complicated by such factors as fluctuations in the composition of the student sample taking the exams (Wirtz, 1977). Attempts to make change comparisons regarding educational achievement based on the number of students earning high grades have been difficult where the assignment of grades for equivalent work may itself not be constant over time (Ohmer, Pollio, & Eison, 1986). Attempts to make change statements by comparing the cost of living for the poor over time have been complicated by the fact that available indexes are selective and fail to keep track of certain living costs that may be nonrandomly related to socioeconomic status (Innes De Neufville, 1975). Attempts to compare levels of helpfulness at different points in time have been made difficult by the limited and haphazard nature of the record base available (House & Wolf, 1978). In essence, attempts to keep track of the rate of activities have often varied over time. Definitions of the critical activities may well have been subject to flux. The upshot of these problems is that in many cases we cannot be certain to what degree change has taken place. Such methodological problems are not inevitable; it is simply that it is often difficult to ascertain after the fact the extent to which a particular case is free of the aforementioned problems.

The limits of post hoc assessment are now fairly well understood (Innes De Neufville, 1975; Yarrow, Campbell, & Burton, 1970), and the heightened awareness of measurement problems has led to increased methodological sophistication. There is now greater recognition of the importance of developing data bases that will allow for change assessments in the future. Shifts in practices of data collection have occurred that reflect that sophistication. More advanced ways of collecting information in a systematic, time-consistent fashion are now often employed. Intended to eliminate all difficulties in interpreting change, they have not. Instead these efforts have exposed a rich new set of methodological perplexities. This emergence of new methodological issues about change can be illustrated in some of the longitudinal work in the life span developmental area.

Methodological Issues in Assessing Change Across the Life Span

Like those who study social change, researchers who study person change across the life span have encountered interpretational difficulties when using the data at hand to assess change. For example, attempts have been made to draw conclusions about the changes that occur in individuals as they age by simply comparing people of different ages at a single point in time. But rather than providing reliable evidence of change, such studies have instead often highlighted the problems with these methods of assessing change (Baltes, 1968, 1979; Nydegger, 1981). Where attempts were made to measure intellectual deterioration with age, for example, what appeared to represent an age-related decline was found in part to reflect exposure to different educational experiences in cohorts born in different decades (Horn & Donaldson, 1976).

Increased sensitivity to the weaknesses of cross-sectional and other simple designs for advancing the understanding of person change has resulted in greater interest in more refined methodologies that appear able to provide more reliable information about individual change. Methodologies are now employed in which data collection over a span of years is planned in advance and provisions are made for the collection of information in a uniform manner over time (Block, 1971; Bloom, 1974; Costa & McCrae, 1980; Mednick, Harway, & Finello, 1984; Schaie, 1983). These methods include a variety of innovative techniques designed to enhance the accuracy of change comparisons, such as the use of relative comparisons (rather than attempting to make absolute judgments of change) or the use of different judges to make assessments of individuals at different life points (rather than using the same judges which may prejudice the comparisons). There is no question that these varied attempts to eliminate problems have contributed to progress in conceptualizing and understanding change. In particular, planning data collection in advance and making the collection procedures uniform have improved the quality and completeness of change-relevant information. However, even where high-quality data sets are in hand, there remain many difficulties in knowing if available evidence should be treated as an indication of change.

Consider, for example, the difficulties that arise from attempts to assess individual change by means of the individual's relative standing in a reference group. With this strategy, assessments of stability and change are based on the extent to which individual rankings within a cohort remain the same or change over a period of years (e.g., Block, 1971). This comparison of ranks is intended to overcome several problems. It is intended to avoid the difficulties of attempting to gauge the absolute amount of change on the basis of measures that can never be made fully reliable; thus, this method has the advantage of being less dependent on having measures that directly map onto the actual change. More importantly, it also attempts to overcome the problems raised by the fact that people engage in qualitatively different behaviors at different ages. But the method of judging change relative to the amount of change in a reference group introduces certain problems, even as it addresses others. With the rank-comparison method one has to abstract up from concrete behaviors to some dimension of comparison that is presumed to hold over time and across different kinds of behavior; theory-based choices must therefore be made about what constitutes the appropriate level for comparison for capturing the relevant events. Furthermore, certain sorts of change may be inadequately captured as a result of adopting the rank-comparison method. Upward or downward movement in the cohort as a whole may not be seen or, if detected, can add substantially to the interpretational problems (Kagan, 1980; Rubin, 1980). And, to the extent that members are subject to similar rates and directions of change, individual change may not be apparent or may not be easily disentangled from the change of others (Baltes et al., 1977). As Block (1977) has noted, questions of continuities and change are beset by methodological difficulties.

The failure of the rank-comparison method and similarly sophisticated methods of studying change to resolve fundamental issues concerning the scientific study of person change points to the irresolution of these issues in the field as a whole. Without doubt, difficult questions remain of how to operationalize change and how to conceptualize what constitutes true change (Gergen, 1977, 1980; Kagan, 1980; Nesselroade & Baltes, 1979). For example, how should one categorize psychological movement that, on the one hand, appears to follow a predictable trajectory and thus suggests a kind of sameness in the individual but, on the other hand, also clearly shows that the person is now at a different point than in the past, thus suggesting that the person has changed? Similarly, in trying to assess change and constancy in characteristics over the life span, investigators are still faced with the problem that people engage in quite different classes of behaviors at different ages. Adolescents often engage in behaviors that are different from those of adults; and even in cases where the behavior of adolescents and adults are highly similar, their meaning may be quite different (e.g., the same act of giggling on a first date that may be typical of adolescent behavior could represent a deterioration of social skills when carried out by an adult). As Moss and Susman (1980) point out, it is no easy matter to select a level of analysis for observations that will accurately measure and reflect underlying patterns of change and stability. Questions have been raised as to whether it is even possible to develop measures that are independent of a particular theory of what constitutes change (Brim & Kagan, 1980; Gergen, 1977; Kagan, 1980, 1984).

In addition to these general conceptual issues, there are a variety of quantitative issues that have remained problematic in the assessment of change. Numerically, it is still far from clear what would constitute the best or most appropriate measures of change in the life-span area. Indeed, as Bryk and Raudenbush (1987) have remarked, methodological problems have led to "a bewildering array of well-intentioned but misdirected suggestions about the design and analysis of research on human change" (p. 147). Many of the proposed methods of mathematically defining life-span change have come under criticism (Baltes et al., 1977). The problems with many commonly used statistical measures for assessing change have been enumerated by a variety of authors (Blomqvist, 1977; Cronbach & Furby, 1970; Dielman, 1983; Harris, 1963; Linn & Slinde, 1977; Nesselroade, 1983; Nesselroade & Reese, 1973; Plewis, 1985; Rogosa, Brand, & Zimowski, 1982). These include well-documented problems with the still common practice of relying on difference scores as evidence of change (Cronbach & Furby, 1970). Errors in measurement have been found to complicate the quantitative analysis of change. For example, because observed change over two occasions is often negatively correlated with the subject's initial status, the impact of errors on measured change may not be independent of initial position (Byrk & Raudenbush, 1987). Variability in responses has been found to create problems in change measurement. For example, on many psychological variables, variability tends to increase with age (Baltes, Reese, & Lipsitt, 1980), complicating attempts to make comparisons from one age to another. Substantial problems have also arisen because much of the work on change depends on looking at measures at two points in time (Furby, 1973; Labouvie, 1982), yet many of these measures were not designed for this purpose. As Bryk and Raudenbush have pointed out:

> Studies of change typically use tests that are developed to discriminate among individuals at a fixed point in time. Their adequacy for distinguishing the rate of change among individuals is rarely considered during the instrument design process. Further, statistical procedures routinely applied to these instruments, such as standardizing the scores to a common mean and variance over time, effectively eliminate the essence of individual growth. (1987, p. 147)

Furthermore, even when full recognition is given to the fact that two time points provide an inadequate basis for studying change and data have been collected on multiple occasions, researchers have typically analyzed the data as a series of separate designs with two time points (Bryk & Raudenbush, 1987). How to handle multiple occasions in the analysis of change remains an issue of some debate (Bryk & Raudenbush, 1987). There remains much disagreement on methodological specifics.

Researchers have also become sensitized to the problems of attrition, such as those that commonly occur when studying aging populations or other groups where there is likely to be much natural attrition (Baltes et al., 1977; Schaie, 1965). With longitudinal designs, the difficulties that selection strategies may cause in terms of regression toward the mean have become evident (Nesselroade, Stigler, & Baltes, 1980), and the subtle possibilities for rater and response bias over time have been analyzed (Block, 1971). In all, a sobering array of serious methodological questions has emerged from attempts to measure change across the life span.

Concern with comparable sorts of methodological issues has arisen in other areas where investigators are immersed in the measurement of change. In the social indicators field this is quite evident (Innes De Neufville, 1975; Rossi & Gilmartin, 1980). In evaluation work, concern with methodological issues involved in assessing program-related change has been prominent (cf. Cook & Campbell, 1979; Forehand, 1982; Nunnally, 1975; Tuchfeld, 1979). Researchers doing trend analysis and studying time series have articulated similar sorts of problems in the measurement of change (cf. Bauer, 1966; Glenn, 1970, 1976, 1980; Kessler & Greenberg, 1981; Taylor, 1980).

In sum, the study of change assessment has generated an extensive body of findings both about change and about the methodological problems connected with its measurement. As we have seen, an important outgrowth of this research has been the increasing recognition among researchers of the methodological problems likely to be encountered in any serious attempt to measure change. It has become fully evident that attempts to draw conclusions about change must be approached with considerable caution. The impact of this realization is apparent in the ways professional observers refer to their findings about change. On those occasions when researchers venture an estimate about change, their conclusions are typically couched in tentative terms and accompanied by some disclaimer regarding the inconclusiveness of the data. The possibly spurious nature of findings on change rarely goes unacknowledged in formal assessments.

The inescapable complications that arise in the course of formal assessment of change are not without their implications for intuitive judgments of change. On the face of it, intuitive judgers of change would seem to be hampered by a daunting array of problems as they confront their task. Do intuitive perceivers of change experience anything like the qualms expressed by their professional counterparts, as they arguably ought to? Without preempting the analysis offered in the following chapters, it is possible to note for now that the change judgments made by intuitive perceivers take on quite a different character from those made by professionals. In contrast to the cautiousness that marks formal assessment, intuitive judgments are often made with great alacrity and confidence. Laypeople frequently begin intuitive change assertions with phrases such as "I'm certain that . . . ," "I'm sure . . . ," "It's clear to me . . . . " Intuitive impressions of change are reported with little reluctance or uncertainty. The possibility that intuitive change judgments differ from formal assessments in important respects is intriguing and raises fundamental questions about the underlying processes that govern the intuitive interpretation of evidence about change. In light of the methodological difficulties that have become apparent in the formal assessment of change, the question of how informal change judgments come to be made with such eagerness and assurance will be a point of continuing interest throughout the chapters that follow.

Intuitive Change Judgments and the Impact of Change

As the points in the previous section suggest, the measurement of change can raise questions about how individuals perceive everyday changes—how people decide what has changed and how they overcome various difficulties in making these assessments. A substantial body of work on change has looked at change from the perspective of the individual, yet little of this work has been concerned with how people generate their impressions of change. The focus has largely been on the impact of change on the individual—how change feels to the person, how disruptive it is, what kinds of consequences it has for people's lives. Left open is the question of how people come to perceive these same changes.

Efforts to document change have usually been closely tied to an interest in understanding the impact of change on those experiencing them. A great deal of attention has been given to the question of how change affects us—an interest that has resulted in a substantial, though widely dispersed, literature concerned with analysis and interpretation of the possible impact of change. As we look at the literature linking measurements with impact, we return once again to intuitive judgments and to the question of their place in the experience of change. The literature reveals an unresolved tension between the attempt to move away from intuitive change judgments in the belief that they are poor reflections of real change and a vague awareness that the impact of change may sometimes be mediated by intuitive perceivers' impressions of change.

Widespread speculation about the potential effects of change can be seen in a variety of domains. For example, interest in changes in the family and family life has elicited a steady flow of commentary about the impact of such changes on people's lives (cf. Bernard, 1981; Kimmel, 1987; Seward, 1978; Somerville, 1982). Significant changes in the number of females in the workforce has sparked intense speculation about the impact of those changes (Bernard, 1984; Hobfall, 1986; Sales & Frieze, 1984), while changing patterns of employment in the workforce as a whole have prompted debate about how those changes are affecting individual lives (Glenn & Weaver, 1982; Kanungo, 1982). A focus on increases in crime, particularly in violent crime, has been accompanied by considerable discussion of the social impact of those changes (Russell, 1984). Recognition that patterns of sexuality and sexual behavior may be changing has led to speculation about the effects that will follow from those changes (Chilman, 1979).

Across these different domains, several themes have emerged from the concern with the impact of change. The impact of social change has often been looked at in terms of the kinds of fears and concerns that laypeople express. The rate at which change is occurring has been treated as an important determinant of reactions to change (Lauer, 1974; Lauer & Lauer, 1976; Lauer & Thomas, 1976), with consideration being given to the ways that the rate of change may contribute to social ills and to psychological problems of various sorts (Bellak, 1975; Keniston, 1965; Toffler, 1971). Researchers have also concerned themselves with issues of control, particularly with the question of how the feeling of control may mediate reactions to and fears of change (Lauer & Lauer, 1976; Watson, 1976). There has been an accompanying concern with issues of dislocation, feelings of powerlessness, and the sense of alienation (Faunce, 1968; Finestone, 1976; Keniston, 1965; Marris, 1986). Sometimes concern with impact has involved looking at change at the individual level, as seen, for example, in attempts to relate the number of changes taking place in a particular individual's life with their impact on his or her psychological and physical well-being (Dohrenwend & Dohrenwend, 1974, 1981). Other work has addressed the impact of social change in a global sense. Here the focus has been on the combined consequences of various sorts of social change, with researchers posing questions about how social change in general is having an impact (Campbell, 1980; Campbell & Converse, 1972; Meyrowitz, 1985).

The interest in psychological impact of change is represented in its most vivid form in Toffler's popularized and well-publicized analysis of impact. In his several works on the topic (1971, 1980), Toffler has written at length on the negative consequences of rapid social change. To highlight the supposed impact of social change, Toffler juxtaposes various findings that purport to show a rapid rate of change in American society with evidence of aberrations in current social behavior so that the latter then appear to be responses to the rapid rate of change. Summarizing the rapid change, Toffler writes: "Western society for the past 300 years has been caught up in a fire storm of change. This storm, far from abating, now appears to be gathering force. Change sweeps through the highly industrialized countries with waves of ever accelerating speed and unprecedented impact" (1970, p. 9). Throughout his book Toffler then describes the impact this change has on the individual:

> [The individual] experiences a deepening sense of confusion and uncertainty. Caught in the turbulent flow of change, called upon to make significant, rapid-fire life decisions, he feels not simply intellectual bewilderment, but disorientation at the level of personal values. As the pace of change quickens, this confusion is tinged with self-doubt, anxiety, and fear. He grows tense, tires easily. He may fall ill. As the pressures relentlessly mount, tension shades in to irritability, anger, and sometimes, senseless violence. (1971, p. 363)

Comments like Toffler's often approach hyperbole, yet his broad assumptions about the connection between actual change and psychological consequences are not greatly different from those held by investigators who have more cautiously described the changes taking place (Bellak, 1975; DeVos, 1976; Harris, 1973). In analyzing the impact of change, researchers (e.g., Russell, 1984) can often be seen moving interpretationally back and forth between change evidence culled from their own sensitive scientific assessment (evidence, for example, that points to a moderate increase in crime) and the statements about change made by laypersons during that same period (for example, fears about crime being out of control); the magnitude of such fears is assumed to be a function of the rate of change uncovered by researchers. Similarly, having themselves come to a clearer understanding of the actual magnitude of change taking place in gender roles, researchers have sometimes taken as a given that people's expressions of concern about changes in gender roles are in direct response to that rate of change (Eakins, 1983; Lewis & O'Brien, 1987; Russell, 1983). Or, guided by their own work on possible increases in the incidence of family violence in recent years, researchers have speculated about the ways in which the supposed level of change has resulted in the heightened fears now seen;

it has been suggested that fears about this change lie behind calls for social programs that would deal with this problem of worsening proportions (Lystad, 1986; Pillemer & Wolf, 1986).

The common assumption that perceivers' assessments of the rate of change correspond to actual change is surprising when considered in light of the rationale for concerted efforts to supplant informal judgments with more reliable formal assessment. Formal measures have been of interest precisely because informal speculations were themselves suspect. Given the possibility of wide discrepancies between the results of formal assessments and those of informal judgments, the formal assessments may well be uninformative about how much change people perceive. As things stand, the exact nature of the relationship between actual change and perceptions of change remains unclear, but we shall see in the chapters below that there is ample reason to doubt that informal judgments map directly on to actual rates of change. To the extent that informal assessments hold the greater validity for perceivers, intuitive judgments will often mediate between change as it actually occurs and whatever responses people have to change (see Ryff, 1984, for an interesting discussion of this point from a phenomenological perspective).

Intuitive Change Judgments and the Study of Social Perception

Despite the professional emphasis on formal change assessment, the majority of conclusions drawn about change are not formal assessments, but rather informal judgments. Those aspects of modern life for which a formal assessment has been carried out represent a very small subset of the topics about which change assertions are made. Most attempts to formally document change have been limited to large-scale change, to change in social institutions and social practices. Yet, intuitive change judgments are made about all sorts of local, ordinary, and individual events. Formal assessments of change are sometimes available for the political stances of a public figure, such as a president or a member of congress; the same is generally not true for private individuals. Still, assertions are often made about changes in political (or other) views of spouses, parents, friends, employers, and the like. Likewise, conclusions about change in one's neighborhood, local schools, or community are made with great frequency, but typically in the absence of parallel results from scientific assessment. Even lacking access to relevant formal information, laypeople express strong opinions about things having changed. Intuitive impressions are a very common source of change conclusions.

We have seen that those interested in change have not generated a body of work seeking to account for the processes by which intuitive change judgments are made.*

---

*The kind of subtlety and richness of analysis underlying the explication of methodological niceties has often been missing in the consideration of informal assessments of change. By their comments, some in this area seem to have regarded change judgments as epiphenomenal—to the extent that change judgments occur at all they are of relatively little importance because they have little impact and few consequences. Others seemed to have assigned a

We might turn instead to research explicitly concerned with how people intuitively perceive their social environment for an understanding of intuitive perceptions of change. The most extensive literature devoted to the analysis of intuitive judgments is the large body of work on social perception. This research on the perception of the social environment has been enormously productive, having led to extensive work carried out under such rubrics as person perception, attribution processes, and social cognition. What once consisted of simple demonstrations of the effects of trait expectancies and the like has developed into sophisticated and increasingly technical analyses of underlying factors that account for social judgments. Throughout, there has been very much of an emphasis on process, that is, on questions of how people think about and use information in ways that account for the sorts of judgments they make and the conclusions they draw.

Given the inherent concern for intuitive perception reflected in this work and the broad reach of this concern, it would seem likely that the interest in social perception would have naturally encompassed the study of change judgments, but this has generally not been the case. What we find, instead, is that the major focus of this work has been on the problem of explaining how people go about finding stability in their social environment. In particular, we see that the field has adopted a predominant working assumption that social perception operates in ways that lead to stability.

Early theorists as well as more recent students of the perception process have focused on stability. Asch wrote early about social perception as operating in ways that emphasized stability:

> Out of the diverse aspects of an individual we form a view of him as a particular kind
> of person with relatively enduring qualities. . . . Ordinarily our view of a person is
> highly unified. Experience confronts us with a host of actions in others, following each
> other in relatively unordered succession. In contrast to this unceasing movement and
> change in our observation we emerge with a product of considerable order and stability.
> (Asch, 1952, p. 206–207)

Heider, too, referred to the fact that social perceivers operate under an "ideal of the invariance of the behavior of the other person" (1958, p. 55), a belief that leads to stability in impressions because the perceiver assumes that commitment to an early impression is justified by the stability in the characteristics of individuals. Recent authors have reiterated the stability theme: "The most general and encompassing lay theory of behavior—so broadly applied that it might more aptly be termed a 'meta'—is that behavior is caused primarily by the enduring and consistent dispositions of the actors" (Nisbett & Ross, 1980, p. 31). Elsewhere these authors

---

somewhat greater role to these judgments, but have not viewed them as in need of, or even amenable to, empirical investigation. In some cases, intuitive judgments of change seem to have been regarded as transparently simple and predictably errorful and thus there has been little about them that has been seen in need of systemic explication and analysis. Their characteristics are believed to be self-evident, as are their problems (i.e., laypeople are simply poor at making change judgments and little is to be said beyond that basic fact). For illustrations of these points see Lauer (1977) and Zollschan and Hirsch (1976).

refer to perceivers as having a "superordinate goal of the importance of stability to beliefs and belief systems" (p. 191).

The extent to which stability has been emphasized is apparent throughout much of the work on social perception. In their processing of information about the social environment, perceivers are said to be guided by an underlying search for stability and regularities (Monson, Keel, Stephens, & Genung, 1982; Nisbett & Ross, 1980; Schneider, Hastorf, & Ellsworth, 1979). It is believed that perceivers seek to form coherent, stable impressions of others (Hamilton, Katz, & Leirer, 1980). Impressions are assumed to be formed quickly and, once formed, to remain stable and be resistant to change (Cantor & Mischel, 1982; Nisbett & Ross, 1980; Schneider, Hastorf, & Ellsworth, 1979; Nisbett & Ross, 1980; Schneider et al., 1979). Early impressions and prior beliefs are believed to channel the gathering, processing, and interpretation of later information, so that new information is interpreted in ways that are consistent with earlier information (Bell, Wicklund, Manko, & Larkin, 1976; Carlston, 1980; Hayden & Mischel, 1976; Rothbart, Evans, & Fulero, 1979; Snyder & Cantor, 1979). Perceivers are assumed to rely on the types of cognitive categories that lend stability to impressions, such as dispositional trait categories (Cantor & Mischel, 1979) and encoding strategies (e.g., person schemas; Taylor & Crocker, 1981; Wyer & Srull, 1981) that lend stability to impressions. Recall and reconstruction of prior information have been interpreted to occur in ways that create and maintain a view of others and self as stable (Greenwald, 1980; Snyder & Uranowitz, 1978). The search for invariance has been assumed to be powerful; the perceiver not only focuses on those aspects of the social environment that are stable but even constructs stability where it does not exist. Perceivers are believed to be sufficiently imbued with a stability-oriented world view that they often reinterpret, nonstable events to conform to a stability model. Thus perceivers' readiness to see stability leads to seeing it even when the evidence for it is not compelling: "despite the fact that people sometimes behave in inconsistent and unpredictable ways, we form remarkably stable impressions of what other people are like" (Crocker, Hannah, & Weber, 1983, p. 55).

The extent to which stability has been emphasized is also seen in the use of a stability metatheme to interpret otherwise puzzling effects in social perception. In explaining why perceivers persist in seeing traits when the evidence for traits is so weak, Mischel (1968, 1973) argued that the perception of traitlike impressions was the result of perceivers' tendency to construct stability:

> How does one reconcile our shared perception of continuity with the equally impressive evidence that on virtually all of our dispositional measures of personality substantial changes occur in the characteristics of the individual longitudinally over time and, even more dramatically, across seemingly similar settings cross-sectionally? . . . In my appraisal, the overall evidence from many sources . . . shows the human mind to function like an extraordinarily effective reducing valve that creates and maintains the perception of continuity even in the face of perpetual observed changes in actual behavior. Often this cognitive construction, while not arbitrary, is only very tenuously related to the phenomena that are construed. (1973, p. 1012)

In other words, Mischel held that although stability and consistency can no longer be assumed to be fundamental attributes of people, without a doubt they can be assumed to be fundamental attributes of person perception.[†] In accounting for puzzling attribution effects, researchers have posited a stability bias to explain why perceivers tend to weigh person information more heavily than would be expected on the basis of what is known about the power of situational determinants. Thus the tendency to attribute causes to persons, what Ross (1977) has termed the "fundamental attribution error," has been described as an indication of a stability bias in perceivers. According to a standard treatise on the topic (Taylor & Crocker, 1981), the fundamental attribution error represents "a bias toward perceiving stability and consistency in the person's behavior" (p. 120). Puzzling findings from research on how people react to discrepancies in another person's behavior have been interpreted as further evidence of a stability bias (Crocker et al., 1983; Hayden & Mischel, 1976). The fact that perceivers often ignore, downplay, or reinterpret discrepancies has been assumed to reflect the workings of a stability orientation in the perceiver.

Through much of this work a formidable view of the preeminence of stability in social perception has taken root—a view in which stability has been assumed to reflect the essence of the social perception process and for which compelling evidence has been thought to exist. It is not surprising, then, that change judgments have received only limited study because change judgments take on the appearance of unlikely events when the intuitive perceiver's ongoing interpretation of the social environment is believed to be stability bound. In effect, questions that might have been raised about the processes by which perceivers infer change have been rendered irrelevant by the fact that people are not even expected to look for change. As a consequence, the kind of detailed attention to process that has marked the work on other aspects of social perception has rarely been applied to the study of change judgments.

Against the general backdrop of stability work, only a scattering of studies have investigated the processes by which intuitive judgments of change are made. Wagenaar and Timmers (1979) studied how people go about judging exponential growth by providing subjects with pictorial information showing the growth of duckweed on ponds, a natural situation in which an exponential growth rate occurs. Agostinelli, Sherman, Fazio, and Hearst (1986) investigated the process of judging change by adding and deleting features in a complex visual stimulus to determine whether people are better at noticing changes when features of a stimulus set are added or when they are eliminated. Shaw and Pittenger (1977) studied intuitive judgments of changes in aging faces by asking whether such judgments are chiefly a result of information in the stimulus array or a result of detailed higher-order processing on the part of the perceivers (see also Todd, Mark, Shaw & Pittenger,

---

[†]Mischel's assertion about the lack of stability in traits aroused great controversy (e.g., Epstein, 1977; Epstein & O'Brien, 1985) and in recent years he has somewhat modified his initial position. For our purposes what is interesting is that the controversy was brought about by the claim that people are not stable and not because of the assertion that perceptions are stability oriented. Few, if any, have challenged the idea that social perception would lead to a stability bias.

1980). Mackie and Allison (1987) investigated the effects of a group attribution error on the perception of group change. Conway and Ross (1984, 1985) investigated people's use of information when making judgments of self-change in a context where subjects had just undergone an improvement regimen. Reinke, Holmes, and Harris (1985) and Ryff (1982, 1984) conducted descriptive studies of the intuitive impressions of change people form about themselves over the course of several years. Although such studies point to intriguing directions for the study of change judgments, they stand as rare exceptions to the dominant stability orientation in the social perception literature.

The social perception literature and the issue of its emphasis on stability will be considered again in Chapter 4 when the literature is scrutinized for process-related findings that may be germane to the study of change judgments. There we will find that some lines of work on stability provide possible insights into the process of judging change once the basic findings in the literature are separated from their traditional (but, as we shall see, unnecessary) stability interpretations.

In the present chapter we have seen that much research has been directed at the separate tasks of understanding change and understanding social perception. Yet, despite the prolific work in each of these areas, there has been very little work that brings together the content and process to look at change from the perspective of the intuitive perceiver. The intent of the present work is to begin bridging this gap.

Chapter 3

A Framework for the Study of Change Judgments

The chief aim of this chapter is to lay out a framework for the selection and analysis of problems in the study of everyday change judgments. This framework developed out of three general assumptions about the kinds of change judgments that are important to understand and about the underlying character of the intuitive perceiver's approach to change. In the following section, these assumptions are discussed, along with their implications for the choice of a suitable approach to the topic of informal change judgments. The framework will then be outlined.

Some Orienting Assumptions

The present program assumes that the study of change judgments should be approached by analyzing change assessment, not as a process to be understood in the ideal, but as a form of judgment characterized by the use of across-time information in the real world. The interest here is not so much in how people use statistical reasoning to infer change under ideal conditions but rather in what they conclude about change when faced with the kinds of fragmentary information ordinarily available for comparing the past with the present. Thus, emphasis will be placed on understanding the character of everyday change-related information—what's available for different times and for different areas of interest—and then using that knowledge to investigate the change impressions that arise under these different information conditions.

Second, the interest here is not so much in studying what inferences of change would be like when people know beforehand that they are going to be asked to assess change as in analyzing what change judgments will be like when they arise in an unpremeditated way. A basic assumption is that most intuitive concerns with change are not preplanned and do not occur with the kind of foreknowledge that goes into formal assessment. It is assumed that concern with change often does not precede the gathering of relevant information and does not occur prior to the events having taken place; instead, interest in change often develops after events have already taken place, or after something has happened that engenders a retrospective interest in the issue of change. The contention here will be that many of the distinctive features of intuitive change judgments are a consequence of their unpremeditated character.

A third assumption shaping the choice of research questions is that intuitive judgers are often opportunistic in using information that presents itself when they are forming impressions of change. The use of information when looking for change is not expected to be constrained by a strict adherence to conditions in which commensurability of information is assured. It is assumed that there is a tendency on the part of perceivers to view each item of information without suspicion and not to treat it as a datum that must first be scrutinized for its suitability to enter into meaningful comparisons with other data.

The foregoing assumptions have clear implications for which kinds of approaches to the study of change judgments will be likely to prove fruitful and which will not. Given that change judgments basically involve difference perception (i.e., that things are different now than in the past), it might seem useful to adapt the traditional framework and procedures for investigating difference perception in the laboratory—namely, the framework of psychophysics that is commonly used to study just noticeable differences (*jnds*). In psychophysical analyses, the problem of difference perception is framed in terms of perceivers' sensitivity to subtle differences in directly experienced discrete stimuli or objects, and the focus is on the factors that influence whether two physical objects are judged to be the same or different along some predetermined dimension, usually that of physical magnitude. The task for the perceiver in these studies is highly circumscribed. Typically all of the comparison information is provided by the experimenter and all of it is available in the same brief experimental session. Over short intervals, participants subjectively compare the magnitude of an earlier-presented stimulus with the magnitude of the stimulus currently presented. Such work has been important in uncovering interesting perceptual regularities in the judgment of differences.

Although the task of inferring change in everyday life is like the traditional jnd task in that it involves the detection of differences, the task of judging change in the everyday world has crucial features that prevent it from being readily assimilated to the psychophysical paradigm. This is perhaps best seen by considering examples of intuitive change judgments: the perception that child abuse has increased, or that family life in America has changed, or that life was once simpler than it is today. (1) In such cases, the information people use and how they use it is likely to be less a function of the mere detection of differences and more a function of how change-related information is gathered, stored, and interpreted. The making of such inferences of change involves some sort of sifting and comparing of evidence, the nature and origin of which is not immediately apparent (e.g., what sorts of information might be drawn upon in an intuitive assessment of change in families?). (2) Unlike the case of the psychophysical task, the change comparison in everyday life covers long, perhaps even ambiguous, time frames (e.g., which of the various time periods in the past serves as the implicit reference point when we assert that life was once simpler? *Is* there a specific reference point?). (3) Some of the comparison periods that figure in intuitive change judgments probably have not been directly experienced by the person making the inference (e.g., we may not ourselves have been around in those so-called "simpler" times). (4) The information about the past in everyday judgments probably comes to the perceiver from different sources and in different forms than the information about the present (e.g., our sources of knowledge about child abuse in the distant past may be quite different from our sources for the present). (5) Even the metric of comparison used in intuitive change inferences is not self-evident (e.g., when life is referred to as having once been simpler, along what dimension is that simplicity presumed to have changed?). Factors such as these suggest a situation whose complexity goes beyond that of the perception of differences in discrete, readily available objects.

With the more complicated situation presented by everyday change judgments, the sorts of questions that are of interest shift in focus. Here we become concerned with questions about the sorts of information available for the different comparison periods, about how well informal "facts" represent past actions and events, about how people choose from among the wide variety of possible points of comparison, and about how perceivers make sense of the heterogeneous information about trends that is available. For everyday change judgments to be fully explicated, the study of change judgments requires a model that goes beyond the simple perception of difference to take into account the more varied nature of the information as well as the less controlled and more fluid comparison situation.

This concern for understanding intuitive judgments in terms of the less circumscribed, more ecologically varied conditions of everyday life has precedence in work in other areas of social perception. In recent years, much of the early research on person perception has come under criticism for having been based on an impoverished model of person perception, a model that treated person judgments as simply the result of discrete judgments of distinct items of information and that failed to recognize person perception as a process that is extended over time (Hastie, Ostrom, Ebbesen, Wyer, Hamilton, & Carlston, 1980; Higgins, Herman, & Zanna, 1981). In the person perception area, this belated recognition of person perception as a complex process has been fruitful, resulting in a shift in and broadening of issues and models underlying much of the current work (Higgins & Bargh, 1987; Wyer & Srull, 1984). The study of change judgments is also an area that is likely to be best understood through a broader, more ecologically oriented approach.

The broad-based, multifocused approach to the study of change judgments that will be outlined here draws on ideas from the various areas where broadened approaches have previously been found to be useful. Paralleling the heruistics approach and work on decision theory processes (Einhorn & Hogarth, 1978, 1981; Hogarth, 1987; Kahneman, Slovic, & Tversky, 1982), the present approach will attempt to understand the everyday rules used in analyzing information in different kinds of change judgments. The Gibsonian focus on the way the environment structures information will also figure in the present analysis (Baron, 1980; McArthur & Baron, 1983), although the concerns here depart from the Gibsonian emphasis by including a focus on the ways in which limited and sometimes impoverished environmental representations of past events shape change impressions. Although

the environment clearly provides much information to be "picked up," the peculiarities of the available information about the present and past may seriously complicate
the process of making change judgments. Paralleling the focus found in social cognition work (Wyer & Srull, 1984), an interest will be shown in how the processing of
information contributes to the shape and veracity of knowledge; here the concern
will be with the consequences for change inferences of relying on personal knowledge about the present and the past as the basis of change-related facts.

Four Basic Themes in the Study of Change

The discussion presented thus far can be brought together and systematized by lay-
ing out four themes that have guided the investigations reported in the chapters that
follow. Each theme is designed to capture a factor or family of factors that govern
how everyday change judgments are made. The themes may be stated as follows: (1)
Informal change judgments depend crucially on the "facts" about different times that
come to the perceiver from outside sources—that is, on the pool of outside information that is typically available for the present and the past. The historical and cultural factors governing what information is typically available in the environment
will play an important role in the formation of change judgments. (2) Being comparisons of information about the past and the present, change judgments are dependent
on how perceivers make sense of their own experiences of change-related events. In
other words, personal factors, including (often idiosyncratic) personal histories and
reconstructed memories, govern what information is typically available to and used
by the person who contemplates change. (3) Different types of intuitive change judgments call for different types and uses of information; and particular kinds of change
judgments will prove problematic to the degree that the environment induces them
without inducing attention to the appropriate types and uses of information. An
analysis of simple and complex change judgment tasks will indicate the information
components relevant to particular kinds of change judgments and will direct attention to whether those information components are salient in available information.
(4) How and when intuitive change judgments occur will depend critically on the
perceiver's intuitive definition of what constitutes change. An understanding of this
definition and its effects on the perceiver's readiness to see change in various contexts will be important in accounting for the range of contexts in which change is
judged to have occurred.

It will be noted that three of the four themes stated above concern the role of information in the intuitive judgment of change. Often in the study of inferences the
focus has been primarily on the processes by which people use information (e.g.,
Wyer & Srull, 1984) and only secondarily on the character of the information itself.
In the present approach, the information will frequently take center stage. Indeed,
it is the unique character of the informal information base that may account for
many features of change judgments—why, for example, certain overstated informal
conclusions about social change occur with great regularity and why informal
change conclusions deviate in regular ways from those that arise out of formal
assessment where commensurability of information is assured.

Knowing something of the facts themselves as well as their comparability will provide an indication of the change judgments that are likely to arise. In the case of a formal assessment, for example, much is known about the comparison information that serves as the basis for conclusions about change. Not only is the nature of the information usually stated explicitly in describing the basis for a specific change conclusion but it generally adheres to a predictable form. Across time, information is gathered in such a way as to ensure its comparison value. Events are measured in the same way over time so that information from different times is in comparable numeric form. The information does not have to be retrieved from memory because it is recorded in some written form. Thus, in the case of formal assessment the data have known qualities, including a known degree of reliability. In the case of intuitive judgments, the pool of potential information, though less well known, is no less important. Just as formal assessments are shaped by the information on which they are based, intuitive judgments are likely to be shaped by the information on which they rest. It is important then to look at the kinds of everyday comparison information that ordinary perceivers have available for forming impressions of change about events in their lives.

In the sections on information that follow, the change-related information provided by the environment is first considered and then attention is turned to an analysis of comparison information that is derived primarily from the perceiver's personal experience and is thus shaped by perceiver processing. In each case specific examples will be cited to illustrate how informal information provides the materials out of which change impressions emerge. The discussion as a whole will serve as an introduction to the questions that are the focus of research reported in later chapters in the book.

Theme 1: Information that Comes to the Perceiver

In many areas of change assessment some of the most interesting questions involve the ways in which the information array is shaped by various forces before it even reaches the individual making the change judgment. Thus, an approach that treats environmentally generated information about the past and present as initially independent of the individual judger's personal experience will have value in suggesting possible sources of the all-important differences between past and present information.

As a way of introducing the environmental information issue, it is useful to begin with a simple example. Consider the case of someone making a change inference about the quality of motion pictures having deteriorated. Someone might remark that movies in the 1980s are not of the same caliber as movies made in the 1930s (e.g., "they just don't make movies like they used to"). In order to understand this change judgment, it will be important to know what the environment provides to the perceiver in the way of relevant data and to look at how the peculiarities of those data might shape the resulting impression of change. In the case of movies, it is probable that certain aspects of the information transmitted by the environment become altered or even lost with the passage of time, resulting in essentially incommensurable sets of comparison data for different periods. In the case of movies, those films from the 1930s that are currently available for comparison will have been highly selected for their lasting viewer appeal, and hence will no longer be representative of the population of 1930s movies as a whole. Marketplace forces operate such that for the past we are likely to have available not only a smaller information set but also a more select, and perhaps more uniform, one as well. The possible consequences for change impressions are obvious: If the "better" movies are selected from the past, a change – a deterioration – may be perceived in the overall quality of movies. Likewise, if the data set is more uniform for the past than the present, movies today may be perceived as having become less consistent in quality. Thus, the pattern of the data preserved by the social environment may encourage or provoke certain conclusions about change on the part of the perceiver.

Consider another example. When the claim is made that people in our society are no longer as helpful as they once were, it is reasonable to consider such a claim in light of the "facts" about helpfulness in the past and the present that would be available to intuitive perceivers. The available information is likely to be in some form other than actual statistics on levels of helpfulness. Much of the information about helpfulness may be of the anecdotal or incident-based variety, with the information often emphasizing people's failures to help others. Furthermore, that information may often emphasize present incidents where people failed to help whereas past failures to help may less often be reported in present accounts. The asymmetrical nature of the available information is likely to shape the resulting interpretations of change in levels of helpfulness.

These brief examples illustrate the way in which an analysis of environmental information might proceed. The approach emphasizes uncovering the way data for the past and the present are made available by the environment. Analyzing the data characteristics in this way, particularly in terms of the potential complexities and ambiguities in the data, will not only indicate some of the difficulties that must be surmounted for veridical assessments of change to occur but also provide an indication of the limits likely to be imposed on intuitive judgments by the kinds of information available.

By applying analogous analyses to concrete situations whenever possible, the information conditions that hold in specific cases of interest can be understood. Thus, attention to the characteristics of the information "out there " in specific cases is likely to be enlightening for understanding change claims. When political beliefs are perceived as having changed in recent years, an analysis of the nature of the cues in the environment about political preferences would be an important step in anticipating the form such claims will take. When it is said that heroes are different now relative to the past, the nature of the existing information from which people could draw conclusions will give an indication of the range of change impressions that could occur. The fact that teenagers are often perceived as more disrespectful now than in the past and that this conclusion is recurrent from generation to generation highlights the importance of taking into account what is knowable about levels of respect from one period to another. When claims are made that people change when they become famous, an analysis of the information in the environment about celebrities before and after they move into the public eye may provide insight into such conclusions. Through such analyses, one can begin to characterize the information in individual cases and relate the structure of that information to the outcomes of the change judgment task.

Attempts to identify the structure of the environmental information could be organized by (1) topic area, (2) time, or (3) source. Beginning with topic area, one could try to ascertain the completeness of accounts for particular areas of interest in change and find out what features are systematically left out of the accounts. One might, for example, ask what details of information now exist about the past for groups and individuals, for public versus private events, for attitudes versus behavior, and so forth. If the concern were with judging change in group performance, one might examine how current group behavior is reported in comparison with how group behavior is reported for past times: Is information about the diversity within earlier groups or organizations retained and, if so, how is this information about past diversity conveyed? For example, do we receive information about diversity in entering college freshmen classes in earlier years and, if so, in what form is this information communicated? Is the information we have about the past likely to be about the typical member of earlier groups, or perhaps about the best member, rather than about the range of members in terms of their skills, characteristics, and performance? Which aspects of day-to-day behavior are likely to be highlighted in the available information? Are there consistent differences in what we know about past public activities versus past private activities? For example, are we likely to have less information about the private conduct of members of Congress in the past, and perhaps more about their voting records, than we have for current members of Congress? If such area-related asymmetries in information do exist, one could expect certain kinds of change judgments to be made—for example, about change in the propriety of legislators' conduct.

Questions generated by a focus on topic area could also be asked about the nature of information that would be available about topics that are less salient. If past attitudes rather than actions are of interest, how would details about underlying attitudes be represented? Would past attitudinal stances be represented at all in current accounts? If fears existed in the past about child safety, what remnants of information about these past attitudes would exist in the information we have today? What information would be available about prior impressions of the world as a complex and unpredictable place? Questions can also be asked about records of mundane areas and events. What information would still be available, for example, about prior levels of boredom in the workplace? Is information regarding the absence of events preserved as well as information about events that took place? Is information about times when little was going on available for comparison? As these examples are intended to suggest, organizing questions by topic in this fashion could be useful in uncovering crucial features of change-related information in particular areas.

The identification of questions about the information base can also proceed by focusing on the passage of time as a factor shaping and limiting the information available from outside sources. Some characteristics of the loss of change-relevant information are likely to be predictable from knowing the length of time intervening between the past comparison events and their present counterparts. The greater the passage of time, the more fragmentary and more selective the information about the past is likely to become. The information available about past political life may be increasingly condensed with each passing decade and may be more likely to be conveyed in terms of certain symbolic images or events than in terms of information about day-to-day activities. In the area of education, the level of detail in the ordinarily available information about what learning was like in earlier schools and about the nature of early classroom experiences will likely become increasingly limited with the passage of time. The information that would be available about disaffection in families during our grandparents' generation could well be different from that available about disaffection in our own generation or that of our parents. In sum, the information about the distant past that is made available to perceivers by the environment may be smaller in amount, less representative of diversity, or substantially different in form than the information about the present. As these examples suggest, organizing the analysis of information in terms of how long ago the events occurred is likely to be useful for understanding intuitive judgments of change.

Questions about information could also focus on identifying particular environmental sources and characterizing how those outside sources structurally represent and convey information for the period or topic in question. Among the different sources that provide change-related information about the past, some are current sources conveying information about past times (e.g., current news reports referring to earlier events, weather reports reporting earlier averages, historical books and documentaries), whereas others are sources from that time (e.g., clippings from newspapers, class yearbooks, personal letters, archival documents). Current sources about the past are likely to present information that is selected for its relevance to present concerns, whereas past sources about the past are likely to selectively preserve information that was of concern in the past or that was projected to be of concern in the future. More generally, outside sources will differ in numerous ways in terms of the features of the past that they highlight. Some will highlight average information and typical events, and some will provide cues to prior variability or diversity, whereas others will focus on extreme cases or on one tail of some distribution of prior events. Some sources will provide detailed information about actual behavior or events in the past, perhaps even in direct numeric form. Others will provide information primarily in the form of conclusions, without any clear specification of the data on which they were based.

An analysis of sources will be useful not only in indicating those aspects of the past for which information is transmitted to the present, but also in identifying those features that go unrepresented in information sources. To take a simple example, old photographs are available that preserve something of the visual character of cities in earlier times, whereas information about, say, odors, noises, and pollution levels will not be so directly represented. This makes possible a more immediate sense of the visual changes in urban life than of how the levels of noxious odors or noise may have changed. In many sources, the absence of certain kinds of information may be routine. For example, information about past outcomes are likely to be more available than information about developments that led to the outcomes: the fact that wars were won or lost may be more available than information about the individual campaigns, steps, or setbacks that culminated in victory or defeat. In government affairs, information about final decisions may be more available than evidence about any uncertainty that existed prior to the decision. The individual political compromises that are so often critical to the formation of a political system may be conspicuously represented as faits accomplis, or even as inevitable outcomes of rational deliberations, while the ambiguities and fortuities that routinely mark political processes in such cases may go unrecorded in all but the most esoteric sources.

Joining together area, time, and source, one can begin to identify systematic differences in the structure and availability of information, and to envision the implications of these differences for intuitive change judgments arising out of various informational contexts. Consider the seemingly different cases of judging changes in the weather and in the performance of a sports figure. Although different in many respects, the two cases are similar in that information about the past is regularly provided along with the information about the present. As a part of weather reports, we are reminded of the average and record temperature for this date in the past; as we watch an athlete's performance on television, commentators routinely provide us with details about how well the player has performed in the past. Yet cases such as these are unusual in the extent to which they include detailed past information for comparison. In other areas the relevant information about the past is neither cited as regularly nor made as publicly accessible to the intuitive judge of change. For example, a politician's day-to-day fluctuations in mood, behavior, and performance may become visible only once that person comes into the public eye, with prior fluctuations not being reported in the same structured way as are past fluctuations in a sports figure's performances. In the nightly news reports covering incidents of crime, past comparison information may not be structured into the presentation or be regularly reported. Such situations mean that intuitive perceivers of change will often be operating under markedly different informational contexts. The sports fan who would resist concluding that an athlete's skills have dramatically improved on the basis of one outstanding performance may nonetheless accede to conclusions about the rapidly worsening problem of crime upon hearing of one particularly gruesome murder.

However, even in the relatively favorable cases such as weather and sports, where relevant past information *is* often provided, the available information may be far from complete. It is often a highly condensed summary, and what is highlighted in the summary can vary considerably. Sometimes summaries present relevant comparison information in the form of averages, as would be the case in the reporting of a baseball player's past batting average. Sometimes a summary presents reference information in the form of extremes: in New England in the last decade the comparison point for every winter storm is the blizzard of 1978. Thus, change inferences, even in generally favorable information conditions, may be expected to be sensitive to such variables as the particular forms in which information is summarized by the environment.

In other information contexts, the information for the past is likely to be available in original nonsummarized form. This might be the case for old television episodes, songs from the past, and earlier movies. On television reruns each individual episode is typically shown in its entirety. Because the episodes occur in original, complete form — as opposed to some abstract summary — the information they convey may offer the impression of being quite complete and of not having been selected. Despite the highly selected nature of what is shown in reruns, we may come to view these vivid, individually complete examples as indicative of television episodes in the past and perhaps even as indicative of what life was like during the pst period portrayed in the episodes.

In still other judgment contexts, the form of available information for the past is neither that of raw but selected data nor that of summarized but simplifying numbers. Rather, the available information takes the form of narrative summaries or written conclusions. For example, we are often exposed to capsule summaries of what life was supposedly like in particular decades (in the "turbulent 1960s" or the "Me Decade of the 1970s"). Such "snapshot" summaries purport to represent the essence of earlier periods (e.g., summaries of the sort found in books like Peck's [1985] *Uncovering the Sixties*). What is highlighted in the narrative summaries can be either concrete or quite abstract, but in either case it is highly culled and the overall summary is often so grandly thematic that its relation to clear numeric or frequency data is neither straightforward nor self-evident. Again, the way the information is presented may belie the degree of selectivity involved.

In summary, the information about the past that is reported and perceived cannot represent every relevant aspect of what has occurred, and so must represent only some subset of past events. What is represented in this subset will naturally be different in different cases. What is highlighted will often be the most frequent instances of past events or the most typical or average of them. But other times what is represented will be extreme instances, symbolic instances (e.g., student deaths at Kent State), "best" instances (e.g., outstanding performance of a singer), most "talked about" instances (e.g., bizarre serial murders), most elaborated upon instances, most understandable instances, or instances that were the most important to the sources reporting the events. The general availability of information can vary greatly, as can the structure of information and its translatability into numeric data. The characteristics of the resultant information are likely to be an important determinant of the change judgments that are made.

This first section has been intended to stress the importance of treating change judgments not in the abstract but rather as grounded in particular, often problematic, bases of environmental information. Change judgments cannot be understood without examining the nature of the environmental information available and analyzing the kind of basis for making change judgments it would provide. Once the scrutiny of the change-relevant information available to intuitive perceivers has proceeded at the level of specific cases, it should be possible to address several of the more general issues pertaining to the information base used in judging change. Taken across a number of different areas, what features of the past tend to be poorly documented over time? Which tend to be well documented? What general kinds of slippage occur in information over time? Questions of this general sort will be useful in providing a broader picture of the usual kinds of outside data available to the intuitive perceiver of change.

Theme 2: Personal Knowledge of the Present and the Past

As we have seen, the analysis of how the environment preserves, reduces, and structures the change-related information reaching the perceiver will figure prominently in the explication of intuitive change judgments. However, the information base used in perceiving change also sometimes comes directly from the perceiver's own experience. A comparable analysis could be done of how intuitive knowledge of the present and the past depends on the perceiver's own experience of relevant events and occurrences, as well as on how that experience is preserved, reduced, and structured at the individual level. In this section, the outlines of such an analysis will be sketched, with particular emphasis on how comparisons of temporally dispersed information from personal knowledge could result in data features of a predictable sort.

It is once again important to remember that the comparability of information for the present and the past is central to the change judgment task. Because perceived differences in information are the basis for imputing change, differences that reflect the effects of individual cognitive processing or shifts in personal perspective are potentially significant sources of change impressions. To the extent that the perceiver is unable to distinguish between impressions of change created by differences in cognitive processing and those due to real differences in events, the transforming effects of cognitive processing on what is known about the past will have important consequences for intuitive change judgments. In this section possible sources of these differences will be considered.

Knowledge about different times will sometimes vary because the perceiver starts out with different background knowledge and skills for each of the periods. The viewer taking in events over an extended period of time is neither stationary in perspective nor unchanging in cognitive abilities or social roles. Through time the cognizer may grow up, grow old, take on new roles while leaving others behind, and in various ways change life goals and vantage points that influence how information about people and events is perceived and processed. Thus, marital partners who sense changes in their relationship are likely to have experienced subtle changes in goals, expectations, and personal agendas that have influenced their perceptions and interpretations of the behavior of their spouses at different periods. The college teacher who is convinced that graduate students have become less disciplined and committed since he or she was a graduate student is, as a professor, in a different role that affords access of a different kind to information about the range of graduate student behavior and performance. Similarly, the office worker who is promoted to supervisor may quickly come to have a very different perspective on the performance of former co-workers, and this difference, in itself, may engender change judgments even in the absence of actual performance changes. Our opportunities to observe other people, our access to certain kinds of events and behavior, even what we take an interest in, is likely to fluctuate and shift over time.

In many cases there is an asymmetry between the information available for the present and that available for the past. Certain occupational roles, for example, may routinely entail differential access to "before" and "after" information, that is, to past and to present information. The crisis counselor who has direct personal experience with a target only after a crisis occurs is unlikely to have equivalent personal experience for the pre-crisis period. The kind of information a therapist has for a client prior to therapy may be quite different in form than that available during the course of therapy itself. It will be important to identify sources of such shifts in the type and richness of the available "before" and "after" data, and to consider their possible effects on the personally derived data base from which change judgments are made.

Two assumptions are made in viewing these sorts of shifts in perceiver status as important to change judgments. First, it is assumed that such shifts often complicate the comparison of intuitive data across time by introducing incommensurability into the information that the intuitive perceiver has for different periods. Second, it is assumed that this incommensurability is not highly visible and therefore not readily corrected or compensated for during the formation of impressions of change. Because perceivers so often move directly from information to drawing conclusions and because they fail to see their conclusions as tempered by role-bound limitations or as having a situationally specific character, their personal knowledge about different periods is treated as readily comparable. In essence, the information provides ease of comparison yet without being entirely appropriate for comparison.

Perspective shift is just one perceiver-derived source of complexity in the intuitive data base. Another important type of source to consider will be the effects of individual information processing, including the organization, reduction, and recall of relatively complex social data. Clearly, the character of our recollections of complex events will sometimes figure in change judgments. In deciding whether political leadership has become less competent over the years, we read about a leader's handling of a recent crisis and compare that performance to memories of how other recent leaders have handled similar crises. We are told what college is like now and compare that information to our memories of what undergraduate years were like, and then use this comparison as a basis for deciding whether the college experience has changed. We are told that a patient is now doing well and compare this to what we recall of the patient's behavior in the past to decide if the patient has improved sufficiently to be released. As these examples suggest, processing effects that are likely to result in the data base for one period being incommensurable with that of another period will be important to identify and incorporate into our analysis of change judgments.

Consider some of the phenomena of social information processing studied by researchers in social cognition that may have important implications for the nature of the personal data bases used in making change judgments. Memory for naturalistic information has been shown to operate as a process of abstraction, perhaps leading to recall for summary conclusions and judgments as opposed to exact memory for the individual, concrete events that formed the basis on which the original judgment was made (Hastie et al., 1980; Higgins et al., 1981). The events themselves may be poorly recalled or recalled less easily than the perceivers' conclusions about the events and about what those events meant or represented (Wyer & Srull, 1984). Perceivers have been shown to use certain types of categories as a basis for organizing naturalistic information—for example, there has been an interest in use of schemas in person memory and how use of schemas influences encoding and retrieval of information over time (Wyer & Srull, 1984). Some work has applied a heuristic analysis to recall for naturalistic information. Broadly conceived, this approach assumes that retrieval of frequency-related information is mediated by everyday rules of thumb (Einhorn & Hogarth, 1981; Kahneman et al., 1982). Rather than retrieving all information, the perceiver applies some shortcut processing strategy that allows for the easy (if at times misleading) assessment of frequency. Other work has been concerned with providing an account of the dimensions along which simplification and loss of information occur or providing an account of the nature of the information that is retained (Fong, Krantz, & Nisbett, 1986; Kunda & Nisbett, 1986; Nisbett, Krantz, Jepson, & Kunda, 1983). Over time certain aspects of information may be progressively more poorly recalled or lost in terms of accessibility, and an analysis of what is retained and what is lost has been a direction for research (Quattrone & Jones, 1980).

Specific memory effects have also been found in social perceivers. Work has been done on what has been termed "flashbulb" memories, that is, memories for highly salient occasions. Many people, for example, have especially vivid memories for what they were doing at the time they learned that President Kennedy had been assassinated (Brown & Kulick, 1977). People have also been found to have difficulties distinguishing between multiple reports of a single instance (e.g., the same instance reported in several different news accounts) and reports that represent actual multiple instances (Bacon, 1979; Johnson, Taylor, & Raye, 1977). A large body of work has considered whether people recall specific aspects or features of events that were not in the original account (Loftus, 1979), and there is work on whether there is an asymmetry in recall such that positive events are better recalled than events that were negative (Bower & Gilligan, 1979; Holmes, 1970). In conjunction with the study of the nature of recollections, attention has sometimes been directed to the question of whether there is awareness on the part of the perceiver of the effects that selective processing and recall can have on the information base. To a large extent the question of awareness has been concerned with how its presence or absence might influence willingness to use information under less than ideal conditions (Bargh, 1984; Nisbett & Wilson, 1977).

This brief overview gives an indication of the kinds of research that may have important implications for the processes by which change judgments are made. Concepts and findings from these lines of work may be particularly germane for understanding the character of the data base available for inferring change. One might, for example, look for findings relevant to questions about the overall information base: Is central tendency information an important part of personal recollections? Is variability well represented? How well do people recall past frequency information and how well do they retrieve past rate information? In what ways is memory for events simplified relative to what is known about events at the time they took place? To what degree is memory for long past information simplified relative to memory for information about the more recent past?

The above questions concern the overall character of the personal data base; it will also be important to consider features of the personal data base as it is used for judging change in specific areas and topics. Consider the case of judging person change (for example, judging change in an old friend encountered at a reunion or judging change in one's elderly parents when they are seen on an irregular and infrequent basis). Here it might be useful to consider the character of the data base that results from reliance on specific memory-organizing strategies for person information. Much of the growing body of literature has focused on trait constructs as an important organizing strategy in person memory (e.g., Cantor & Mischel, 1979; Markus & Zajonc, 1985). If perceivers do rely on traits to recall what a person was like in the past, what sort of information is likely to be available for retrieval when judging change (central tendency information versus variability information; trait consistent information versus trait inconsistent information)? If others' pasts are recalled in terms of their traits, will a trait data base make it difficult to see person change because of the assumption that traits are unchanging? Or will traits have just the reverse effect, increasing the ease of seeing change because they simplify the information about a person at an earlier point in time and thus provide a consistent but perhaps artificially homogeneous past with which to contrast the present?

In like fashion, the character of the personal data base about broad social trends could also be a focus. One might want to consider the nature of the organizational categories for social trends, and here the relevant categories would probably be different than in the case of person information. It might, for example, be found that people rely heavily on such organizing rubrics as "decades," and so organize their knowledge about social trends in terms of what went on in the 1960s versus the 1950s and so forth. Organization in terms of dominant decade-related themes or some similar thematic organization could serve as a simplifying scheme to help make sense of heterogeneous information; thus it would have systematic effects on the information base. There may be important events that are not encoded in terms of a decade-based organization, and thus would not be easily retrieved when such an organization is relied upon. One might ask whether it is largely political and lifestyle information that is highlighted when recalling particular decades. Perhaps events that were newsworthy in their time but are not history in any traditional sense are not so readily recalled when such global schemes are used. The cases of Bernhard Goetz, Kitty Genovese, or Richard Speck were news stories taken in their time to be powerful "signs of the times," but perhaps they are not incorporated into the dominant temporal theme and thus are not readily retrieved when change-related judgments are based on something like a decades organization. The organization of the information could have other effects. Attempts during the past to find meaning and order in events could lead to recall of the past as having been meaningful and coherent when in fact the past was largely unstructured and difficult to understand. There may be a loss of recall cues that could act as reminders that a process of making sense of events was undergone and that this process has potentially affected the information now available.

The purpose of this section has been to point out why perceiver factors will be important to analyze if we are to understand the informal information base used in judging change. Together with the previous section on the first theme, the approach taken here treats change perceptions as critically dependent on the ways past and present information come to the perceiver from the environment and are structured by the perceiver's own processing. In addition to its other benefits, such an approach can perhaps be useful in helping us make sense of certain otherwise curious features of everyday change perception. For example, analyzing change judgments in terms of their data base may offer clues as to why certain classes of change perceptions are so common as to have become clichés of sorts. Such platitudes about change include the oft-heard remarks about things having gone downhill over the years (Davis, 1979, 1981). Statements about things as having once been better occur across very different areas: helpfulness, family life, education, etc. We also encounter clichés regarding earlier times as having been much simpler and less sophisticated than the present. Such perceptions of deterioration and loss of simplicity in our society— perceptions so commonplace as to have been dubbed "the nostalgic fallacy" (Robinson, 1985)—may lend themselves to an analysis that contrasts the structure of the information available for the present with that available for the past. Thus, if positive information is generally found to be better retained over time than negative information (controlling for level of extremity), then the end result would be a tendency for things to appear to have deteriorated over time. Or, if variability information can be shown to be more poorly retained for the past than the present, this informational effect will contribute to the past appearing to have been simpler and more predictable than is the present. In this way, an informational analysis of change -related judgments that constitute our cultural nostalgia could be carried out, and similar kinds of analyses could be applied to other common examples of change perceptions. Many common change perceptions may yield to an informational analysis of the sort recommended here. By applying such an analysis and testing its implications, we are likely to find ourselves with a better understanding of some otherwise rather puzzling, but recurrent, sorts of change inferences.

Theme 3: Differences in Change Judgment Tasks

Not all change judgment tasks are alike. Different classes of change judgments make different demands on perceivers and call for use of different kinds of information. To illustrate this point, three classes of change judgments of varying complexity will be considered: frequency judgments, rate judgments, and variability judgments. The relevance of the differing sorts of information conditions discussed above will become more explicit as we consider information use in conjunction with different change tasks. The examples that follow will indicate how analyzing the nature of the change judgment tasks themselves can contribute to an overall understanding of inferences about change.

Frequency-change judgments. Perhaps the simplest form of change judgment that people make involves the comparison of frequencies. In judging changes in friends' relationships, we might, for example, look at the number of arguments a couple is having now and how many they had when they were first dating in order to decide if they are fighting more often. As employers, we might look at the number of times an employee is late for work this year relative to last year in order to decide if he or she has shown an improvement in punctuality. This class of change tasks is a relatively simple one in that the perceiver need not be concerned with more complex sorts of considerations such as rates and proportions. It is sufficient to count and then compare the number of times a particular kind of event happened. The analysis of these judgments requires looking closely at how frequency information is used and also whether frequency comparison is in fact the underlying basis for intuitive judgments that take the outward form of a frequency comparison. Even in this apparently simple comparison, a variety of complications can arise in the ordinary course of events, making the question of how the change task is actually carried out of particular concern.

Intuitive comparisons of frequencies will sometimes occur under conditions where the meaning or significance of frequencies has not remained the same over time. For example, the number of robberies in which more than $1,000 was taken for different years might be compared as a way of deciding whether there has been a change in the seriousness of robberies. Or the number of dollars people donate to religious organizations might be used as a way to draw inferences about change in religiosity or in commitment to organized religions. Given the facts of inflation, however, the meaning of the frequencies in such cases will not remain the same. In many areas, shifts in meaning can occur due to inflation, changes in measurement, changes in definition, and the like. What happens to the process of comparison in these cases? Do people tend to compare frequencies without regard for such complications?

When making frequency change judgments, the extent to which people rely on explicit numeric information as opposed to implicit frequency cues is open to question. As suggested in previous sections, various implicit cues are available in the environment that could be used as an alternative to explicit frequencies. We may not know how many child abusers there are, but we do know that there are many television dramas about abuse; we do not know how many people actually fail to help in situations calling for helping behavior, but we do hear many admonitions from our elders that people should be more helpful; we may not know how many people live below the poverty line, but we encounter considerable information about the plight of homeless people these days. Where there is a willingness to make frequency judgments on the basis of implicit cues, one might expect frequency change conclusions to be more common than would be expected on the basis of actual frequency information.

In cases in which frequency change conclusions are drawn, it could be instructive to examine the extent to which information is evaluated simply in terms of all-or-none dichotomies as opposed to in terms of specific frequencies. A common reaction to news reports of such events is to say, "it never happened in the past but we have seen an example of it now," or, "this sort of thing simply never would have happened in the past." Consider such cases as a mother murdering her own child or neighbors failing to help in a serious emergency. In some cases, then, even a single occurrence in the present is considered sufficient grounds for concluding that change in the frequency of some type of event has occurred. Whether the conclusion is actually stated in explicit frequency language would be of added interest.

The conclusion that something is more common now than in the past would seem to indicate that an explicit comparison has been made between the frequencies of events at two different times. Yet the extent to which people have a specific period in mind when they compare present frequencies with the past is open to question. Many change conclusions are characterized by a kind of fuzziness about the past periods used for comparison, as for example, when people assert that these days there is less interest in school than there used to be, or more Americans are now feeling good about their country. An examination of frequency change judgments in terms of the use or neglect of actual frequency information from some clearly specified comparison period will be important.

Frequency change judgments that appear to be based on actual comparisons of frequencies may often turn out to be conclusions based primarily on perceived cause and effect. In other words, people's conclusions about change may sometimes be dictated by first encountering change-related causal information—that is, information about events perceived as likely to cause changes in the frequency of certain kinds of behavior—and then making change inferences by looking for confirming evidence in subsequent frequencies. Parents discover drugs in their teenager's bedroom. After that discovery, will they then more readily judge the frequency of insolent behavior to have increased or that the frequency of poor grades has increased? Change-related causal information could come to us in the form of learning that a child's parents have just recently divorced. Will we look for and perceive an increase in behavior problems and hence judge a change to have occurred even without adequate comparison of the frequency of misbehavior during the predivorce period? Causal information could come in the form of finding out that a friend has been awarded a major prize or won a major competition. Will we perceive an increase in the frequency of self-serving or egotistical statements by the individual? Will we conclude that the person has changed on the basis of the causal information? The use of causal information as a substitute for frequency facts would enlarge opportunities for seeing change and perhaps give those conclusions a different character.

As these brief examples suggest, frequency change judgments make questions about certain kinds of information use important. Many of these same questions are also relevant for more complex change tasks such as rate judgments, which also involve added difficulties.

Rate-change judgments. A second and more complex kind of change judgment involves the assessment of whether the rate of events has changed. Thus one might be concerned with questions of whether the rate of high-technology business failures has increased, whether there has been a change in the rate of successful female leadership, or whether there has been a change in the rate of child abuse in day-care centers. Judgments of rate change call not only for taking into account shifts in frequencies but also for controlling for shifts in underlying population size. Fluctuating populations are a part of many contexts and situations, such as in corporations, schools, cities, and the country as a whole; population shifts occur with declines or increases in the number of students entering college or with the immigration of more individuals from another country. Whether people take into account both frequency and population information in various areas will undoubtedly influence the change judgments that are made. Whenever there are shifting populations, reliance on sheer frequency would have predictable consequences for intuitive change judgments. For example, dramatic increases in the size of the population of day-care centers will tend to make the comparison of absolute numbers of cases of abuse across the years misleading.

In typical sources, population information (i.e., facts about the number of people or items in a population) is poorly conveyed and often de-emphasized. Instead, the focus is often on sheer frequencies: the number of children who disappear each year, the number of people who die in car accidents in various years, the one million pregnant teenagers in the United States. Information about raw numeric frequencies is usually the kind of information most readily available to be picked up by the informal perceiver. Accordingly, it will be worthwhile to consider the conditions under which people making rate judgments take this readily available frequency information at face value and those under which they seek out population information even when it is relatively inaccessible or difficult to comprehend.

Like other kinds of change judgments, rate change inferences will sometimes depend on personal knowledge and recollections of the frequencies and rates with which events occurred in the past. How people draw on memories for rate information when making change judgments will be of interest. It will be useful to consider whether people distinguish between frequency and rate in the information drawn from memory, as well as whether people rely on heuristics or rules that call for rate information when making rate change judgments.

The information people receive from the environment could also include various kinds of rate cues that may be used in judging rate change. Although some of these cues accurately capture rate details, others provide rate-like information that will likely be misleading when used in judging change. For example, time-referenced statistics represent a widely used but problematic rate cue in the media. With these time-referenced statistics the number of crimes—such as the number of children who have disappeared—is reported in terms of the number of such events that take place every hour or minute (e.g., every hour, six children in America disappear). Thus, an increase in population will by itself make the rate appear higher if perceivers are not careful to distinguish time-based rates from population-based rates. Subtle rate cues can be provided in a variety of other ways, and the influence of such cues on change judgments is of special interest when statistics give the appearance that a problem has worsened because of a failure to control for changes in the underlying population size.

Problems for rate change judgments are also posed in cases where the frequency information and population information are on different dimensions, a not infrequent situation in everyday life. In the case of judging whether rate changes have occurred in air travel fatalities, the number of passenger deaths must be considered in terms of the number of passenger miles flown rather than the number of passengers. Whether people seek out and use appropriate kinds of population information when the comparison information is on different dimensions would be of interest.

Change judgments using variability information. A third class of change judgments are those that rely on the use of variability information. These judgments are sometimes conclusions that variability has changed. We may perceive our favorite restaurant to have become less consistent in quality of food or service in recent months; an athlete is perceived to have become more erratic in performance over the last year; it is concluded that college freshmen classes used to be more homogeneous in ability than they are today. Such statements are conclusions about changes in the level of consistency or diversity across different time samples. Perceptions of variability will also figure importantly in conclusions, not only about things having become more or less consistent, but also about things having improved or declined relative to a variable past. For example, a student who has been highly variable in past performance has just performed exceptionally well; will this be interpreted as an improvement or merely as further fluctuation? What conclusion about change will be drawn following a similar outstanding performance by a student who has been consistently mediocre in the past? Or consider a case in which the number of car accidents is down this year and a new drunk driving law just went into effect; will the low number of accidents be interpreted as real change in light of past variability?

Such questions raise all-important issues about the use of variability information by intuitive perceivers of change. Are people ordinarily in possession of variability information? Do they have equal access to variability information for the present and the past? When variability information is not readily available, is its absence missed? If so, is it sought out? Are conclusions about change made under low-variability baseline conditions viewed differently or held with greater confidence than those made under high-variability baseline conditions? In sum, do perceivers recognize the importance of variability information and use it appropriately when making change judgments?

The question of whether use of variability information is short-circuited under certain circumstances is also of interest. What happens when change-related causal information is available? Is the concern for having past information lessened, or is concern with information about central tendency heightened at the expense of concern with information about past variability? Under causal circumstances, do people take information that is due to regression toward the mean and interpret it as real change, ignoring degree of prior variability in the baseline?

In this section an attempt has been made to indicate how analyzing the nature of change judgment tasks themselves may be a productive way to uncover important points for study. In subsequent chapters this focus on the nature of change judgment tasks will recur in many of the studies that are reported.

Theme 4: Change as an Intuitive Category

All of the themes introduced thus far have had to do in one way or another with information—where it comes from and its importance for particular change judgments tasks. In contrast, the fourth theme is intended to point to the ultimate indeterminacy of the data for providing a full account of when people will characterize something or someone as having changed or stayed the same. In order to understand change judgments – particularly complicated change judgments – we must understand how people intuitively define change. In this section the case of person change will be used to show why the explication of intuitive definitions is important for our overall understanding of change or, in this case, why judgments of person change cannot be separated from the intuitive view of when it is appropriate to label shifts and flux in behavior as person change.

The readiness with which the label "change" is applied to a person depends on the underlying conception of what constitutes change. Personality psychologists, for example, have come to define and use the term "change" in a very narrow fashion. According to their very strict definition for applying the label "changed," the ascription of change to an individual is warranted only when one can be thoroughly satisfied that personality structure itself is now different from what it was. Change, once defined as something deep-seated, is seen as something that rarely occurs. Most behaviors that give the outward appearance of change can, with careful scrutiny, be seen as merely new manifestations of the same underlying nature. A child who was formerly starting fights with other children is now the popular class clown. Although the child might appear to have changed, the underlying characteristic is still the same – the child continues to have high attention-seeking needs (which merely express themselves in different ways at different times). In the stability-oriented approach of personality psychologists, outward flux can be reframed to maintain internal coherence.

Whether laypeople hold a similar view of change, one that excludes many events from being change but treats those few cases that fit into the category as having enormous significance, is a question of considerable importance for understanding instances of change judgments. Perhaps laypeople think in terms of a broad, inclusive definition, one that is not fully consonant with the personality view; on the other hand, perhaps intuitive perceivers apply an equally narrow view – one that treats change as very significant when it does occur but as extremely rare. As noted above, the basic problem facing the intuitive perceiver of change is the indeterminacy of the data with regard to establishing change and stability in individuals. Except in the rare case where there has been no shift at all in a person's behavior, the data themselves are indecisive as to whether the person should be regarded as having changed or as having stayed the same. Depending on the nature of one's definition, a small shift could be regarded as an instance of change, or it could be seen as representing no change at all. Similarly, a large shift could be seen as representing a significant change or no change at all. The problem, in essence, is that the data cannot speak for themselves. Whether shifts are taken to represent stability or change is largely a matter of underlying conceptions of what constitutes change and stability.

By studying the ways in which the term "change" is used in reference to various patterns of behavior in another person over time, it should be possible to begin to explicate the underlying conception of change. In the area of person perception, whether people intuitively apply the terminology of change across all areas of personal functioning is of considerable interest. Is the use of the term "change" restricted to personality-related events? Is the term used broadly in everyday discourse about individuals? Is the term used for quantitative change or only for what are taken to be qualitative changes? Is its use reserved for "core" characteristics, or is it also used more broadly for "surface" characteristics? Is it used equally readily for behavior and for traits? Questions about whether the overall use is consistent across situations, or whether it is context-specific will be useful to pursue. From the analysis of such issues we may begin to get a sense of the broad outlines of the category and how its use differs or remains the same across areas.

The complexities in the information situations people face in applying the term "change" to another person's behavior are of many sorts and make the issue of understanding intuitive definitions particularly important. Consider, for example, the situation in which teachers have observed the same small group of students over the course of several years and each student has consistently maintained his or her same rank within the cohort while the cohort as a whole has improved in performance. Would the teachers treat the differences in these students as change or, in this context, is the ascription of change limited to cases where one student surpasses his or her peers? Consider the analogous case of an elderly individual who is now in poorer health than in the past but who has maintained the same place among those in her age cohort in terms of health — is this person perceived as having changed in terms of wellness? More generally, how do people set a criterion for judging when change has occurred? If an individual goes from being a moderate drinker to becoming a heavy drinker, is that person regarded as having changed? What kinds of assumptions and background knowledge might influence the setting of a criterion for change in such a case? Examining the willingness with which people ascribe change to others under different conditions will be important for beginning to build a model of the underlying concept. That model, in turn, will be instrumental in helping to predict the use of the term "change" in ways that do not follow simply from the data alone.

Although the foregoing examples have been drawn from the area of person change, questions of an analogous sort can be raised about the conception of change that underlies change judgments in other areas. How do we intuitively define group change, or change in a family, in a country, or a culture? What are the rules for ascribing change and how might they influence and shape our willingness to apply the concept of change under various circumstances? As we have tried to suggest in this section, analysis of underlying conceptions will be an important direction for work if we are to fully understand intuitive judgments of change. In subsequent chapters we shall periodically return to this issue of the intuitive definition of change in our search for an understanding of the properties of change judgments.

Chapter 4

Stability Reassessed: Finding Opportunities for Change Judgments

Is it indeed the case that social perceivers look for change, as has been assumed in the foregoing chapters? Everything that has been said here so far—the anecdotes, the assertions, the analysis—suggests that perceivers frequently see change, that they see it in other people, in themselves, and in social events. It has even been suggested that perceivers are often so ready to see change that they judge it to have occurred even when the available facts are ambiguous and there is little basis for the change impressions in the formal evidence. But there is another view of social perception, one that holds instead that perceivers are stability-oriented, that they look for stability, that their cognitive processes operate to maintain impressions of stability, and that the kind of evidence to which they most readily respond is that which supports a stability perspective. This latter view—the standard one in the field—draws support from a sizable body of literature.

Given the large amount of apparently contrary evidence, any view that holds change judgments to be a common occurrence may seem to rest on a faulty reading of the social perception literature. Are the anecdotes presented here about change simply misleading in their suggestion that people are often focused on change and that there may even be an overabundance of change impressions? Or is the existing literature that gives considerable weight to stability in the social perception process perhaps amiss or incomplete in the picture of social perception it presents?

In the preceding chapters we have encountered good reason to believe that change judgments do occur and even that many factors operate to increase the likelihood of seeing change. One might proceed directly to the systematic study of change judgments except for the existence of the countervailing literature. On the basis of that literature, it might well be argued that people will have serious difficulties in seeing change and would exhibit, at best, limited tendencies to perceive change in their social environment. If one assumes that change judgments are real and even commonplace, the problem becomes one of how to show that this can be so in view of the existing literature. It is not enough to simply embark on studies on perceptions of change; one must come to terms with what is already known about stability in social perception.

Although it may seem counterintuitive to do so, the stability literature will be used in this chapter to show how change judgments might arise—sometimes from the very processes usually said to contribute to impressions of stability. The ways in which findings have been construed as evidence of stability will be examined and consideration will be given to how the interpretation applied to these studies is not always fully supported by the nature of the studies or their results. Much of the work will be found to be neutral with regard to the question of whether people perceive stability or change. Once the findings have been separated from their usual stability interpretations, it will be shown how the existing literature might be tapped to explain the processes underlying judgments of change as well as of stability.

As noted in Chapter 2, a concern for stability has been central to much of the existing social perception work. Early researchers often emphasized the perceiver's search for stability and invariance in the social environment, and more recent investigators have addressed the ways in which cognitive processes may operate to maintain stability in impressions. Many of the distinctive features of social perception examined in various lines of research have been seen as by-products of stability in social perception. As a consequence, widely different lines of evidence have contributed support to the stability viewpoint. One source of evidence is the literature on primacy effects, which suggests that the earliest information received in the course of impression formation is weighted the most heavily. A second is the finding that impressions and beliefs persevere and that processes operate to maintain original expectations even in the face of subsequent evidence disconfirming the original premise or basis for the belief. A third is the attribution-bias research showing that attributions are often made to dispositions, traits, and similarly stable entities even when actions and outcomes may be more readily explained by other factors. Different as these lines of research are, they are seen as providing a common basis for concluding that stability predominates in the social perception process. Interwoven throughout much of the stability literature are interpretive statements concerning what this sort of evidence shows about change and its perception, about the existence of processes inimical to change, and about perceivers as being reluctant to update beliefs and perceive change. Typical of such statements are the following: "Despite the fact that people sometimes behave in inconsistent and unpredictable ways, we form remarkably stable impressions of what other people are like . . . . Our impressions are highly resistant to change" (Crocker et al., 1983, p. 55); "Our prior beliefs and impressions of the person tend to endure, some would argue to an unwarranted degree. . . . Biased information seeking, labeling, and recall processes all may serve to maintain our beliefs about others" (Kulik, 1983, p. 1171). The social perception literature has frequently been seen as indicating that perceivers have propensities that work against their seeing signs of change in the social environment (McFarland & Ross, 1987).

In evaluating the basis for the stability view (and hence its implications for change judgments), the aforementioned lines of work representing different themes in the stability literature will be scrutinized. The literature on primacy effects will be examined first. The interpretation of it as evidence for stability will be assessed by looking closely at the purported temporal analogues designed into the studies and at the appropriateness of such analogues for supporting conclusions about stability and change. We will then turn to studies of belief perseverance as examples of research on confirmation processes and consider what these studies indicate about stability and change in social perception. Finally, the research on dispositional biases in attribution is examined in terms of its interpretation as evidence of a stability bias. Each line of work illustrates in a different way the difficulties with treating the available data as support for the view that perceivers are stability oriented. Across the different areas, a number of conclusions concerning the evidence for stability will emerge: that the data for confirming a stability model of social perception are inconclusive; that stability interpretations are applied to studies that do not directly address stability questions; that evidence of stability in underlying processes has not adequately been distinguished from evidence of stability in the content of beliefs; and, finally, that the existing studies fail to provide conditions appropriate for capturing whatever interest perceivers may show in change.

In some cases, these points will be illustrated by reporting results from studies on change judgments that fall within these "stability" lines of research but that are intended to challenge the link between the underlying processes and the perception of stability. For each line of research, the analysis begins with consideration of the evidence for some process that has been construed as stability-inducing and a reexamination of this evidence to show its neutrality with regard to stability. Studies are then introduced to demonstrate how these processes can contribute to impressions of change as well as to impressions of stability once the appropriate conditions are created. The aim of such studies is to suggest that the absence of change judgments in the literature is not so much a reflection of their limited place in the everyday world as it is an outgrowth of the ways in which studies have been constructed and issues of stability and change have been framed in the social perception literature.

Primacy Effects: "First Impressions are Lasting"

Setting the stage for much subsequent work, early research in person perception and social cognition concerned the question of how people use information in making judgments about others. The study of order effects was undertaken to see what effect, if any, the sequencing of information would have on impressions, and whether the impressions would most closely follow earlier-presented information or later-presented information. In the investigation of this important issue, an early study by Asch (1946) established the now familiar pattern. In the context of a single experimental session, subjects were provided with a set of trait terms that remained the same across conditions but in which the order of presentation of terms was carefully varied. What Asch discovered, and what others have subsequently confirmed for many different kinds of stimuli, is that order indeed makes a difference. The impressions that were formed were most heavily influenced by the earlier-presented information; thus, primacy effects predominate. In summarizing this large literature Nisbett and Ross (1980) have noted that "although order of presentation of information sometimes has no net effect on final judgment, and recency effects sometimes are found, these are the exception; several decades of psychologi-

cal research have shown that primacy effects are overwhelmingly more probable"
(p. 172; see Jones & Goethals, 1972; Nisbett & Ross, 1980; Schneider et al., 1979,
for reviews of the literature).

These finding of primacy effects have been widely interpreted in terms of stability
of person impressions. In the secondary literature and in textbooks (e.g., Myers,
1983; Schneider, 1988; Worchel & Cooper, 1979; Deaux & Wrightsman, 1984),
studies of order effects are commonly cited as evidence that first impressions are
lasting. Students are reminded that such studies show that first impressions will be
difficult to revise at later points in relationships and thus that making good first
impressions will be important. In the scholarly literature, interpretations of primacy
effects have also emphasized their implications for everyday judgments. In making
judgments of others, primacy effects have been regarded as showing that older information will bias and color the interpretation of newer, more recent information
(Jones & Nisbett, 1972; Nisbett, 1980). Primacy effects have been seen not only as
providing support for stability-oriented processing but also as arising out of a stability view of others: "If we regard people's behavior as invariant then this gives license
to the mechanisms underlying the primacy effect" (Nisbett & Ross, 1980, p. 175).

Even the infrequency with which recency effects are found has been regarded as
indirectly supporting the stability perspective. The difficulty that researchers have
encountered in their attempts to induce recency effects, according to this view,
serves to highlight the greater robustness of primacy effects. "To be sure, recency
effects, in which later-presented information has undue influence on final judgments, are sometimes found, but these are rare and appear to depend on the existence of one or more potently manipulated factors" (Nisbett & Ross, 1980, p. 172).
Extraordinary or artificial means are seen as necessary to reduce the supposed
natural tendency to weight most heavily whatever information comes first.

Not surprisingly, the studies of order effects have been criticized on various
grounds: for the artificiality of the stimuli used, for the failure to investigate the
retention of information beyond the confines of a brief experimental session, for the
lack of attention to various kinds of complex judgments that might be made on the
basis of the stimulus items provided (Jones & Goethals, 1972; Schneider et al.,
1979). Efforts have been made in some cases to overcome one or more of the objections, such as through the use of more complex stimuli or by building into the study
more sophisticated assessments of the underlying judgment processes.

Central to these studies and their interpretation is their analogue nature. To
preserve the similarity of information across the different orders, the investigations
have relied on controlled laboratory analogues. In creating these laboratory analogues, researchers have abstracted from everyday situations those features believed
to be important to the judgment process: the character of the information and the
order in which that information is received. The stability interpretation given to the
studies implicitly assumes that varying the order is comparable to varying the
passage of time, and in certain ways, it undoubtedly is. In other respects, varying
order may inadequately evoke the interpretation of information that will arise when
the events are clearly perceived to have taken place over time. Others have pointed
out that such studies, by virtue of their design, are incapable of providing details on

the effects of passage of time on retention and recall of presented information or on related processing factors that could alter subsequent judgments (Hamilton, 1981). Of interest for present purposes, the order analogue also fails to reproduce information about the passage of time in the target person's life—the fact that the early and late behaviors occurred at separate points in the person's life. Possible meaning perceivers may derive from knowing when the events took place across time cannot be tapped.

In a few cases in the literature information about order has been presented as if it were representative of different periods or times in the target person's life. One such study was reported by Jones and Goethals (1972), in a paper more generally known for its summary of the evidence for primacy effects and the stability of impressions. Jones and Goethals reported in passing one study in which subjects were led to believe that the behavioral sequence being observed had unfolded over the course of a semester. Relative to subjects who believed these behaviors were being presented in random order, the subjects with the temporal cues intact were found to treat the most recent behaviors as the most informative. Participants in the unfolding condition apparently entertained the possibility that the person had undergone a change. In describing the result, Jones and Goethals noted its suggestion of the relevance of knowing when the perceiver is interpreting a behavioral sequence as unfolding. But despite the insightfulness of this remark, its overall value for understanding social perception was regarded as limited: for the unfolding aspect to be important, perceivers must believe that the property in question is capable of change, and it was assumed that perceivers infrequently entertain this possibility. It is interesting to note in this regard that when Nisbett and Ross (1980) referred to the supposedly rare and unusual circumstances needed to induce recency effects, they included in their list the "presentation of information about an object or process which can be presumed to be capable of changing over time" (Nisbett & Ross, 1980, p. 172).

At this point, it should be clear that traditional order-effects studies simply fail to recreate the conditions under which perceivers might judge change or stability to have occurred in a target's life, and hence cannot be said to have yielded any clear evidence for the stability-oriented nature of person perception. One way to dissociate studies of order effects from the stability interpretations usually given them is to reproduce such studies but with the addition of suitable temporal cues to make them more appropriate as grounds for interpreting subjects' judgments as perceptions of stability or change in others. One study that lends itself to this sort of modification is a classic experiment by Luchins (1957) that has been widely cited as showing that first impressions are lasting. In the study, Luchins improved upon the traditional order manipulations, which relied on simple lists of trait terms, by providing subjects with more naturalistic information in the form of narrative descriptions of a young man's activities. In one passage, the young man—"Jim"—behaved in an introverted fashion: he left the classroom alone, he crossed the street when he saw someone he met on the previous evening, he drank alone in a crowded restaurant. In a second passage he behaved in an extraverted way: he walked with friends, he conversed with an acquaintance, he was friendly toward someone he had met the night before. In later investigations (1958; Luchins & Luchins, 1986), the study materials were used in a variety of ways to produce both primacy and recency effects (the latter by inserting rest periods and the like), but the most commonly cited result, and the one to which the stability interpretation has been attached, is the finding that whichever passage is encountered first has the greatest impact on the overall impression.

In a modification of the original study (Silka, 1984), subjects (223 students in General Psychology and Introduction to Personality classes) were given Luchins's original stimulus materials, and were also provided with cues about the passage of time in Jim's life. Some subjects were led to believe that the two behavioral episodes occurred very close in time (two weeks apart) whereas other subjects were led to believe that the episodes occurred further apart in time: in one condition they were told that the episodes occurred two years apart and in another condition that the first occurred in high school and the second in college. Some subjects received no temporal information as in the original study. Within each condition the order of the passages was counterbalanced.

In the original study, Luchins demonstrated the primacy effect by showing that subjects selected a trait term matching the first passage rather than selecting a descriptor that contained trait terms representative of both passages. In that study, no options were included that would have allowed subjects to describe Jim as having changed. To give subjects the opportunity to register impressions of change as well as of stability, while maintaining the same overall form of the original dependent measure, subjects in the present study were given seven possible choices: "Jim is basically friendly," "Jim is basically more friendly than unfriendly," "Jim is basically unfriendly," "Jim is basically more unfriendly than friendly," "Jim has changed, he has become friendlier," "Jim has changed, he has become less friendly," "Jim is moody, sometimes he is friendly and sometimes unfriendly." Of interest was the number of subjects in the different temporal conditions who selected either of the two change descriptors. It was expected that perceivers in the no-temporal-information condition and in the short-term condition would readily ascribe traits to Jim and show little evidence of seeing change in him, just as interpretations of the original study suggest. But how perceivers interpret behavior in the short run was not expected to be indicative of their responses when substantial time was believed to have elapsed. In the long-term conditions, it was anticipated that a greater tendency to ascribe change to Jim would emerge.

The results of the modified Luchins procedure showed that how people interpret the behavior does depend on the information they receive about the passage of time. When subjects received no temporal information, 3 of 56 described Jim as having changed. When subjects were led to believe that the behaviors occurred close in time, 6 of 56 described Jim as having changed. When the time was longer (two years) or when the first behavioral episode occurred in high school and the second in college, 28 of 55 and 25 of 56 subjects, respectively, described Jim as having changed. A chi-square analysis comparing selection of a change descriptor to selection of other labels across the conditions was significant, χ^2 (3, $N = 223$) = 44.85, $p <$ .01. Not everyone in the long-term conditions comes to the conclusion that Jim has changed, but many do and their responses to the two passages are not reflected in the results of the short-term condition.

In view of the claim often made that the original study indicates that first impressions are lasting, a separate control group of 16 subjects was asked to estimate the amount of time that had passed between the first and second passage when those passages were presented without temporal information. The mean estimated length of time between the two behavioral episodes was 6.8 hours ($SD = 7.3$), with responses ranging from 2 to 24 hours. People apparently believed that they were being provided with information about behaviors that occurred very close in time. Although the traditional order-effects studies such as the Luchins (1957) experiment may tell us something interesting about how perceivers resolve inconsistent information over the short run, they fail to adequately address the issue of whether first impressions are truly lasting.

As in Luchins' original study, subjects in the replication study were asked to write short descriptions of their impressions of the target person prior to responding to the dependent measure. Those essays provide additional support for the contention that the short-term conditions simply fail to capture the readiness to see change that is evident in the long-term conditions. The essays were coded for inclusion of references to Jim having changed (i.e., inclusion of phrases such as "changed," "has grown," "has become a different person," in describing the target person). Comments about change were found to be more common in the two long-term conditions, where 55 of 111 essays included such comments, than in the two short-term conditions, where 14 of 112 essays included such comments, $\chi^2(1, N = 223) = 35.81$, $p < .01$. Typical of the essays describing Jim as having changed was the following:

> In high school Jim was a very friendly person. He liked walking in the sun and talking to his friends whenever he saw them. When Jim made it to college he changed totally. Everything he did is easily the opposite of what he would normally do in high school. Jim is not as friendly as he used to be.

In a later study using the same stimulus materials (with one two-week and one two-year condition), the attributions made for the two episodes of behavior were investigated to obtain a better sense of how subjects were interpreting the behavior and to see if different attributional strategies were being used to account for the later behavior when it occurred shortly after the first than when it occurred long after the first. Subjects made person and situation attributions on 7-point scales. The person question read, "To what extent was the behavior due to something about the person?" (endpoints "Not at all" and "Very much"). As expected, whereas subjects in the two conditions equally attributed the first instance of behavior to person causes, subjects in the long-term conditions attributed the later behavior significantly more to person causes ($M = 5.7$) than did subjects in the short-term condition ($M = 4.7$), $F(1,48) = 4.46$, $p < .05$. No differences were found on the situational question. Hence, subjects in the long-term condition—where, as we have seen, change is more likely to be judged to have occurred—tend to view Jim's later "inconsistent" behavior, not as a quirk of situational forces but as a sign of genuine change in him.

Obviously, the present demonstration shares the limitations of the line of studies on which it is based. The amount of information provided was limited and both the context and information were somewhat artificial. With the addition of more information, would subjects draw the same conclusions? Would people respond in the same way, for example, if the information concerned a friend rather than a stranger or if the information focused on some dimension other than friendliness? This study was not intended to address such questions, but in later investigations we will see that change judgments also arise in more complex contexts, including those where familiar others are being described. Change judgments will also sometimes be observed even under short-term conditions in cases in which change expectancies are high.

This study is by no means the first to show that recent information can be very important to the impressions perceivers hold of another person; other studies, including work by Luchins and Luchins (1963, 1986), have sometimes conveyed this same message (Crano, 1977; Dreben, Fiske, & Hastie, 1979; Freund, Kruglan-ski, & Shpitzajen, 1985). Why then have such studies been given so little promi-nence in interpretations of social judgments? Perhaps the difficulty in incorporating such findings into accounts of social judgments lies in having cast the processing of later information in terms of the construct of recency. The recency concept focuses on order variations and has not usually been linked to any intuitive rationale for why perceivers should make use of later information. On the other hand, the construct of primacy, although also originating in order variations, has readily been linked to a clear rationale for why the perceiver might heavily weight early information— primacy effects make sense because perceivers are assumed to think of others as hav-ing stable traits and dispositions that will be reflected in early behavior. In the absence of a comparable rationale for why perceivers might rely on later informa-tion, most interpretations of recency effects have continued to treat them as fragile effects to be studied by tinkering with the mechanics of how the information is presented. However, once we have recognized that social perceivers do concern themselves with change, we can easily appreciate that they may sometimes have compelling reasons for making use of later information.

Several responses to the present results might be made. It might be argued, for example, that the conclusion of stability was never intended to entail the claim that impressions would remain the same over considerable lengths of time. Yet it is exactly this ambiguity in what the stability claim represents that poses a problem for what we are to conclude about temporal duration and stability. Interpreters of the literature have often referred to the perceiver's belief in stable personality traits and the like in conjunction with the evidence for lasting impressions (e.g., Nisbett & Ross, 1980; Ross, 1977); such comments would seem to indicate that lengthy periods of time are included in the frame of reference. Another line of argument might be that the important evidence for stability takes a form altogether different from the primacy effects that have been the focus here. The evidence for stability in impressions might depend not so much on how people view others over time as on the processing that induces perceived stability and that may have gone untapped in the limited situation investigated in the present study. In the next section, we exa-mine some evidence that has been interpreted as showing that processing is stability-oriented and inimical to change.

By way of conclusion then we might say that central to the interpretation problem has been a failure to acknowledge important evidentially relevant differences among different patterns of time-based information: (1) the presentation of information at different times in the perceiver's life: (2) the provision of information to perceivers about different times in the target person's life: and (3) the order in which information is received. There has been a tendency to treat time in ways that are insensitive to the differential implications of these different sorts of manipulations. Further, this interpretational ambiguity has in certain respects paralleled the inexactness in translating "real world" time concerns into laboratory analogues. In designing manipulations intended to recreate critical temporal aspects of the real world, researchers have not always chosen a temporal dimension appropriate for the intended conclusions nor have they operationalized the intended temporal dimension in ways that adequately recreate the temporal feature they set out to study.

In typical laboratory studies, change judgments cannot easily arise because these studies present only a slice of time in the target person's life and thus do not provide appropriate conditions for expecting change. What appears to be contrary stability evidence is therefore inconclusive: at best, it shows the effects of receiving information about target persons without the benefit of temporal information about them. The "evidence" of stability is evidence of stability in the absence of any progression of time in the target person's life.

Belief Perseverance as Evidence for Stability

In recent years, investigators of social perception have more closely considered the ways in which perceivers are active cognizers. Perceivers have been viewed as actively working to make sense of the behavior and actions of others even when those behaviors resist interpretation or are difficult to integrate. One of the outgrowths of this work is the finding that perceivers often make limited use of subsequent information that is inconsistent with or disconfirming of their prior views (Fiske & Taylor, 1984; Nisbett & Ross, 1980). People do not easily discard their views. An important line of research supporting this generalization is the literature on belief perseverance. Here, beliefs have been found to persevere and to do so even when subsequent information discredits the very basis for the original belief (Anderson, 1983; Anderson, Lepper, & Ross, 1980; Anderson, New, & Speer, 1985; Jennings, Lepper, & Ross, 1981; Ross, 1977; Ross, Amabile, & Steinmetz, 1977; Ross & Anderson, 1982; Ross, Lepper, & Hubbard, 1975; Ross, Lepper, Strack, & Steinmetz, 1977).

Although these results are similar to those found in studies of primacy effects, the processes underlying the perseverance effects are thought to be different (Ross, 1977). In the context of perseverance, the effect of relying on earliest information is believed to be the result of perceivers having gone through cognitive work to arrive at their view of events. Having invested cognitive effort in explaining events in a particular way and having marshalled facts to suit that view, people then come to interpret subsequent information in ways that support that initial impression, and do so even to the point of discounting otherwise plausible information that is inconsistent with those entrenched views.

Interpretations of these findings have often focused on their implications for the stability-prone nature of person perception. For example, evidence for belief perseverance has been seen as important because it helps to explain why perceivers maintain a view of others as having stable traits and personalities. Ross (1977) has argued that the workings of belief perseverance and related cognitive strategies may account for why the perceiver "remains committed to concepts of broad, stable, heuristically valuable personality strategies" (p. 209). The mechanism of belief perseverance has been seen as explaining the undue perseverance of dispositional attributions and the tendency of perceivers to interpret subsequent behavior to make it fit their initial dispositional impressions (however awkward the fit may be):

> Once formed, initial impressions structure and distort the attributional processes through which subsequently considered evidence is interpreted. Specifically, the relevance, reliability and validity of dubiously relevant, reliable, or valid information is resolved as a function of its consistency with the attributor's initial impression. This information consistent with a first impression tends to be attributed to corresponding dispositions of the actor. (Ross et al., 1975, p. 889)

Thus, the process of belief perseverance in seen as enhancing the tendency to regard subsequent behaviors as similar to earlier ones.

Certain of the studies in this area, by virtue of their stimulus materials and design, have lent support to the idea that perseverance is instrumental in maintaining views that future behaviors are similar to past ones. In some cases, subjects have been given the task of identifying threads of continuity linking past behaviors to future ones; once having done so subjects continue to act as if such links exist regardless of whether this is in fact the case. For example, in one study (Ross et al., 1977), subjects were provided with case history materials to be used in explaining one of various critical events in a person's later life. After having explained the later event, subjects learned that it was purely hypothetical and that no information was available on the later life of the person whose history they read. The expectations that had come into being concerning the future behavior of the person were found to maintain themselves even when the rationale for the original expectations was undercut, and these perseverance effects occurred even when the subjects were asked to engage in cognitive work, knowing at the outset that the event being causally explained was hypothetical. By furthering an account of the future in terms of the past, processes of perseverance are seen as helping to perpetuate beliefs that the future will be like the past.

The stability interpretations given to such findings often link them to stability in content—that is, it is often assumed that the belief is itself *about* the stability of persons—but in point of fact these studies have demonstrated only that perceivers rely on processes that yield perseverance of beliefs, regardless of what the beliefs are about. Because the stability-producing processes are neutral with respect to content, the beliefs that are being maintained might well involve either stability or change. Once process has been distinguished from content, it can be seen that the stability processes may contribute to the perpetuation of expectations for change as well as for stability. In other words, there is no inherent reason why stability processes could not contribute to beliefs about change. If perceivers begin with the expectation that someone has changed, then devoting cognitive effort to explaining why this would be the case should lead perceivers to believe that a person will change even after the reason for the original belief has been removed.

In an experiment designed to look into this possibility, the perseverance of general expectancies for change and stability was investigated. The intent was to see if perseverance effects are limited to perceptions of others as stable or whether they also occur for change expectations. Forty-four students in introductory personality classes participated in a study that reproduced in essential outline the belief perseverance paradigm used by Ross et al. (1977). After reading a case study, subjects were asked to explain a future outcome; the true outcome was then said to be unknown, and the subjects made predictions about how likely the explained outcome was to occur.

All subjects read a case study of approximately 500 words adapted from Medved and Wallechinsky's *What Really Happened to the Class of '65?* (1976, pp. 241–248). The case described in some detail a young man's high school years, and provided information about his academic performance, his interests during that period, and his relationship to his father. Before reading the case, subjects were given either a set to explain why the person would change in the future or a set to explain why he would stay the same in the future. Subjects were told that they were to compose either (1) a detailed account explaining why this person in later life would radically change, or (2) a detailed account explaining why he would remain largely the same in adult life. In a control condition, participants read the case study but were not asked to go through an explanatory process.

After subjects had read the case study and written an explanation of why the young man would change or stay the same, they learned that information was in fact unavailable about his life beyond high school and thus it was not known whether he had changed or stayed the same. Participants in all three conditions were then asked to answer several questions estimating the likelihood that the target individual would change or remain the same. As in the original Ross et al. (1977) study, the questions called for the subjects to compare the individual to other American males of his age; responses were made on 9-point scales (ranging from -4 to 4) with endpoints "Much less likely than the average American male" and "Much more likely than the average American male." Subjects were asked "How likely is it that this person will undergo some kind of large change in adult life?" An analysis of their responses revealed that subjects in the change condition saw the person as more likely to change ($M = +1.35$) than did subjects in the stability condition ($M = -1.41$) or those in the control condition ($M = +0.28$), $F(2,41) = 8.17, p < .005$. In terms of stability, subjects were asked: "How likely is it that this person will remain relatively the same during adult life?" As predicted, participants in the stability condition viewed stability as more likely ($M = +1.71$) than did subjects in the change condition ($M = -0.29$) or in the control condition ($M = +0.29$), $F(2,41) = 4.41, p < .05$. Once having explained why a person would have changed or remained the same, subjects apparently found it easy to envision that such an outcome was likely to occur even though there was no longer any special basis for assuming that such an outcome had a high likelihood.

In a second study following a similar format, subjects read another case study adapted from the Medved and Wallechinsky book (1976, pp. 160–168). In the actual case in question, the individual became a Hare Krishna after receiving a mechanical engineering degree in college. In the study itself subjects learned that the person had become a Hare Krishna (in the change condition) or had gone on to have a career in the same area as his mechanical engineering major (in the stability condition). Subjects were asked to explain either what would lead a person to undergo such a dramatic change or what would lead a person to stay the same. Control subjects did not go through the explanatory task. After the explanatory task, subjects learned that in fact no information was available as to the behavior of this individual after college.

Subjects were again asked questions about the likelihood of stability and change, as in the first study. When asked whether they believed that the target person would undergo some large change, subjects in the change condition were more likely to expect change ($M = +1.62$) than those in the control condition ($M = +0.18$) and those in the stability condition ($M = -0.18$), $F(4,86) = 3.54$, $p < .01$. Similar effects were found for the stability question. Stability subjects expected more stability ($M = +1.53$) than did change subjects ($M = -1.00$) or control subjects ($M = +0.14$), $F(4,86) = 8.21$, $p < .001$. The results showed that broad expectations for change were induced; as to the specific kind of dramatic change presented, subjects did not come to conclude that this would be a likely outcome. Even after having explained why dramatic change would take place, subjects rated the outcome of becoming a Hare Krishna as an implausible outcome ($M = -2.08$).

In a later study dealing with unexpected turns in a target's life, Tversky and Kahneman (1982) provided subjects with a personality description and information that the person had chosen an unexpected career choice. Subjects were asked to outline the theory that most likely explained the relationship between the person's personality and choice of careers. Tversky and Kahneman found that subjects readily discovered links. From that result they went on to conclude that social perceivers hold strong beliefs in the stability of others. The present studies indicate that such effects are not limited to beliefs that others are stable.

Although the body of findings on belief perseverance has sometimes been interpreted as evidence of bias on the part of the perceiver (Nisbett & Ross, 1980), the present studies are not intended to highlight some demonstrably flawed processing of social information. Rather, what they suggest is that change beliefs, like their stability counterparts, can create expectancies that give meaning to subsequent events. Moreover, this is an observation of considerable significance given that everyday life presents numerous occasions on which such presumptions of change might arise. Very often, the first question reporters ask lottery winners concerns change: how do they think winning large sums of money will change them and their lives? In cases where children have undergone distressing experiences (having their parents divorce, for example, being the victim of sexual abuse, suffering a prolonged illness), the initial presumption often is that the children will be changed. For example, the mother of an ill child writes, "I kept thinking Nicky's time in the children's ward would irrevocably change him" (Johnson, 1986, p. 66). So too with adults; the expectation is that certain kinds of experiences cannot help but change the individuals involved—suddenly becoming successful, being the victim of a serious crime, losing a loved one. Fears that people cannot avoid being changed can be seen in the case of families of hostages (Hostetler, 1987). Imagining how someone might change and anticipating that they will change—in major or minor ways—may well be an important part of our ongoing experience with others.

The belief perseverance literature has served as a point of departure in reconsidering the stability interpretations that have been given to the phenomena of active social processing, but the argument developed here is likely to prove germane to similar approaches carried out in related parts of the literature. For example, discussions of the belief confirmation literature have often focused on their implications for stability in impressions (Snyder, 1981, 1984). Here, too, such conclusions are not surprising given that salient belief manipulations have generally concerned traits and stable attributes. In the Snyder and Swann (1978) study, for example, subjects were first given trait prototypes and were then provided with an opportunity to ask either confirmatory or disconfirmatory questions to learn whether a person matched or did not match the prototype. The fact that perceivers were found to select questions confirming of the trait prototype might seem to indicate that perceivers are trait- and stability-oriented, but again it shows only that people can be confirming of initial expectations (although even this conclusion has been contested, e.g., Trope & Bassok, 1983). The range of beliefs to which this confirming process extends may go well beyond that suggested by the usual conclusions drawn from the findings.

In referring to processes that allow us to protect our beliefs from disconfirmation, Nisbett and Ross (1980) have asserted that "the mechanisms of premature commitment and insufficient revision are probably aided and abetted in most real life contexts by people's adherence to what we have called the dispositional metatheory." They go on to say that from the perceiver's viewpoint, "theory revision is rarely necessary because, again, characteristics are invariant and later information seldom will be truly inconsistent with earlier information" (p. 175). The present results would suggest that the theories that people hold and the beliefs that are difficult to disconfirm can be about change just as well as about stability.

Dispositional Bias as Evidence for Stability

Recent findings in the attribution literature have been regarded as an additional source of evidence that people demonstrate a strong bias toward perceiving others as having stable, enduring dispositions. Indeed, the supposition that stability is important to the perceiver has been woven into various accounts of the attribution process and a stability interpretation has been given to some of the more salient results that have come from the study of attribution processes.

Early on, Heider (1958) alluded to the possibility that perceivers may be especially concerned with stable attributes in assigning causes to events. The search for regularity was seen as a search for stable aspects of the environment—for the stable characteristics of the person (traits, attitudes, needs, beliefs, personality structures) and the permanent properties or structures in the environment (Heider, 1958, p. 79). More recent interpretations of the attributional search have also portrayed perceivers as stability emphasizers. Watson (1982) notes that the standard view throughout much of the literature regards perceivers' attributions as linked to an underlying concern with stable, dispositional characteristics of others: "It is important to be able to understand and to predict the behavior of those with whom one interacts. Other-raters are thus motivated to identify stable internal characteristics of others, and will selectively attend to their characteristics" (p. 683). Jones (1979), in his aptly titled article, "The Rocky Road from Acts to Dispositions," succinctly summed up the effect that seeing others as having stable dispositions is assumed to have on willingness to make attributions to others' characters on the basis of behaviors that are situationally determined: "The journey from acts to dispositions is apparently often taken in unthinking haste and leads commonly to unwitting error" (p. 116).

Various kinds of evidence have been assimilated to this view, but perhaps the most important has been the robust finding that perceivers attribute actions to persons, apparently to the neglect of situational factors (for reviews see Harvey & Weary, 1981; Jones, 1979; Jones & Nisbett, 1972; Ross, 1977; Watson, 1982). In many contexts, situational determinants are given relatively little weight by perceivers, an effect that has been found even where the situational pressures have been made quite explicit. This neglect of situational factors has often been taken to reflect the perceiver's tendency to see behavior as flowing from an actor's personal qualities and enduring characteristics. The presumed centrality of this tendency to overattribute acts to persons is suggested by Ross's (1977) widely cited reference to it as the "fundamental attribution error." Ross's analysis has been accorded an important place in both scholarly and text book accounts of attribution processes, with the fundamental attribution error usually being treated as a central finding about person perception (e.g., Carroll, 1978; Jones, Riggs, & Quattrone, 1979; Miller, Baer, & Schonberg, 1979; Myers, 1983; Schneider et al., 1979; Worchel & Cooper, 1979). This effect is presumed to be more than a mere person bias. The effect represents, according to Taylor and Crocker (1981), not only a person bias, but also "a bias toward perceiving stability and consistency in the person's behavior" (p. 120). Similarly, Nisbett and Ross (1980) have argued that the fundamental attribution error "encourages people to assume that outcomes reflect stable dispositions of the actor and hence that future outcomes generally will resemble past ones" (p. 268).

Despite attempts to offer clear interpretations of this literature, there is still considerable doubt as to what the heterogeneous body of findings has shown. That these findings are capable of supporting a wide variety of conclusions about the intentions underlying the attribution choices has been noted (Funder, 1982; Herzberger & Clore, 1979; Ross & Fletcher, 1985; Watson, 1982), as has the fact that there are various points of looseness in recent interpretations of this literature, particularly in claims that the results unambiguously represent bias on the perceiver's part (Funder, 1987; Harvey, Town, & Yarkin, 1981; Harvey & Weary, 1981; Kelley & Michela, 1980; Ross & Fletcher, 1985). Of particular concern to us here are the ways in which the studies fall short of providing the sort of unambiguous evidence for stability searching that they are often claimed to provide.

For the most part the studies to which stability interpretations have been given were not originally intended to address stability questions. What has generally been done in such studies has been to provide a stimulus context in which some situational factor has been made to powerfully affect the behavior of a target person, and participants are then queried to see if the strength of situational pressures is fully recognized. In such studies, subjects have been found to "underestimate" the strength of situational forces; when faced with a situation that powerfully influences behavior, they perceive the behavior as being due to something about the person rather than to constraints in the situations.

It has been assumed that people's concerns with stability can be read directly from the attributional choices that are made, with evidence for a stability orientation emanating from both the "overweighting" of the person choice and the "underweighting" of the situation choice. Heavily weighting the person choice carries an implication of stability because that choice is seen as representing a dispositional inference on the perceiver's part (see Miller, Smith, & Uleman, 1981, for comments). Likewise, the failure to weight the situation, because it represents an underweighting of something that is unstable from one situation to the next, is taken as further confirmation of the perceiver's greater concern for stability and the tendency to see others as invariant in behavior (Jones, 1979). Further confirmation is seen as coming from the fact that behavior *is* attributed to the situation when the behavior is inconsistent; thus, it is assumed that the view of others as stable is further preserved by explaining away apparent inconsistencies through attributing them to situational causes (Crocker et al., 1983).

However, the reading of person-focused attributional choices as evidence for stability is problematic on various counts. For one thing, the exact meaning of the person attributions varies from one study to the next and their relationship to stability is often unclear. For example, to make a person attribution could mean that a particular essay (the event for which the attribution was to be made) was rated as reflecting the writer's true opinion (e.g., Jones & Harris, 1967); it could mean that relatively great weight was assigned to personal characteristics, defined for the subject as a person's personality, character, personal style, attitudes, and mood (e.g., Storms, 1973); or it could mean that, given a choice between the alternative of two opposing trait labels and the phrase "depends on the situation," subjects chose one of the trait terms (e.g., Nisbett, Caputo, Legant, & Marecek, 1973). Such choice alternatives are perhaps meaningful when framed in terms of the relative importance given to situations and persons (see, however, Goldberg, 1981; Miller et al., 1981; Monson & Snyder, 1977; Watson, 1982); they less clearly can be brought to bear on the stability question. The person-choice alternatives do not refer directly to stability; at best they *imply* stability and they do not even always do that. As is evident from the above cases, the person choices have not always been designed to represent only stable attributes (e.g., mood generally would not be considered a stable attribute).

Furthermore, the majority of existing studies do not allow subjects to express both a preference for making person attributions and a view that people's attributes are not inevitably immutable. To the extent that perceivers are interested in making attributions to persons, they have had to express that interest in the person language that is provided. Because the person choice provided can be construed in stability terms by researchers, it has been assumed that the selection of that choice by perceivers also signals a stability preference on their part. The dispositional feature of the choice may, in effect, be a red herring in that, given the options, perceivers cannot show a penchant to weight person information heavily relative to situational information without also being seen as having a stability bias.

Attempts to read stability from the underweighting of situational information are similarly problematic. The failure of perceivers to make situational attributions indicates merely that they fail to appreciate how behavior might vary from situation to situation and that they fail to recognize the extent to which situations are plausible and potent causes of others' behaviors. Yet being unable to conceive of situational factors as potent forces is far from an indication that perceivers are unable to conceive of behavior as undergoing alteration. In particular, whether one expects behavior to be the same in different situations is quite different from whether one expects behavior to be the same across time.

Focusing on situations emphasizes what it is about situations that affect behavior; focusing on time, in contrast, emphasizes those forces occurring with the passage of time that could affect behavior. People could have relatively impoverished notions about situational pressures, and at the same time have detailed expectations for how the passage of time can powerfully change behavior ("growing up," "growing old," "going to college," "getting a job"). Existing studies suggest only that if one introduces powerful causes that are situational in nature, people do not forego a view of constancy in behavior; such studies tell us little about whether the expectation for constancy holds when powerful across-time forces are introduced.

Together, the considerations raised in this section have pointed up the difficulties with interpretations linking person attributions to an underlying conception of others as stable. The contention here is that connecting this attributional pattern to a stability worldview is misleading in that person attributions do not always carry with them stability assumptions. Indeed, if attributors focus on persons in assigning causes and do so to the neglect of situational factors, then this so-called "fundamental attribution error" should *heighten* the tendency to perceive someone as having changed rather than seeing changes in situations as responsible for the differences in the person's behavior. People do not necessarily give up person attributions in order to maintain stability; rather people may give up assumptions that others are stable in order to maintain a person attribution.

It is possible to illustrate this point experimentally. Consider the case of someone whose behavior is very different when seen at one point in time than when seen several years later. If perceivers focus on situations, they should be less ready to believe that the person has changed when they have seen that person in two very different situations than when they have observed the target in two very similar situations. On the other hand, if perceivers focus on persons to the neglect of situational information, this difference in situations should make no difference in the readiness to make strong inferences of person change when the person's behavior changes from one time to another.

To examine this possibility, 44 General Psychology students were provided with an account of an individual who behaved very differently at one time than she did several years later. The situational context was varied so that for some subjects the two behaviors occurred in the same kind of situation and for other subjects the behaviors occurred in quite different situations. In addition, some subjects were given instructions designed to enhance their likelihood of attending to situational contexts; the other subjects received no such instructions. Thus, the study was a 2 × 2 design varying situation similarity and focus on context. Of interest was the question of whether perceivers would attribute the behavioral differences to the person having been in different circumstances or whether they would judge that the differences indicated that the person had changed.

After first being asked to describe someone in their own lives that they see infrequently (specifically, to describe the person's behavior on the two most recent occasions of contact), participants were given what was ostensibly another student's account in which she described her two most recent visits with an elderly aunt living in another part of the country. On the earlier visit the niece saw the aunt either alone in the aunt's home or at a family reunion. During this earlier visit the aunt seemed very alert:

> My great-aunt is 73 and lives in the midwest so I don't get to see her very often. A few years ago when I saw her I spent an afternoon with her at her farm. She talked a lot about her children and about the other relatives. She had lots of funny stories to tell about old family gossip and about who doesn't get along with whom in the family. She asked me questions about my friends and about how school was. She talked a lot about current events. She was really enjoyable and very alert.

Some subjects learned that the aunt had been seen at a family reunion instead of alone at her farm. Several years later the aunt was seen at a family reunion. On this occasion, the aunt was described as being forgetful and somewhat confused:

> Last summer we flew out to the midwest for a family reunion (it was my grandparents' 50th wedding anniversary). My great-aunt was there. I hadn't seen her for a long time and she seemed very forgetful. She couldn't remember the names of some of the relatives. She even called one of my cousins Harriet instead of Susie. At one point, she lost her car keys and at another point she misplaced her purse. We were afraid that she wouldn't be able to find her way home so one of my cousins drove her home. She looked confused.

Following a manipulation used by Quattrone (1982), some subjects were primed to attend to the character of the situations in which the events took place. These subjects were asked to note possible similarities and differences in the two situations in which the aunt's behavior was observed.

After having read the account of the aunt's behaviors, subjects were first asked to describe briefly their impressions. Following this, participants were given an opportunity to make attributions for the changes in the aunt's behavior. Separate person and situation attribution questions were included and were phrased so as to be appropriate for the attribution of differences. The person question asked, "What is your best judgment of how important this factor was in causing the aunt to behave differently now than she did a few years ago: The aunt's mental functioning has probably deteriorated since her niece last saw her." The situation question asked, "What is your best judgment of how important this factor was in causing the aunt to behave differently now than she did a few years ago: The situations caused the differences." In both cases, responses were made on 9-point scales, with endpoints "Not a very likely cause" and "A very likely cause."

Responses on the person attribution question were consistent with the "fundamental attribution error" notion that unless explicitly instructed to do so, people generally do not attend to situational contexts in accounting for behavior. In judgments of person change, a significant interaction was found, $F(1,40) = 10.65$, $p < .01$, and there were no significant main effects. As confirmed by a post-F analysis (Duncan's Multiple Range Test), subjects in the primed condition who first observed the aunt behaving coherently in a quiet home setting and then as forgetful and confused at a family reunion were less likely to attribute the change in behavior to the aunt having changed ($M = 5.91$) than subjects in all other conditions, including those who saw the aunt in the same situation both times ($M = 7.64$ unprimed and 8.37 primed) and those who saw the aunt under different circumstances but who were not primed to attend to situations ($M = 8.36$). The pattern of means on the situation question was the reverse of this, and thus similarly supportive of the hypothesis, but the effects were not significant. It would be misleading to assume however, that subjects in the different conditions did not respond somewhat differently on the situation question. Scrutiny of the results revealed that subjects reacted in a dichotomous fashion seeing the situation either as not at all responsible or as very responsible, thus increasing the within-cell variance. In the case of the two dissimilar-situations conditions, for example, the primed and unprimed subjects responded quite differently. When students were not cued to attend to the situation, only 2 of the 11 subjects were at or above the scale midpoint in attributions to the situation, whereas in the condition in which students were primed to the situation 8 of the 11 subjects were at or above the scale midpoint. A test of differences in proportions confirmed that this difference was indeed significant (2.60, $p < .05$).

The responses on several additional questions substantiated the effects found on the attribution questions. Subjects uniformly regarded the aunt's memory in the past as quite good ($M = 7.18$). With regard to evaluations of the aunt's present memory, an interaction was found, $F(1,40) = 6.75$, $p < .05$, again with no significant main effects. A Duncan's Multiple Range Test showed that when subjects had been primed, those who had read about the aunt's behavior in two different situations were less likely to assert that the aunt's memory had become poor on the basis of differences in behavior ($M = 3.82$) than were subjects who observed the aunt under similar conditions ($M = 2.36$). When subjects had not been primed, they uniformly concluded that the aunt's memory was now poor regardless of differences in the situation in which she had been seen ($M = 2.91$ similar situations; $M = 2.27$ dissimilar situations). Manipulation checks showed that subjects did indeed view the family reunion setting as more likely to induce confusion than the home setting.

Subjects' responses to open-ended questions provide some sense of their impressions of change in the target person. In the condition where the observational settings had been different, one of the subjects not primed to attend to the situation summarized her impressions of change in the aunt:

> Apparently she has become senile, as most older people do. It would hurt to see her so forgetful with obvious failing health at a family reunion when in the past she would have loved being with the family she spoke of so frequently.

In the condition where subjects attended to the difference in situations, participants sometimes described their concerns about the impact of the different situations. One subject wrote:

> It would be hard to form an opinion without having the chance for another long talk in a relaxed atmosphere. Initially, she could be thought of as becoming senile, but this is not a fair judgment to make after a brief meeting.

The case of the aunt in the present study exemplifies the kind of case in which perceivers are likely to have strong expectations of person change and show a readiness to draw inferences from limited amounts of information. Such cases are far from infrequent in modern life. As a part of living in a mobile society, many members of one's social sphere are seen infrequently—relatives, old classmates, former neighbors, former spouses, one's own adult children. Former friends and colleagues are encountered at occasional conventions or class reunions, and relatives may be seen only at infrequent family gatherings. From these brief behavior samples we may form impressions of what friends are like now as compared with what they were like in the past. The present situations in which we encounter our friends differ in subtle and not so subtle ways from the situations in which we knew them in the past. Rather than asking ourselves how a class reunion or a convention might elicit different behaviors than a high school class or a graduate school seminar, we may use the information to decide how our old friends have changed. Indeed, the willingness to draw inferences of change from brief samples and an apparent lack of concern with the situations in which old friends are encountered were revealed in subjects' responses in the study just described. For example, when asked about the two most recent visits with an old friend, one subject wrote:

> The first time that I met her was in my organic chemistry class 3 years ago. She was a smart, easy going type of person and she seemed to be happy with her life. Her only problem was that she had no self-confidence, she was insecure. The last time that I saw her was back in the summer of 1985. She had been accepted at the Tufts Medical School. I felt that she had been through a big change in her personality. She was not the insecure person any more. Now she felt strong and she knew what she wanted from her life.

In a sense, the fact that people readily attribute change to persons as opposed to situations should not be surprising, despite countervailing themes in the literature. Just as language and events generally focus attention on persons (Taylor & Fiske, 1978), they may also focus attention on persons as the locus of change. The finding that subjects made equally strong attributions when the situations were different and when they were not should not be taken as evidence of a bias on the perceiver's part; among other things, it may be yet another example of the person focus in language and the consequences that can follow from that focus. Given that we can only surmise to what extent situations influence behavior (Kelley & Michela, 1980), the discounting of situational factors during social information processing may not be erroneous after all. Perceivers may be stability oriented to the extent that, having no other information to go on, they expect others to behave in the same way in the future as they did in the past (Gifford, 1975; Miller et al., 1981). However, even if perceivers have a "default" option of this sort, we should not jump to the conclusion that social perceivers will fail to see change when presented with evidence of it or even rule out the possibility that they will have a default option for change under certain circumstances.

This idea that dispositional attributions can contribute to seeing change may be a novel one for many social psychologists, but it is not without some support in the literature. Consider the intriguing set of experiments recently reported by Mackie and Allison (1987). In these studies subjects read about voters in a small town whose bid to recall commission members failed at one time but passed six months later. The bid succeeded the second time, not because of any change in the vote (the actual percentage of voters supporting the recall remained the same), but only because the required proportion of votes needed for the recall had changed from 65% to 50% during the six-month period. Nonetheless, subjects perceived that the underlying attitudes of the group had changed from the first vote to the second, and the amount of perceived change was related to the degree to which subjects made dispositional attributions about typical voters in the community. Apparently, the tendency to make dispositional attributions contributed to the tendency to perceive change.

The general neglect of attributions of person change as a topic of research has resulted in missed opportunities to pursue interesting insights and findings already in the literature. Lord and Gilbert (1983), for example, investigated how subjects perceived the effectiveness of change-inducing stimuli as a function of whether the change was gauged on the basis of a within-person comparison or a between-groups comparison. Although Lord and Gilbert's concern was with what they term the "same person" heuristic, the study also raises interesting questions about the relative salience of individual change and its role in intuitive reasoning about potentially change-inducing events. There are also several studies on the perceived impact of events on attitudes that indicate that perceptions of an actual change in a person's attitudes may be necessary before perceivers initiate an attributional search (Layton & Moehle, 1980). Together, these findings suggest that judgments of person change may mediate other important inferential processes in the course of social perception. An awareness of perceivers' concerns with person change can also give a new perspective on standard ways of conceptualizing attributional phenomena. In some areas of attributional theorizing, the tendency has been to frame the perceiver's choice in terms of a continuum running from stability to instability (Kelley, 1967, 1972; Weiner, 1974; Weiner, Russell, & Lerman, 1978). If person characteristics are not stable, they have been presumed to be unstable, with the latter alternative seeming unpatterned and unpredictable. For perceivers, the alternative to stability may sometimes be change (often patterned, predictable change), with the consequence that they readily make a variety of person attributions that are not well represented on the stability-instability continuum as it is currently construed.

Social Cognition and Judgments of Change

Before leaving this chapter, it will be useful to briefly consider how recent social cognition studies have handled temporal information, along with the implications of this handling for capturing the perceiver's interest in person change. The long-neglected fact that person perception is extended over time has become an explicit focus of recent research (e.g., Hastie et al., 1980; Higgins, Herman et al., 1981; Fiske & Taylor, 1984; Wyer & Srull, 1984). Much of the recent social cognition work has attempted to shed light on the recall and reconstruction of person information and the effects of memory for persons on the kinds of conclusions that perceivers draw about people over time. Although a considerable amount is now known about processing over time, much of it has been learned without having time pass in the target's life.

With regard to the perceiver's experience, subtle temporal variations have been employed. Perceivers have been provided with information at several different times, they have been asked to recall at later points the information that was received earlier, and they have been given new information at a later point to be used in conjunction with whatever they recall from an earlier point. Yet, despite concern for subtle nuances in when the information is received and used, the target itself has frequently been presented in a "timeless" fashion, as if time-related changes in the target were nonexistent or irrelevant. A few investigators have noted that the use of information might be different when details of temporal information about the target are provided (Fiske & Taylor, 1984; Higgins, Kuiper, & Olson, 1981; Hintzman, 1974), and studies focusing on such temporal details have occasionally been completed (e.g., Snyder & Cantor, 1979; Snyder & Uranowitz, 1978). For the most part, however, the work has continued to focus on the problem of how perceivers organize incoming information to maintain the same overall impression of a person (Hamilton, 1981; Higgins & Bargh, 1987).

How an understanding of perceivers' interest in change might reorient our approaches to studying the processing of specific kinds of information is illustrated by the case of memory for inconsistencies. Recall of inconsistencies has been a major focus of work because of its implications for various models of processing (Hastie, Park, & Weber, 1984; Higgins & Bargh, 1987); that same interest intersects with present concerns because there may be occasions where change is the preferred explanation for inconsistent behavior, as earlier studies in this chapter suggest. The research to date has shown that inconsistent information is sometimes better remembered than information that is consistent with prior impressions, but that the inconsistent information is sometimes more poorly remembered; it appears that inconsistent information sometimes receives more processing and sometimes less (for reviews of findings see Hastie, Park, & Weber, 1984; Markus & Zajonc, 1985). Attempts to make sense of these mixed and complex results (Hastie, 1980; Markus & Zajonc, 1985; Srull, 1981) have related them to perceivers' existing categories and cognitive structures. According to these interpretations, perceivers' categories for interpreting information about persons lead to expectations that people will be the same. Consistent information is basically more easily processed and recalled; but because perceivers are motivated to maintain the same view of the person, inconsistent behaviors may receive more attention and processing as perceivers work to reinterpret them so that they will fit with their preexisting views of the person (Crocker, Hannah, & Weber, 1983; Stern, Marrs, Millar, & Cole, 1984). This theoretical account is based largely on findings from the "timeless" case, where inconsistencies have been presented with little or no temporal information. Although these findings have been treated as readily generalizable (because the timeless case is treated as the generic case), perceivers operating with an intuitive category of person change may process the information in ways that are not indicated by the existing research, which assumes that the perceiver is trying to reduce, rather than fully acknowledge, the inconsistencies. In cases where the perceiver's processing goals include the assessment of behavior for the possibility of genuine change, the handling of inconsistencies may be very different from what is currently envisioned.

Remaining central across many areas of social cognition are the traditional social perception questions having to do with how perceivers maintain their stable views of others. The inclusion of more explicitly cognitive approaches seems not to have dampened the reliance on stability assumptions: the categories perceivers are said to use and the processing goals that are assumed to underlie their search for information are still widely believed to represent, at their core, concerns for stability.

Chapter 5

Judging Change with Informal Data

When informal data serve as the basis for comparing the present with the past, what sorts of conclusions about change are likely to emerge? What characteristics of everyday information account for the features that are common to change judgments in different areas? These questions will be the focus of the present chapter as we examine how the character of change impressions can be understood as an outgrowth of the kinds of informal facts readily available to the intuitive perceiver.

Much of the research presented here builds on the analysis of everyday information begun in Chapter 3. It was noted there that change judgments differ in the demands they place on perceivers and in the kind of information about the present and past that will be crucial for making those judgments. In some cases what is needed are facts about variability in the past and present, whereas in others the requisite information might concern frequency and population; but whatever the relevant kind of information, it may or may not be readily available in everyday sources. In this chapter, we will examine the consequences—first for rate change judgments and then for judgments of change in variability—that follow from the way in which past and present information germane to the judgment is made available to intuitive perceivers. Some common information conditions will be identified and studies of the change impressions that emerge under various constellations of information will be discussed. The studies reported here are intended to illustrate the more general approach of situating intuitive change judgments within particular informational contexts.

Rate Change Judgments

Change judgments frequently involve claims that an activity or outcome has changed in how common it is now relative to the past. We hear it said that there are now more acts of violence, or fewer acts of helpfulness, or that more people are engaging in illegal business activities. There are said to be fewer people reading books, more people going to college, and so forth. Judgments of rate change occur across many different areas; they can concern change in an individual, a school, a business, a community, or even the country as a whole. As such, rate change judgments represent a very general class of judgments. Regardless of content area, people making implicit rate comparisons begin with some knowledge about the frequency with which the target behavior has occurred at different times. But if the only information available is about the sheer frequency of the target behavior, the change impressions that result will often be problematic because differences in population size cannot be taken into account. What is typically needed, then, is for perceivers to have information about population sizes at the two comparison times along with whatever information they have about frequencies.

The question of how well represented population information is in everyday accounts will concern us in the studies to be described in this section. Some of the ways that population information might be made available in everyday information are examined and the consequences for change impressions are considered. To illustrate the importance of population information and its method of presentation, three sets of studies will be presented involving different kinds of population information (number of high school students in a community, number of friends, and number of day-care centers) and different ways of bringing population information to the perceiver's attention. After examining judgments of teen pregnancies at a high school, we will look at judgments of change in the health and relationships of a group of friends and, finally, at judgments of change in rates of abuse at day-care centers.

Judging Change in Teen Pregnancy

Consider the case of perceivers deciding that teen pregnancy has become more common. In making such judgments, perceivers need to be cognizant not only of the number of pregnant teens—a fact likely to be salient—but also of the relative sizes of the teen cohorts at the two comparison points. A failure to take into account shifts in population could potentially lead one to conclude that a rate change has occurred simply because the number of pregnant teens has changed. The higher number could be treated as an indication that sexual activity among teenagers has rapidly increased or that a "loosening of the moral fabric" has occurred (see Silka & Albright, 1983); similarly, a decline in sheer frequency might be interpreted as showing that programs intended to reduce the number of teen pregnancies have been effective when, in point of fact, the overall rate may have stayed the same while the size of the teen population underwent a decline.

Although it is often important to take population into account, it may be difficult to do so if population information is not readily available or not very salient. Indeed, population information is frequently not salient in informal accounts, and is sometimes not presented at all (see Silka & Albright, 1983, for examples). In newspapers, magazines, and television shows, accounts of the problem of teen pregnancies often focus on the number of pregnant teens, with little or no information provided about crucial population details. To begin to look at intuitive change judgments as a function of what is known about population information, three studies will be described (Silka & Albright, 1983) that investigated conclusions about change in teen preg-

Table 5-1. Mean Judgments of Pregnancy Rate Change.

Number of pregnancies in	Population size in 1980 relative to 1970		
1980 relative to 1970	Half	Same	Double
Same	20.71	16.50	9.94
Double	24.18	22.75	18.67

Note: 1 = Rate is much lower now; 15 = No change; 29 = Rate is much higher now. From "Intuitive judgments of rate change: The case of teenage pregnancies" by L. Silka & L. Albright, 1983, *Basic and Applied Social Psychology, 4,* p. 342. Copyright 1983. Adapted by permission.

nancy rates under conditions where population information was salient, not salient, or not available.

In each of the studies, subjects were presented with information about a high school in 1970 and 1980. Under the guise of placing themselves in the role of peer counselors and imagining how they might handle different issues at the school, subjects reviewed detailed information about the school, including data about school size and number of teen pregnancies in 1970 and 1980. The school size and the number of pregnancies were varied. All subjects learned that in 1970 the school size was 1200; the school size in 1980 was said to be half that size, the same size, or twice that size. The number of pregnancies was said to be 25 in 1970, and the number for 1980 was said to be either the same or double that for 1970. The design of the study was thus a 3 × 2 factorial (School Size × Number of Pregnancies).

In the first study, the population information was made salient. School size information was presented early in the stimulus materials and subjects were asked to answer a question as a part of the peer counselor activity that made them attend to the size information (i.e., they were asked to describe ways that the school was similar to and different from their own high school).

As a part of the cover story, participants were asked various questions about their reactions and opinions throughout their reading of the case study materials. Several direct and indirect questions about rate were included among these questions: "How does the pregnancy rate in 1980 compare to the pregnancy rate in 1970?" (29-point scale, endpoints and midpoint "Rate is much lower now," "No change," "Rate is much higher now"); "In your opinion, how common has the pregnancy problem become at this high school?"(29-point scale, endpoints "Much less common" and "Much more common"); and, "In your opinion, how serious has the pregnancy problem become at this high school?" (29-point scale, endpoints "Much less serious" and "Much more serious").

All three questions elicited a similar pattern of response. Table 5-1 shows responses to the first question about rate. An analysis of variance demonstrated clear effects for both population information and pregnancy information (main effect for population information, $F(2,89) = 16.36$, $p < .001$, main effect for pregnancy information, $F(1,89) = 27.63$, $p < .001$). The interaction was not significant, $F(2,89) = 1.66$. The array of means is as would be expected if both population and pregnancy information were taken into account by subjects. When population had decreased and pregnancies had stayed the same (or increased), subjects perceived an increase, as they did when the population stayed the same and pregnancies doubled. When population and pregnancies similarly fluctuated, subjects saw little change. And when population declined and pregnancies remained the same, subjects appropriately perceived the rate as having declined. When asked how serious the problem had become, subjects again used both population information and pregnancy information (population main effect $F(2,89) = 9.01$, $p < .001$, pregnancy main effect $F(2,89) = 21.98$, $p < .001$, interaction $F(2,89) = 1.73$, n.s.), as they did when asked how common pregnancies had become (population main effect $F(2,89) = 9.45$, $p < .001$, pregnancies main effect $F(2,89) = 10.18$, $p < .01$, interaction $F(2,89) = 3.72$, $p < .05$).

In brief, these results show that population information is readily incorporated into change judgments when that information is made salient. More often than not, however, population details are not highly salient in everyday sources. In the case of articles on teen pregnancy, for example, much emphasis is placed on the number of pregnancies while little is placed on population information. Headlines herald the fact that there are now 1,000,000 teen pregnancies (e.g., Wexler, 1979); only much later in the articles are relevant details about population provided (see Silka & Albright, 1983). The next study examines the impact of population information on change judgments when population facts are not salient.

Subjects in the second study were provided with the same statistics about school size and number of teen pregnancies as in the first study. Again, under the guise of acting as peer counselors evaluating the need for sex education in high schools, participants reviewed case study materials in which the increase or constancy in number of pregnancies was presented at the very beginning of the materials. Prior to receiving the school population figures, readers were asked some open-ended opinion questions about the pregnancy numbers related to the cover story. Following this, participants received background information about the characteristics of the school in 1970 and 1980 that included the population figures. In this study, unlike the earlier one, participants were not asked to compare and contrast this school with their own; thus, case study questions did not direct subjects' attention to school size or implicitly suggest that variation in size might be important. After reading all the materials, participants were asked two questions related to the rate issue: a general rate question, "Compared to 10 years ago, how would you describe the rate of pregnancy at this high school now?" (29-point scale, endpoints and midpoint "The rate is much lower now," "The rate is the same," "The rate is much higher now"); and a specific rate question in which participants were asked to select a specific rate change (1 = Current rate $\frac{1}{6}$ of the previous rate, 6 = Same rate, 11 = Current rate 6 times previous rate).

Similar effects were found on the general question and the specific rate question. Responses to the general rate question showed that, regardless of change in population size, subjects were much more likely to infer that the pregnancy rate had increased when the number of pregnancies had doubled ($M = 23.84$) than when the number had stayed the same ($M = 15.67$), $F(1,66) = 34.42$, $p < .001$. The main effect for population size was not significant, $F < 1$, and there was no interaction,

$F < 1$. On the specific rate question, a significant main effect for pregnancy information was found ($Ms = 6.15$ for same number of pregnancies and 6.95 for increased number of pregnancies), $F(1,66) = 4.00, p < .05$. Again, the population information had no effect, $F = 2.23$, and there was no interaction, $F < 1$. Participants who learned that the raw number of pregnancies had increased were much more likely to say that the rate had doubled than were subjects who received the same number of pregnancies, regardless of compensating changes in population size. This is perhaps best seen in terms of choices of specific categories on the question: 26 of 38 (68%) who received the same number of pregnancies selected the rate choice of "Same," whereas 23 of 34 subjects (68%) who received the double number of pregnancies selected "Twice" as their choice.

These results indicate that background population details have a more limited impact when they are conveyed with little emphasis. The findings suggest that population shifts will not always be given much thought, perhaps in part because a satisfying impression of change can be formed without drawing on population figures. Although population information was aptly used by perceivers when their attention was drawn to it, relevant population data may not be inevitably sought out. Because informal sources often omit population details entirely, the question of how people evaluate the adequacy of their knowledge base when population details are omitted is important for understanding the readiness with which people infer change. The next study investigates subjects' requests for population details when those details are not available in the information provided.

Under a peer counselor guise similar to that used in earlier studies, participants were again provided with information about teen pregnancies at the target high school. Here, the teen pregnancy information consisted of the number of pregnancies in 1970 and 1980, together with brief vivid descriptions of four of the young women who had become pregnant. The descriptions, averaging 150 words, were adapted from an article on the teen pregnancy "epidemic" that had appeared in a popular magazine (*McCalls*, 1978), and were used here to reproduce a typical context in which incomplete statistics occur. The information about number of pregnancies was identical to that used in the previous two studies. Again, half of the subjects were led to believe that the number of pregnancies had doubled over a 10-year period, whereas the other half were led to believe that the number of pregnancies had remained the same. After reading the case studies and the statistics, participants were asked a number of open-ended questions related to the cover story of peer counseling. The critical information question asked: "In order to decide the extent to which teenage pregnancy has become more of a problem in the last decade at this high school, is there any additional information you would like to have?" Participants were given an opportunity to list as many different kinds of information as they wished.

In response to this question, only 11 of the 47 subjects requested information about school size, and the number of such requests did not significantly differ as a function of whether the number of pregnancies had increased or remained the same (seven in the Pregnancies-Doubled condition and four in the Pregnancies-Constant condition). Although requests for population information were infrequent, those that were made were clearly distinguishable from other sorts of information requests. For example, several subjects in the Pregnancies-Constant condition asked, "Has the population at the school changed?" and "Has the enrollment increased or decreased since 1970?" Two subjects in the Pregnancies-Doubled condition stated their concerns this way:

> You have to look at the number of students (has it increased or decreased?) in the past decade, then the number of students who are pregnant. Compare the number of students in high school and the number of teenagers who are pregnant . . . . I think that percentage increases are necessary to determine this. Just because there are 25 in 1970 and 50 in 1980 does not mean the problem has grown. There might be twice as many kids attending the school now than in 1970.

Given that requests for population information were rare, with 77% of participants not requesting any sort of information related to population size, it is of interest to examine what sorts of information *were* requested by these subjects. Interestingly, the information they felt they needed was often of a numeric sort but concerned with event frequencies and their possible causes. For example, five subjects requested information about hidden pregnancies (abortions, unknown pregnancies, etc.). Two subjects requested information about hidden pregnancies in each year between 1970 and 1980. One requested information about pregnancies at other schools in order to make comparisons. Many wanted more specific qualitative information about students (had attitudes changed, what were their morals like, what were the ages of the pregnant students?) in order to assess the growth of the problem. Some requested information about family background and changes in the families (economic status, sexual attitudes within the family, behavior of older siblings that might contribute to early sexual activity), and some requested additional information about the school (changes in student composition, the nature of the discipline, the student/teacher ratio). Significantly, some responses indicated the extent to which readers simply accepted the frequencies at face value. For example, one participant in the Pregnancies-Doubled condition accepted that a rate change had occurred and wanted to move on to understanding reactions: "How does the community as a whole react to this epidemic?" Another subject in the Pregnancies-Doubled condition responded that no additional information was needed because "the statistics speak for themselves."

Together, these three studies have provided examples of the kinds of information conditions in which social perceivers encounter population data. The results highlight the sensitivity of perceivers' change impressions to differential emphases on the relevant population data, the willingness of perceivers to rely on frequency information, and the tendency of perceivers to find frequency data meaningful on their own.

The next studies investigate the impact of population shifts in another topic area, one in which the population information comes to the perceiver in a different way than in the preceding studies. In the teen pregnancy studies, information about population was conveyed by providing subjects with explicit population figures. In the studies that follow, information about population size is conveyed indirectly through varying the number of events that subjects are exposed to.

Judging Change In a Group of Friends

Just as large-scale populations can vary, populations can fluctuate at a local, even individual, level. The number of students a teacher has can vary over time. The number of times a person is around a certain friend can increase or decrease. The number of friends an individual has can grow or decline at different points in the life span. Taking into account these changes in "population" size will be important in interpreting the meaning of change—for example, the meaning of having more students complain about one's teaching, or having more arguments with one's friends, or having more friends with troubled relationships. Where no attempt is made to control for shifts in population size, change judgments could sometimes reflect shifts in sheer frequency alone.

In order to examine individual population shifts and their impact on change judgments, subjects were given correspondence consisting of greeting cards supposedly written to an individual by his friends at two times separated by a decade. The number of cards included in the correspondence either changed or remained the same. The rate of certain kinds of events was held constant (rate of health problems in the first study and rate of troubled relationships in the second study), but the *frequency* of the events changed with the number of cards. Of interest were the change conclusions drawn by subjects when encountering the same rate but with that rate represented in a larger population. The studies were ostensibly investigations of acquaintanceship, with subjects being told that the purpose was to see what impressions would be formed of an individual by knowing what his friends were like at different periods in his life. In both studies, subjects knew that they would be participating in a two-part study with the two sessions spaced one week apart.

In the first study subjects read Christmas cards supposedly written to an individual by same-age friends at different points in his life. During the first session, all subjects read seven letters written to "Kevin" when he was 21. The letters ranged in length from 100 to 200 words and discussed general happenings in the writers' lives (e.g., relationships, jobs, school). Of the seven letters, two mentioned health problems. Subjects who returned the following week (all but 3 of the original 35 subjects) read letters written to the same individual when he was 31 years old (with these letters being written by different "friends" than those in the first session). Subjects were randomly assigned to read either seven letters, two of which contained comments about being ill, or 28 letters, 8 of which contained comments about being ill. The letters had been pretested so as to contain similar degrees of illness. Without having access to the original letters, subjects were then asked to answer a series of questions about Kevin and his friends. After a series of open-ended questions addressed to the cover story, subjects answered questions about change in Kevin's friends. Embedded among questions about other possible changes (e.g., more or less settled, more or less creative, more or less athletic) were two questions about changes in health: "To what extent did the rate of ill health change?" (answered on a 10-point scale with higher numbers representing a greater degree of ill health at a later age), and "In general, what do you think Kevin's friends were like now when

Kevin was 31 relative to his earlier friends: more troubled by ill health, less troubled by ill health?" (answered on a 10-point scale with higher numbers representing a greater concern about ill health at a later age).

On both questions, the number of letters was found to have a significant influence on judgments of rate of illness. When subjects read a larger number of letters, they perceived a higher rate of ill health ($M = 7.5$) than when they read the same number of cards ($M = 5.7$), $t(30) = 4.53$, $p < .05$. Also, subjects who read a greater number of letters were significantly more likely to conclude that the older people were more troubled by the incidence of ill health ($Ms = 9.0$ and 6.6), $t(30) = 4.76$, $p < .05$.

In the second study, subjects again read cards supposedly sent to an individual when he was aged 21 and then when he was aged 31. Subjects in this study received a number of cards in the second session that was equal to, greater than, or less than the number received in the first session. Thus, subjects read either seven and seven, seven and 28, or 28 and seven cards in the first and second sessions (letters from the first and second session were again said to be from different friends). As before, the letters discussed many topics; in this study the rate of comments about people being in troubled relationships was held constant. Subjects who read 28 letters learned of eight such relationships; subjects who read seven letters learned of two such relationships. After reading the letters and without access to the correspondence, subjects were asked to judge changes in the rate of troubled relationships: "Did the rate of troubled relationships change as the friends grew older?" (29-point scale, endpoints and midpoint 1 = "Rate of troubled relationships was much lower at older age," 15 = "Did not change," 29 = "Rate of troubled relationships was much higher at older age"). As anticipated, judgments of change in the rate of troubled relationships were influenced by the number of cards read ($Ms = 11.08$, 14.58, 17.83, decreased number of cards, same number of cards, increased number of cards, respectively), $F(2,33) = 3.69$, $p < .05$. Subjects who read a different number of cards from the first session to the second were more likely to perceive a change to have taken place.

Judging Change in Day-Care Abuse

The next two studies investigated the effects of information about the current population on judgments of changes in rates of day-care abuse. Previously we have considered the effects that can follow from having or not having population information for both of the comparison periods; in these studies we consider the impact of adding population details for the present only, in a case where perceivers may seriously underestimate the size of the current population as a result of the dramatic increase the population has undergone in recent years.

In recent years there has been a significant increase in the number of day-care centers and in the number of parents using day-care centers. Although the intuitive perceiver may be aware that more parents are now using day-care centers, information about the exact number of day-care centers currently in operation is not widely available. News stories about day-care centers rarely provide information about numbers, or even describe what the typical day-care center is like so that the reader can form an impression of typicality; more commonly where the topic of day care warrants news coverage it is because of some instance of abuse or alleged abuse. And such reports on individual cases of day-care abuse generally do not include population information or give any indication as to the number of centers in operation that have *not* been sites of alleged abuse. In the absence of salient information about the increased population, the most visible sign of that increase may be the higher number of abuse cases. Work by Nisbett and others (Nisbett, Borgida, Crandall, & Reed, 1976; Slovic, Fischhoff, & Lichtenstein, 1982) suggests that people might overestimate changes when their knowledge consists largely of information about current abuse cases. If perceivers greatly underestimate the number of centers, then hearing about more cases of abuse may easily lead to the view that the rate of abuse has dramatically increased over previous years.

Examining perceptions of change in day-care abuse after exposure to a news article is one way to evaluate the impact of everyday information that omits details about the underlying population size. A recently published article offered an opportunity to examine impressions of change in day-care abuse that arise when population information is not included in the write-up, and to then look at the effect on these impressions of having population information added to the original article. The article (Ball, 1985) had three features that made it useful for exploring these informational issues. Like many articles on day-care abuse, this front-page story focused on a specific incident of alleged abuse (in this case involving sexual molestation of a three-year-old girl by a male juvenile). Second, the original article included a summary of the number of centers in the state that had been closed due to abuse during the year. And, third, like most articles on the topic, this one did not include any population information about the number of day-care centers operating in the state. Thus, it was possible to investigate the kinds of impressions people form from articles that omit population information, and then to see if intuitive change impressions are influenced by the inclusion of relevant population information. Do people bring to the articles they read an accurate sense of the underlying population size that helps them compensate for what is not included in the articles? Or, do people approach the articles with a misleading sense of the number of day-care centers (perhaps as a consequence of recurrent exposure to similar articles in the past), and then come away from them with that view still intact and unchallenged?

In a study using a transcript of the newspaper article, some participants read the account in its original form (without population information), whereas others read the same article but with actual population figures inserted. The inserted population information was presented in two ways. Some subjects learned simply of the existence of 11,000 day-care centers in the state. Other subjects received information that emphasized the number of day-care centers that had *not* been sites of reported abuse. After being told that there were 11,000 centers, these subjects learned that: "Ten are suspected of abuse; the other approximately 10,990 have not had any reported abuse." In its original form, the article contained 11 paragraphs. The inserted population information appeared at the end of the sixth paragraph immediately after the summary of the number of day-care centers that had been closed:

The A and T home became the 10th day care facility in Massachusetts since September
to have its license suspended; the suspensions were the result of allegations of sexual
or physical abuse, Coughlin said. There are approximately 11,000 day care facilities
in the state of Massachusetts.

After reading the article, participants answered several open-ended questions about
their overall impressions of day-care centers and about their view of children's safety
in day-care centers. They were then asked several questions about the current rate
of abuse in day-care centers in Massachusetts and about changes in the rate of abuse
over the last 10 years.

The impact of population information on views of current rates was first assessed.
Subjects were asked, "In your opinion, what is the current rate of child abuse in day
care centers in Massachusetts?" (9-point scale, endpoints "Very low rate of abuse,"
and "Very high rate of abuse"). The population information had a significant effect
on views of the current rate. Subjects in both conditions in which population information was provided viewed the current rate of abuse as significantly lower ($M =$
3.45 in the nonemphasized condition and $M = 2.91$ in the emphasized condition)
than did subjects in the no population information condition ($M = 4.56$), $F(2,75)$
$= 3.65, p < .03$. The two population conditions did not differ significantly from
one another. Of interest was the question of whether seeing the current rate as lower
would lead to a different view of the degree of change that had taken place over the
last decade. Subjects were asked about change in rate of abuse: "In the last 10 years,
what has happened to the rate of child abuse in Massachusetts day care centers in
your opinion?" (9-point scale, endpoints and midpoint "Rate of abuse has greatly
decreased," "Has not changed," "Rate of abuse has greatly increased"). Change
impressions were found to be unaffected by population information. Subjects uniformly gauged the abuse rate to have increased ($Ms = 6.63, 6.43, 6.65$, no population information, nonemphasized population information, emphasized population
information, respectively), $F < 1$.

In all conditions, subjects were asked to estimate the number of day-care facilities
in the state. For participants in the two population information conditions this
question served as a manipulation check; almost all subjects in both conditions gave
the correct figure of 11,000. For subjects who did not receive population information, this question was used to obtain information about their prior beliefs concerning the number of day-care centers in the state. These subjects were found to
underestimate the number of day-care centers in the state, with a mean estimate of
589 (estimates ranged from 5 to 1000). To provide an additional measure of the
salience of population information, subjects were also asked to underline any
aspects of the news article that they found to be important. Of the subjects who
received population information , 37 out of 51 failed to underline that information
even though they generally underlined many other aspects of the story (e.g.,
description of the incident, information about the 10 closings). Thus, the fact that
subjects attended to and remembered population data does not necessarily mean that
they considered it important.

Table 5-2. Current Rates of Abuse.

Control	No population	Population not emphasized	Population emphasized
3.55_{ab}	4.00_a	2.83_{bc}	2.00_c

Note: The higher the mean, the greater the perceived current rate.
Means sharing the same subscript do not differ at the .05 level.

The study was then run again with the original three conditions, plus a condition in which subjects answered all questions without reading the news article. Of interest was the issue of whether people would judge the rate differently without having just read a news story providing vivid information about a case of alleged abuse. Table 5-2 shows mean responses to the question on the current rate of abuse.

A significant effect was again found, $F(3,41) = 3.66, p < .02$. Subjects in the two population conditions differed significantly from the no population information condition, whereas subjects in the control condition did not differ from the subjects who had not received population information. Yet, once again, differences in views of the current rate of abuse had no effect on perceptions of change. In all conditions, subjects uniformly rated abuse in day-care centers to be on the increase ($M = 6.45$). Subjects in the control condition were also asked to estimate the number of current cases of abuse and the current number of day-care centers. On average, they underestimated the number of day-care centers ($M = 652$) and overestimated the number of cases of abuse ($M = 28.3$).

The present studies are interesting in their suggestion that giving people detailed information about the present without accompanying information for the past will do little to alter beliefs about change, regardless of the impact of that information on perceptions of current rates of abuse. As a consequence of reading the article, subjects in the two population information conditions came to perceive the current rate to be lower than they had earlier believed, but perceiving current rates to be lower did not lead them to alter their views that the rate of abuse had greatly increased over the last decade. It might seem reasonable to conclude from these findings that articles on abuse should also include information about the past population and past number of abuse cases; however, it would be difficult to provide comparable figures given that licensing rules and requirements for reporting and investigating suspected abuse have not remained constant.

These studies were carried out around the time of several widely publicized trials for day-care abuse in California and in Massachusetts. The effect of multiple reports of the same incidents on perceptions of frequency here remain unknown, but work by others (Johnson et al., 1977) would suggest that perceivers will infer from multiple reports of the same incident that the number of such incidents is higher than it actually is. More generally, it has been noted (Nisbett et al., 1983) that one major problem faced in making judgments of social events is that of ambiguity in what constitutes the sampling space. The issue of what constitutes the appropriate population for comparisons of abuse cases is an example of how such ambiguity can create interpretational difficulties. Consider the following points relevant to the present studies. The population figure of 11,000 represents the number of centers, not the number of children (which, of course, is far greater). One case of abuse may occur at a day-care center in which there are many other children who are not targets of abuse. Moreover, the figure does not include centers that have not applied for licensure or child sitters with fewer than three children in their charge. In the case of the abuse figures, only those cases are included that have reached the attention of authorities; the number of unreported cases remains undetermined. Furthermore, many of the cases recounted in the news are drawn from incidents occurring nationally rather than simply from those occurring in the state of Massachusetts. As with many kinds of social behavior, there are inherent ambiguities in whatever population and frequency figures are selected to serve as the basis for describing the behavior. Ambiguities such as these may provide a context in which personal beliefs about change can take precedence over problem-laden numerical data, and those beliefs may be difficult to modify even with more detailed information about the relevant populations.

Taken together, the three sets of studies presented here underscore the variety of forms in which population information can appear and the variety of contexts in which population information becomes relevant to judging change. Sometimes the numbers in question are explicit, sometimes not. Sometimes population figures are on the same scale as the frequency information, and sometimes not. The judgments can be about state or national populations in a particular topic area, or about the population of events in an individual's life. When social change is at issue, the concern can be with change in large or small groups. Each of these population situations may carry with it its own set of interpretational difficulties. For example, in the case of drawing change inferences from small data sets (such as might be available for events among one's personal friends), the limited information is more volatile, making interpretations of change especially problem-prone. As Tversky and Kahneman (1982) have shown, people tend to be insensitive to such problems with small numbers and are frequently as willing to draw inferences from small data sets as from much larger ones (but see also Fong et al., 1986). In view of the array of difficulties facing perceivers in the task of judging changes, it will not be surprising if their judgments are often made in the absence of clear-cut evidence for or against change.

Intuitive Judgments Where Variability Is Important

Summarized in the last section were several studies intended to highlight the importance of population details; in this section consideration is given to knowledge of past variability and the role it can play in judgments of change. In the analysis presented here, two cases are considered in which change judgments may grow out of limited knowledge of past variability: (1) where the perceiver is attempting to decide whether a recent instance of behavior represents a change given what is known about the past, and (2) where limited information about past variability is juxtaposed against abundant evidence of variability in the present.

Variability in the past is common to many areas. Political attitudes held by different people may have varied. The performance of a particular actor or sport figure might have been variable from day to day in the past, or the political stances of a politician may have fluctuated. The frequency with which people helped others or were friendly with their neighbors may have varied. College students were probably diverse in what they were like in the past, as were professors. There may have been variability in what a person's parent-child relationships were like or in the quality of one's marital relationship. If perceivers are apprised of past variability, it can be taken into account in making change judgments; in the absence of knowledge of past fluctuations it is difficult to take variability into account without making certain assumptions, and variable and nonvariable past series may be indistinguishable in the condensed information that is available for the past. In some cases, what remains for comparison is, in effect, not a range of points but rather one summary point, and perhaps one whose function of representing central tendency to the exclusion of variability in past behavior is not readily recognizable. For example, the information perceivers receive about political views in a particular period—say, the 1950s—may implicitly convey the impression that people were uniformly conservative in their views rather than simply that the average of the range of opinions was on the conservative side. Similarly, available information may suggest that all students in the 1960s were liberal, not merely that the broad range of political opinion centered at a somewhat liberal point. The information that is available for the past will often fail to mirror the heterogeneity of past events, and may instead convey an image of uniformity.

What is learned about the past is, of course, necessarily limited in comparison with the full extent of what actually happened; but what is known about past *variability* is especially likely to be limited. Many factors can combine to narrow the range of information available about the past. As noted in Chapter 3, the individual items that make their way into current culture as representative of earlier eras often reflect a limited range of the original items and activities. The old hit songs still receiving airplay, for example, capture only part of the range of earlier popular music. The summaries of earlier eras often convey impressions of what was typical rather than of the full range of past behavior. For example, thumbnail sketches of particular presidencies (e.g., Nixon, Ford, Carter) attempt to capture what is deemed characteristic of that presidency, but without necessarily conveying information about inconsistencies that did not fit the overall pattern. The social indicators and statistics that are reported for the past often focus on averages rather than on the range of past behaviors. We hear about the average number of deaths due to drunk driving in the 1970s rather than about how those figures varied from day to day or year to year. Facts are presented about the average income during some period, or the average amount of schooling, average life span, or average length of marriages. Even when the past in question is a period we experienced personally, the ways we think about and remember the past may deemphasize variability. Recalling what a particular period was like may focus attention on what was most characteristic of that period rather than on the broad and complex differences in behavior that occurred during it. Similarly, recalling an acquaintance's past by relying on general impressions is likely to direct interest to what the person was characteristically like in the past rather than to the fluctuations in that individual's behavior.

To the extent that our information about the past is impoverished in details about past variability, what sorts of consequences for intuitive change judgments might follow? Will people avoid making intuitive comparisons when variability information is lacking? Or will the absence of information about variability go largely unnoticed by the intuitive perceiver? If so, might change impressions arise because of apparent differences between the past and the present stemming from the use of a simplified baseline as the point of comparison?

Social perceivers often meet with situations in which they are deciding what to make of some recent instance of behavior. For example, during a recent visit one's retired parents may seem much less energetic than one recalls them as having been in the past; or an old friend encountered at a class reunion may seem less happy than in the past. If the past variability in such cases is inadequately represented in the information for the past, will the present behavior be more likely to appear indicative of change than if the information about the past fully captures the variability?

In a study previously reported (Silka, 1981), the possibility that perceptions of change in others are affected by knowledge of past variability was examined by providing subjects with data sets for past behavior that contained substantial variability and instructing them to attend to and remember either the range of past behavior or the average level of past behavior. Participants were subsequently given information about an instance of current behavior for one of the target individuals and were asked to judge the extent to which the person had changed. Of interest was the question of whether the judgment of change would differ across instructional conditions.

The information about variability was given in the form of psychological test scores for three individuals that were said to have been taken over a period of 12 months. Subjects received 12 scores for each of the individuals, and were told that the scores came from tests that had proved effective in accurately diagnosing mental illness. The values ranged from 1 to 93 with higher values representing greater degrees of psychological dysfunction. The values for the crucial target person (called Person C) had a 20-point range and a mean near the high end of the scale ($M = 85.8$). In addition, the means of the first and second halves of the data series for Person C approximated each other, as did the standard deviations.

Half of the subjects were instructed to remember an average for each individual and the remaining subjects were instructed to remember the range of scores for each individual. Either one week later or immediately thereafter (for subjects in the control conditions), subjects received information about the current mental health of the target person and were asked about their impressions of change. The new information informed subjects that: "Person C has been in a mental hospital. In arguing for his release a psychiatric aide noted that Person C's level of mental illness in the most recent month had decreased. The psychological test score was 76." Without access to the original values, subjects were then asked to judge the significance of the change implied by the new value ("In your opinion, how justified would someone be in believing that Person C's psychological health had permanently improved?," 31-point scale). It was predicted that when knowledge of variability was high (i.e., in both immediate control conditions and in the delayed condition where subjects had been asked to remember variability), the new value would not be seen as indicating a change. However, once recall was delayed, subjects who had not attended to the prior variability would infer from the new value that the person may have changed.

An analysis of variance revealed significant main effects for time of recall, $F(1,49) = 8.26, p < .01$; instructional set, $F(1,49) = 5.80, p < .05$; and a nearly significant Time of Recall $\times$ Instructional Set interaction, $F(1,49) = 3.99, p < .051$. As predicted, these effects were primarily due to heightened ratings of change in the average-delayed recall condition. Subjects in this condition had a mean change rating of 14.23 whereas those in the other conditions had a combined mean rating of 7.07. A Duncan's Multiple Range Test confirmed that subjects in the average-delayed recall condition differed from subjects in each of the other conditions, whereas subjects in the latter conditions did not differ among themselves.

In a second study (Silka, 1981), an additional instructional set was added. In addition to the average and range condition, some subjects were simply instructed to form a general impression of the information they received. The aim was to see whether people would encode variability information in the absence of explicit instructions to do so. Also, the numbers provided in this study concerned a different topic in order to see whether the results from the first study would generalize.

A 3×2 factorial design was employed, varying instructional set and time until recall. Subjects again received several sets of values and were asked to remember (a) the range of values for each set, (b) the average value for each set, or (c) a general impression of the nature of each set. Subjects received additional information either immediately or one week later, and were asked to judge the degree to which the information signified a change from the past.

In the cover story, subjects were told that they would be receiving data on average monthly air pollution levels in several target cities for a 12-month period. The pollution values were ostensibly based on an air quality index that could vary from 0 to 140, with 0 representing negligible pollution and 140 representing a pollution level that is highly hazardous to human health. For half of the subjects in each instructional condition, this concluded their activities for the week. The remaining subjects received additional information about the current pollution level in City C, being told that the present pollution level in City C was 76 (a value 10 points below the mean of the original series). The information was presented in the following way:

> Based on the overall air quality index for each city, some industries in selected cities are being asked to install additional pollution control equipment. In City C, some of the business people are concerned about the possibility of having to install this equipment because of the expense. In arguing their case before the Environmental Protection Agency, they presented statistics that showed that the current month's pollution level was down. The air quality index for the current month for City C was 76.

Table 5-3. Mean Ratings of Change.

Time of recall	Attend to range	Attend to average	Form general impression
Immediate	8.84$_a$	8.53$_a$	5.92$_a$
Delayed	8.33$_a$	14.41$_b$	16.00$_b$

Note: The higher the mean, the greater the perceived change. Means sharing the same subscript do not differ at the .05 level. From "Effects of limited recall of variability on intuitive judgments of change" by L. Silka, 1981, *Journal of Personality and Social Psychology, 40*, p. 1014. Copyright 1981. Adapted by permission.

Subjects were asked to judge the degree to which a change had occurred. The delayed subjects received the additional information and filled out the dependent measure one week later.

Table 5-3 presents mean responses to the question, "How much of a permanent change in the air quality index of City C has there been?" (31-point scale, endpoints "No change" and "Substantial change"). An analysis of variance revealed a significant main effect for time of recall, $F(1,75) = 13.26, p < .001$, and a significant Time of Recall × Instructional Set interaction, $F(2,75) = 4.65, p < .01$. The main effect of instructional set was not significant. A comparison of the means using Duncan's Multiple Range Test showed that the predicted effects were obtained. As in the first study, subjects who were asked to assess change immediately saw little change whether they attended to the range or average; however when recall was delayed, subjects who attended to the average saw greater change than did subjects who attended to the range. Thus, this study shows that the selective effect of time on variability information is reproducible in a different topic area. In addition, the pattern of results in the general impression condition suggests that people are unlikely to encode variability information without being explicitly instructed to do so.

Together these studies indicate that whether people remember variability can be a factor in the impressions of change that are formed. If change judgments are eventually to be well understood, it may be important to study different types of information in terms of their relative susceptibility to the effects of time. From these preliminary results, it appears that variability may be one type of information that is especially vulnerable to the passage of time (see also Mackie & Allison, 1987). Next we consider change conclusions that things have become more variable than they used to be and the way in which limited information about past variability could contribute to such impressions.

One relatively common class of change judgments consists of those in which things today are said to be more variable and unpredictable than they used to be. We may hear it said that an artist's work is more erratic than in the past, that the weather has become more unpredictable, or that business conditions fluctuate more from month to month than they did in the past. Such judgments are sometimes the reflection of true changes in variability. But to make these judgments in such a way that they reflect genuine changes in variability, the available information about the present and the past has to be comparable. There are many instances where this will not be the case, most notably when we have information about day-to-day events for the present but when our information for the past consists of a summary that does not capture past variability.

Information for the present often includes a formal or informal record of individual change-relevant data points: an athlete's current game-by-game fluctuations in performance, the day-to-day changes in the weather, the daily ups and downs in one's relationships. Because the information for the present is readily available in such cases, the range or variability of the data is likely to be evident (see Nisbett & Kunda, 1985, for examples showing accurate judgments of present variability). In contrast, what we know or learn about the past is often of a more limited nature: it may highlight what was true on average, or what was typical, or what was taken to be most symbolic of the earlier time. When that information about the past comes to us from other sources, it may not even be apparent that information about past variability has been left out. What happens to change impressions in cases where this kind of asymmetry is characteristic of the information perceivers have for the present and the past? To examine the possibility that comparisons of variable present data with a past average can heighten impressions of change, two studies (Silka, 1983) were conducted in which subjects were given information about individual items in the present and were asked to compare those items with the average for the past or with past information that included both the prior range and average.

In a study on the topic of the weather, in which the ostensible purpose was to explore better ways to present weather information, participants learned that they would be receiving information about past and present temperatures at an unidentified locale. Based on this information they would be asked to make certain judgments about the weather and to describe their impressions of the adequacy of the presentation format. In one of the conditions, subjects were told that their past information would consist of the average temperature for this time of year in this locale in the past. The other subjects were told that their past information would consist of the average and range of temperatures typical for this time of year in this locale in the past. The average temperature for that month in the past was said to be 68 degrees; the normal range was said to be 47 to 89 degrees. The experimenter then presented 30 temperatures representing the month's daily temperatures. These values had a mean of 68, a standard deviation of 11.22, and a range of 48 to 88. After receiving each value, subjects were asked to compare the value with the average (or range, in the range condition) and to make a note of their comparison in the appropriate space on a worksheet. When the presentation of the values was completed, subjects were asked several questions related to the cover story. Embedded in those questions was a question on change in variability of the weather: "Relative to the past, the weather has become more variable (more unpredictable)" (29-point scale, endpoints "Not at all" and "Very much"). In addition, two open-ended questions were included, the first asking about impressions of current weather, and the second about what additional information participants felt they should have been given to form a more complete impression of the weather in this location.

The main dependent measure asked subjects to assess the extent to which, relative to the past, the current weather was more variable. An analysis of variance showed a strong effect for the kind of baseline used for the past. Subjects provided with only the prior average were more likely to infer that the weather was now more variable ($M = 16.68$) than were subjects who had been given more complete information that included the prior range ($M = 7.41$), $F(1,64) = 31.43$, $p < .01$.

Prior to answering the major dependent variable, participants were asked the open-ended question requesting them to describe briefly their general impressions of the weather now. Statements were dichotomously categorized as either describing the weather as variable or as making no statement about the weather being variable. Proportions of subjects in the range and average conditions making variability statements were then compared. Only 12 of the 34 subjects provided with information about prior range described the current weather as variable, whereas 23 of the 34 subjects given only the prior average did so. A z-test for differences between proportions showed this difference to be significant (z value of 2.67, $p < .01$). The second open-ended question asked subjects what additional weather information they felt they needed in order to form a more complete impression of the weather in this locale. Of the 34 subjects in the average condition, only one requested any kind of information about past variability. Thus, subjects who were not given prior variability information did not request such information when given an opportunity to do so.

This study illustrates that direct comparison of variable information for the present with a past average can increase the likelihood of seeing the present as more variable than the past. Fictitious figures were used in the study in order to hold constant the average and the degree of variability for the past and present data. To eliminate the possibility that the effect was due to the statistics having been different from what the subjects would normally experience, the study was replicated employing local weather information.

The basic procedure was largely the same as in the preceding version. Subjects were told that they would be receiving average (or range) information about past weather and would be asked to compare that information with current weather statistics that would be provided. The weather statistics were taken from U.S. Weather Service reports for the local area (Boston) and were for a recent year during the same fall period in which the study was run. These values had a mean of 60.5, a standard deviation of 10.44, and a range of 48 to 76. As subjects received the temperatures, they were asked to compare each temperature with the average (or range) as to whether or not they felt the temperatures to be unusual. After all temperatures were presented, a series of questions was asked about the statistics. Embedded in these questions was a question asking subjects about perceived changes in the variability of the weather, "Relative to the past, how variable is the present weather?" (29-point scale, endpoints "Not at all variable" and "Highly variable").

Not surprisingly, subjects who compared individual daily temperatures with the average perceived more of the temperatures to be unusual than did subjects who compared those temperatures to the range. Subjects in the average condition described a mean of 17.41 values as unusual, whereas subjects in the range condition described a mean of 3.96 values as unusual, $t(50) = 7.69, p < .01)$. On the primary dependent measure, subjects in the average condition were more likely to describe the weather as having become more variable than participants in the range condition ($Ms = 18.93, 14.56$, average and range conditions, respectively $t(50) = 2.89, p < .01)$.

As the foregoing studies make clear, the informational conditions under which people receive their information for the present and the past can lead to differences in the kinds of change conclusions that are reached. The effects of a few of those information constellations have been illustrated here, including cases where information comes from the environment and cases where the information is drawn from the perceiver's own recall of the past. Other consequences of particular information conditions will be considered in subsequent chapters when we investigate the effects of causal contexts on change judgments and examine the confidence with which perceivers make change judgments when they lack specific information for the past.

Chapter 6

Looking for Change

Intuitive change judgments often arise in an after-the-fact fashion. Perceivers do not ordinarily start out expecting to assess change in the future and so proceed to gather information about events in a uniform manner over time in order to have appropriate information at hand when an occasion for assessing change arrives. On the contrary, it is typically not until some occasion calling for a change judgment occurs that an interest in gauging change in a particular area comes into play.

Concerns with change arise for a reason, commonly with the perception of, or information about, something that is likely to cause change. An intuitive focus on change often begins after an event has taken place that leads the perceiver to anticipate that things will change, and hence the interest often develops after the would-be baseline period is over—sometimes long after. At that point, the perceiver no longer has the opportunity to assemble the appropriate baseline information but must depend in a retrospective way on information about the past. Whatever informal knowledge perceivers possess about different periods may then serve as the basis for deciding whether there has been a change.

On the face of it, the fact that intuitive questions about change tend to arise at times that are inopportune with regard to formulating of data bases for judging the change would seem to be daunting for perceivers. What is available in the way of information can be so lacking in comparability that it would seem difficult for perceivers to come to any view of whether change has occurred. But these incommensurabilities of data may not pose the problem for perceivers that one might expect if perceivers begin their interpretation of the data in a context where they have reason to conclude that change has occurred as soon as their interest is generated. In other words, when making intuitive judgments, the change-relevant context may itself become a source of evidence for change—not only providing the reason for an interest in change but becoming part of the evidence used to conclude that a change has in fact taken place. Indeed, the satisfaction with an impoverished or incommensurable evidence base that perceivers seem to feel in a variety of real-world cases may be a result of the causal context itself adding to the information constellation.

A concern with causal contexts when considering change is not limited to the intuitive perceiver. Even in the professional measurement of change, the causal context often provides the rationale for assessing change. Time-series analysis is not proposed at some random point; the selection of the time frame is often dictated by the need for reliable data about the periods leading up to and following an intervention. Yet, in professional assessment, the existence of causes that might produce change does not, in itself, provide evidence as to whether the change has occurred. The causal context simply makes it of interest to compare the differences in the rate of events before and after some intervention (or other causal event that is expected to produce a change), and it is this comparable before and after information that serves as the basis for the change conclusion. How intuitive perceivers evaluate information in that same kind of context and the extent to which they rely on the before and after information as opposed to information about the intervention itself will be of interest to us here.

The previous chapter focused on some of the ways in which information with different characteristics can shape informal judgments of change. There it was pointed out that asymmetries between past and present information sometimes contribute to the appearance of change, and it was noted that impressions of change can be enhanced by the omission of certain kinds of information for the past, especially when those omissions are not readily noticed by perceivers. Change impressions may not automatically be prompted by such instances of asymmetry or incompleteness, but when the perceiver has reason from the outset to believe that change is in the offing, those same characteristics may combine with information about the cause to promote powerful impressions of change.

The present chapter focuses on the role played by change-relevant causal context in augmenting the information constellations that induce perceivers to make change inferences. We will examine how perceivers use incomplete or "unmatched" information from the past and present both within and outside of some sample causal contexts. The willingness with which people make change judgments in causal contexts, even without past information, will be considered. We will also examine the tendency of perceivers to neglect crucial information about the past (such as prior variability) as a function of whether or not their judgments are being made in a change-related causal context. Together, the various studies presented here will serve as a point of departure for the analysis of information use in cases where the perceiver has some prior reason for inspecting the available information for signs of change.

Expectations for Change

In dealing with specific change-relevant contexts in this chapter, we will of course be dealing with people's actual expectations for change. The notion that people do carry about expectations for change may be counterintuitive in certain respects given the long-standing emphasis in social psychology on perceivers' supposedly dominant (if not totally exclusive) expectations for stability. Consequently, it will be useful and informative to briefly consider some evidence bearing on the nature of people's change expectations. As we shall see, people may show few signs of having change expectations in the abstract, but they seem to be endowed with rich intuitions about the kinds and amounts of change that are to be expected in relatively concrete situations. The evidence about to be discussed suggests that change judgments must be situated in change-related causal contexts if we are to understand the force of change expectations.

In a study designed to examine the nature of people's pre-existing change expectancies, 31 subjects were asked a combination of different sorts of questions: (1) questions about how easy it is for people to change different aspects of themselves (traits, beliefs, emotions, habits, or behavior), (2) questions about how often people actually do change these different aspects of themselves, and (3) questions abut how likely people are to change after different specific experiences (e.g., serving in the military). Subjects were first asked how easy it is for people to change. These questions did not ask about the effects of particular experiences or the impact of any context but were simply worded so as to ask about the general ease of changing traits, beliefs, emotions, habits, or behavior. Responses were made on 9-point scales, with endpoints "Not at all easy" and "Very easy." After answering each question on the ease of changing, they were asked "How often do you think people do change in terms of traits?," with corresponding questions being asked about beliefs, emotions, habits, and behavior. Nine-point scales were used, with endpoints "Happens to few people" and "Happens to most people." Again, these questions did not ask about the effects of any experience or context, but simply asked about change in the abstract. The responses to these general questions indicated that subjects did not see change as something that is easy to achieve or as something that is expected to happen to everyone. The overall ease of changing was rated as relatively low ($M = 3.66$), with the mean rating on individual questions ranging from a low of 2.87 for traits, to a high of 5.16 for behavior. Regarding the issue of whether change happens to most people or to few people, the mean rating across questions was 4.50, with average judgments on individual questions ranging from 3.96 for emotions, to a high of 5.94 for behavior. Again, the overall expectancy of change, at least in the abstract, was fairly low.

In the study, subjects were also asked how likely it is that someone would change after undergoing certain experiences (9-point scales, endpoints "Not at all likely" and "Very likely"). The experiences inquired about were: serving in the military, becoming famous, winning a large lottery, using heavy drugs, surviving a life-threatening illness, having a friend commit suicide, having a parent die when one is young, being a victim of a sexual assault, being a victim of a life-threatening crime. The order of topics was varied. In response to this set of questions, very clear expectations for change emerged. Indeed, there was very little overlap between responses to the general questions and responses to the specific-experience questions. The average rating across the experience questions was 7.18. All of the means on the specific-experience questions were above the scale midpoint, and most were substantially above the midpoint. The mean ratings ranged from a low of 5.90 for the change expected from serving in the military to a high of 7.77 for being a victim of a sexual assault. In a later study in which 44 subjects were asked about the impact of a somewhat different set of experiences (parents' divorce, failing in school, being a rape victim, marrying, getting divorced, crime conviction, breaking up a relationship, combat), high expectancies for change after a variety of experiences were again found. The average change rating was high ($M = 6.90$), with ratings on individual questions ranging from 5.86 (for breaking up) to 8.14 (for rape).

Subjects in the original study were provided with opportunities to write open-ended comments about the kinds of change they expected. These written comments give yet another indication of people's expectations that change will often be the outgrowth of certain kinds of experiences. In describing the impact of serving in the military, for example, participants wrote about a variety of changes that might be expected:

> The person would probably become more disciplined and mature. But they also lose some of their open-mindedness.... More dignified, more respect for people and country, more obedient, high self-esteem.... It might make a person more patriotic or instill confidence or "make him a man." ... Some people are scarred for life as a result of painful memories and fears of military life. Others may now enjoy life much more—be more appreciative.

In describing the effects that might follow from becoming famous, subjects cited various changes that could take place:

> The person may become pompous, snobby, airy as the result of feeling popular and admired. In the other direction a person may become quieter and more withdrawn. Also one may become more thankful and appreciative .... A person's ego would certainly grow if they became famous. They would probably forget who they were and where they came from .... The person would most likely become arrogant and self-centered. Only a special type of person can remain unchanged by fame.

Or, in describing the changes that might occur in someone after the loss of a parent while young, subjects wrote:

> A person would change emotionally, psychologically. The person would feel very upset, as if someone had done this intentionally .... This might make one constantly angry at the world for taking away a loved one .... Having something dramatic like that happen at a young age would usually bring about a personality change. The person would probably be more withdrawn and feel unwanted .... From this point on the individual may become more cold, sensitive, frightened or insecure due to the loss of someone close and special. This could cause the individual to change many things about himself: beliefs, qualities, emotions.

Taken as a whole, the responses in this study indicate that change expectancies are largely tied to specific contexts and that people's expectancies may best be seen when those contexts are the focus of interest. As the results show, subjects' answers to abstract questions about whether change will occur could create the impression that change expectancies are absent in intuitive perceivers. Yet when those same subjects are questioned about change in terms of the impact of experiences of various sorts, a far different picture of their change expectancies emerges. Here, pronounced and widely shared assumptions about change are revealed. How pervasive such contexts are remains an open question, but it is likely that for the intuitive perceiver the environment is rich in experiences that are perceived as capable of bringing about change. Many different events may be seen as instigators of change, some bringing about change at the level of the individual and some inducing change in groups or large-scale social change (for examples in popular literature of assumptions of change stemming from various causes, see LaRossa & LaRossa, 1984; Lenz, 1982; Sheehy, 1977; Sheridan, 1977; *Time*, 1979; Zilbergeld, 1983). In the remainder of the chapter, we identify some forms that these ostensibly change-causing events can take, both for person change and for social change, and consider the impact that knowledge of putative causes of change can have on the interpretation of ambiguous information about change.

Judging Change with Information from Different Sources

One of the difficulties in attempting to infer change is that the information for the present and the information for the past often come from different sources and thus cannot be assumed to be commensurable. In the case of a social problem like child abuse, for example, the source of information about past rates of abuse will sometimes be different from the source of statistics about current rates. Or, in attempting to assess what an individual is like in adulthood as compared with her youth, a perceiver may have to depend on very different sources for information for the two times. Such differences in information may be troublesome to judgers when there is no reason for expecting change; but when a reason does exist, the ambiguity posed by potential incommensurabilities in the information may be less likely to be seen as posing difficulties for the inference of change. To investigate this possibility, 63 subjects participating in a study on community problems were given statistics on child abuse in a particular city. The statistics they received for one period were said to be taken from a different source than the statistics for a second period. Some subjects learned of the statistics together with an ostensible cause of change in the incidence of abuse, whereas other subjects did not. The interest was in whether knowledge of conditions that could potentially lead to an increase in child abuse would enhance perceivers' willingness to make change judgments in the face of incommensurability in the data.

In the materials they read, participants learned that Maine cities and towns were being asked to report statistics on child abuse. They were told that in one of the larger Maine municipalities, one with about 7000 children, the statistics from police records for a certain year showed that 132 cases of child abuse had occurred. They learned that several years later, again with approximately 7000 children in the community, the statistics on child abuse as taken from physicians' reports showed that there had been 211 cases of abuse. Thus, the statistics were reported as being from different sources, with the second source being potentially more inclusive than the first (though this was not pointed out explicitly to subjects). Half of the subjects additionally learned of deteriorating economic conditions in the city. Those learning of the ostensible cause were told that some of the major industries (paper mills and shoe factories) in the town had suffered layoffs during the second time period, and that there had been an upturn in alcoholism in the community.

After reading over the materials and answering several open-ended questions related to the supposed purpose of the study, subjects were asked to judge how much change had occurred and how confident they were that they could be sure from the figures available that child abuse had changed. When asked "What has happened to child abuse in this Maine town?" (9-point scale, endpoints "Probably has not changed at all" and "Probably has changed a lot"), participants who had learned of the deteriorating economic conditions saw more change as having occurred ($M = 6.03$) than did subjects who were asked to make judgments without information about the ostensible cause ($M = 4.71$), $t(61) = 1.99, p < .055$. When subjects were asked "How confident are you that you can be sure from the figures available that child abuse has changed in this town?" (9-point scale, endpoints "Not at all confident" and "Very confident"), participants were found to be more confident when they had information at hand about an ostensible cause ($M = 5.56$) than when they did not ($M = 3.71$), $t(61) = 2.54, p < .02$.

Participants also answered an open-ended question that asked them to describe in their own words their impressions of what had happened to the problem of child abuse in this Maine town. Subjects in the cause condition frequently brought up points about the economic situation in describing what many seemed to treat as a real change in child abuse. For example:

> Alcoholism and unemployment have been directly responsible for the doubling increase in child abuse . . . . The child abuse problem increase is due to the problems the parents were experiencing. I think there should be a support group for the unemployed because they took out their frustrations on their children . . . . When people lose their jobs, they are under a lot more pressure and stress, so it becomes harder to control their emotions, therefore more people abuse their children . . . . I feel that due to the increase in unemployment and alcoholism it has caused the number of child abuse cases to grow.

Unlike subjects in the cause condition, subjects not receiving the causal information sometimes noted the potential incommensurability of the two sets of figures. For example:

> Apparently the number of cases of abuse has risen over several years. An important aspect to note is the fact that the data was gathered from different sources. Perhaps doctors' reports concerning child abuse are always greater in number than police reports . . . . It seems that the number has increased although the first report was from the police and the second from doctors' reports. It's hard to say if it actually went up due to the fact that most cases are not reported to the police . . . . I feel that the problem has not increased. The number of reported cases are a lot less than the real number of child abuses. The doctor reports are more because they do not include the law.

The results of this study are in some ways similar to those reported in Chapter 4 for the study on the "fundamental attribution error," in which perceivers made change judgments even though the target person had been observed under very different conditions at the two times. Just as the data-source differences here were not so important in the presence of an ostensible cause, the differences in situations in the earlier study may not have been important because there was an ostensible reason (i.e., aging) for change to have occurred. Regardless of the source of the incommensurabilities (whether differences in the situations in which observations are made or differences in the sources from which statistics are collected), those incommensurabilities may be of less concern when other features of the context make it plausible that change is possible or even likely.

Judging Change Without Past Information

At times we know about events that could have changed someone even when we do not know what the person was like before those events took place. Intuitive change judgments sometimes seem to be made even when information about the past is lacking. Consider the following examples. The unusual behavior of converts to a "brainwashing" cult seen proselytizing on a city street is sometimes taken as a sign of how much these individuals have been changed by their cult experience, with such conclusions being drawn even though the perceiver did not know the individuals prior to their conversion. Children not known by a perceiver until after their parents' divorce are sometimes seen as having been changed by the experience of their parents' divorce; the mere fact that the children are now badly behaved (or that they show high rates of attention-seeking behavior, etc.) is taken to be evidence that they have changed. Signs of irritability and conservatism in an elderly person are sometimes assumed to be indications that the person has changed with advanced age, even in the absence of knowledge about what the person was like at earlier points.

When knowledge of what a person was like in the past is limited or entirely absent, it will sometimes be a consequence of the roles of the perceiver and target and sometimes a result of receiving information from the media or other secondhand accounts. In certain roles and occupations, experience with unfamiliar individuals typically begins after some potentially change-inducing event has taken place. In the case of police, social workers, and clinical psychologists, certain individuals tend to be encountered only after a significant traumatic event has occurred (after a person has been a victim of a crime, after some family disturbance has occurred, after a suspected case of abuse). Similarly, media reporting on particular individuals frequently commences at the time of a newsworthy occurrence that provokes interest in the possibility that the person has changed or is about to change. Individuals abruptly appear in the news after winning a lottery, after being nominated for an important post, after winning a contest, after being the victim of a highly publicized crime, and so forth. What we know about a person often consists only of a salient change-relevant cause and something about what that person is like afterwards.

The manager of actor Sylvester Stallone (Kubick, 1986) once remarked that people have often thought of Stallone as having changed into an arrogant person after he became successful. But what people do not realize, the manager went on to say, is that Stallone was *always* arrogant; he had not changed. Although it is natural to think of change judgments as based on comparisons of the past with the present, perhaps information about the past does not always figure in intuitive conclusions about change. Indeed, simply knowing about an ostensible cause for which the perceiver has strong intuitions may make it seem unnecessary to know in any detail what the person was like in the past. As in the Stallone example, if an individual's current behavior matches what one would expect in a changed person, this behavior might then be taken as a sign that change has indeed occurred.

Some preliminary findings bearing on the possibility that change judgments can occur in the absence of past information were reported by Silka and Albright (1982). The study in question looked at whether knowing about an ostensible cause, when that information is combined with the kind of behavior expected to follow from the cause, can serve as a basis for seeing change. Under the guise of studying daydreaming habits, participants were given information about a high level of daydreaming behavior in a target individual. Everyone was given information about the target's current daydreaming behavior, but only some of the participants received information about similar behavior in the past. In addition, some subjects also received information about an ostensible cause while others did not. After reading the case study, participants were asked to judge the extent to which the target had become more or less troubled than she had been previously and to judge whether in general she had changed.

After describing some of their own daydreams, subjects received information about the present behavior of a college student named Karen. The information consisted of a passage approximately 250 words long, describing what was purportedly a representative day's activities in her life. Embedded in the passage were descriptions of five brief instances of daydreaming and of failures to attend to immediate surroundings (e.g., Karen daydreaming during a math class). Half of the subjects had also been provided with a similar passage describing Karen's daydreaming a few days before. The earlier passage also included descriptions of five brief episodes of daydreaming. Both passages were designed to reflect substantial daydreaming and were pretested to contain similar levels of daydreaming. In addition to the manipulation of whether participants had information about the past, half of the subjects in each of the above conditions also happened to learn that Karen had been the victim of a recent assault near her apartment. The occurrence of the attack was listed as having taken place between the first and second observations. After reading the case study, participants were asked to answer a number of questions related to the supposed purpose of the study, including several that assessed the extent to which Karen's later behavior was seen as indicating that she had become more troubled and that she had changed.

As a check to ensure that the level of daydreaming was considered high, all subjects were asked to rate the degree of daydreaming shown by Karen. On a 10-point scale (1 = low daydreaming), subjects rated the daydreaming as moderately high (M = 7.78). There were no differences across conditions. Participants were then asked to assess the extent to which Karen had become more or less troubled (10-point scale; 1 = less troubled). An analysis of variance revealed two significant main effects and no interaction. Participants who saw only the present elevated behavior were significantly more likely to infer that Karen had become more troubled than were participants who saw the elevated behavior both times (Ms = 6.77 and 5.30, no past and past, respectively), $F(1,48) = 11.78, p < .01$. Similarly, participants given causal information were significantly more likely to infer that Karen had become more troubled than were subjects not given the causal context (Ms = 6.62 and 5.44, causal information and no causal information, respectively), $F(1,48)$ = 7.30, p < .01. On the more general change question, similar effects were found. When asked the extent to which Karen had changed (10-point scale, 1 = no change), participants without past information were significantly more likely to infer that change had occurred than were subjects who had past information (Ms = 5.77 and 3.00, no past and past, respectively), $F(1, 48)$ = 22.24, p < .01. Participants with causal information were somewhat more likely to conclude that change had occurred than those without causal information (Ms = 5.04 and 3.70, causal information and no causal information, respectively), $F(1,48)$ = 3.71, p < .10. The interaction was not significant. Although participants made heightened change estimates without past information, they were more confident of judgments when they were made with past information. A significant effect for having past information was found, such that subjects with past information were significantly more likely to express confidence in their judgments compared to those without past information (Ms = 7.04 and 5.00, past and no past, respectively), $F(1,48)$ = 5.9, p < .05.

A second study, previously unreported, looked at tendencies to infer a change in a child following a causal event (his parents' divorce or an address change) even though no information about the child's behavior prior to the event (the divorce or the move) was available. To collect information to be used in the study, pilot subjects were asked their impressions of whether grade school children (males and females) would be changed in various ways (aggressiveness, friendliness, etc.) by the divorce of their parents; and in a separate part of the pilot study, subjects were also asked to generate examples of different kinds of behaviors (aggressive, friendly, etc.) that typical third graders might show. The judged likelihood of change in aggressive behavior for boys was high. Based on pilot subjects' responses to these questions, the topic of aggressiveness was selected and the subjects' examples were used to create a set of behavioral descriptions for the study itself.

In the study, ostensibly on how developmental impressions are formed, 66 subjects were given descriptions of behavioral observations of a grade school student that were supposedly completed during his first month in the third grade. No information was given about his behavior prior to this time. All of the observations were said to have been made on the playground. Each was reported by date, and on all of the days the young boy was depicted as highly aggressive (e.g., "He played hard on the playground—he was very aggressive during a game," "Engaged in name-calling"). In addition to the behavioral observations, it was reported in the teacher comments that the boy had either (1) had an address change just prior to the opening of the school year, or (2) had an address change just prior to the opening of the school year because his parents had just divorced and his father had moved to another state; in a third condition, no ostensible cause information was provided. Thus, all subjects had only present behavioral information, and, in addition, some had supplementary information about ostensible causes.

After reading over the materials, subjects were first asked to describe their general impressions of the young boy. They were then asked whether they thought the boy had the trait of aggressiveness (9-point scale, endpoints "Probably does not have an aggressiveness trait" and "Probably does have an aggressiveness trait"). Subjects in all three conditions were agreed that he had an aggressiveness trait ($M = 6.79$), $F < 1$. Subjects were then asked whether they thought his high level of aggressiveness represented a change (9-point scale, endpoints "No, he has probably always been high on aggressiveness" and "Yes, his level of aggressiveness has probably changed recently"). Here a significant effect was found whereby subjects who learned of the divorce were more likely to believe that the level of aggressiveness represented a change ($M = 6.73$) than were subjects who learned that his address had recently changed ($M = 5.64$) or who had received no ostensible cause information ($M = 4.86$), $F(2,63) = 4.10$, $p < .03$. In their open-ended comments, subjects in the divorce condition frequently referred to the boy's behavior as an outgrowth of the family disruption:

> Shawn seems to have had negative effects from the divorce of his parents. It appears that his anger toward his parents' breakup is shown during school time. He is troubled and responds in a violent manner . . . . Shawn is very upset that his parents were divorced. He is angry that his father has moved away. He probably feels rejected because his father left and that his father doesn't love him. He is venting his anger as aggressive behavior toward everyone at school . . . . Shawn obviously has become aggressive due to the loss of his father. He is constantly playing hard and aggressive because he does not want anyone to take advantage of him. Now because his father left, he probably feels he has to be tough and act like a bully.

The daydreaming study and the aggressiveness study together suggest that it may not be necessary to have past behavioral information in hand to infer a change. By relying on knowledge of a change-related cause or by using features of current behavior, the intuitive perceiver can piece together a picture of change. A reliance on current behavior could mean that seeing change will sometimes depend on the extent to which a target's behavior is consistent with change expectations rather than on how different the person has become from his or her own past. Those whose typical behavior happens to be unusual or elevated relative to the norm may more readily give the appearance of having changed. A reliance on information about change-related causes suggests that change can be inferred by virtue of the presumed power of causes to create change rather than simply as a function of comparisons between present and past behavior.

In an intriguing study of the impact of causal information (e.g., participation in a self-help group) on inferences of self-change, Conway and Ross (1984) found that people readily perceived a change that had not occurred when they knew of a salient potential cause. Conway and Ross (1984) went on to note that attributional analyses can provide a variety of insights as to how people might come to see change, once those analyses are applied to the process of perceiving change rather than stability, and once the focus is on how the perceiver uses knowledge of a cause to infer an effect rather than vice versa (as is traditionally done). Studies of causal schemas and of judgments made with incomplete information might be tapped to understand possible inferences of change in the presence of salient change-related causes.

Judging Change with High Past Variability

Knowledge of an intervention (i.e., some program, policy, or action intended to bring about a change) is yet another important form of ostensible cause information. As with other sorts of causal information, knowing that an intervention has taken place could make perceivers more willing to infer change in the absence of past information, or perhaps could help perceivers form an impression of change even when faced with incommensurable information of the sort investigated in previous studies. In this section we consider the question of whether knowledge of an intervention affects the way in which available information about the past is used in judging change. To explore this issue, we return to the theme of past variability and examine the extent to which perceivers take into account degree of prior variability when making change judgments in the presence of causal information.

One of the difficulties in deciding whether things have changed is that the baseline for comparison often consists of a highly variable series of events rather than a uniform one. In the last chapter it was noted that information about past variability will be unavailable in some situations, with the result that knowledge of prior variability cannot figure in change judgments. At other times such information is available to perceivers, and the question of interest becomes one of whether the information about variability is used. The specific issue to be addressed here is whether perceivers will take into account the degree of prior variability when making change judgments in those situations where interest in change may be at its highest— namely, when perceivers have reason to believe that things should change because of an intervention designed to make them change.

On the basis of certain analyses in the extant literature, one might suspect that perceivers would not take past variability into account in intuitively judging change in the presence of intervention information. Campbell (1969; Campbell & Ross, 1968), for instance, provided examples of misleading change inferences that appear to rest on the neglect of information about prior variability. Campbell reported that after a program of stricter laws was enacted in Connecticut to reduce traffic fatalities, then-Governor Abraham Ribicoff claimed that a change had occurred on the basis of a decline in highway fatalities in the year following the enactment of the new laws. Yet, as Campbell noted, this particular drop could simply have represented just one more fluctuation in a series where substantial variability occurred from one year to the next. Just as such illustrative cases suggest that intuitive perceivers may ignore past variability in the interest of seeing change, so too the fact that people often have difficulty with the concept of regression toward the mean (Hogarth, 1987; Kahneman & Tversky, 1973) and tend to underweight other sorts of base-rate information such as Bayesian prior probabilities (Azjen, 1977; Hogarth, 1987; Nisbett & Borgida, 1975; Slovic & Lichtenstein, 1971; but see also Kruglanski, Friedland, & Farkash, 1984) would suggest that intuitive change judgers might not take past variability fully into account in deciding whether or not change has occurred.

Variability is characteristic of many past series in contexts where change judgments arise and where decisions are made to institute interventions. Consequently, the relationship between past variability and knowledge of interventions is of considerable interest. As an initial step toward understanding change judgments in such contexts, studies of several different sorts were conducted to investigate the informal use of variability information in intuitively judging change under different conditions. The first set of studies investigated people's use of variability information in arriving at intuitive change conclusions about traffic fatalities, both in the presence of intervention information and in its absence. The second set of studies concerned the use of variability information about a troubled family's interactions where the causal event could not be assumed to be independent of past variability.

In the first study, supposedly investigating interpretations of state and community problems, 91 subjects received detailed information about an unnamed state in another part of the country. Included in the overall information packet were two sets of so-called in-depth topics about events occurring in the state, the first on the filler topic of sex discrimination in youth sports, and the second on the topic of alcohol-related traffic fatalities. After reading and answering questions on the filler materials, participants received information about the problem of drunk driving in the state. Here participants were given figures said to represent the number of alcohol-related fatalities in the state for each year in the 10-year period between 1974 and 1983. Before the intervention was introduced, participants received fatality figures that were either high in variability or low in variability. The mean was the same in both conditions. In the low-variability condition, the numbers ranged from 25 to 49 with a mean of 37 (the first and second halves of the series had the same average and the final baseline value was at the mean). In the high-variability condition, the mean was again 37 but the values range from 11 to 63 (all high-variability numbers were obtained by subtracting 14 from each low-variability value below the mean and adding 14 to each low-variability value above the mean, with values at the mean remaining the same). In both conditions, the figures were said to have been taken directly from official highway patrol records and were said to reflect the actual number of alcohol-related fatalities in the state.

Some participants also learned of an intervention, introduced early in 1984, that was designed to decrease the number of alcohol-related traffic fatalities; other subjects did not receive this intervention information. The information about the intervention consisted of a description of a new program designed to address the problem of drunk driving; the description was adapted from articles in several newspapers in the New England area that reported on recent programs instituted or proposed in different area states:

In early 1984 the newly elected governor of the state put into place a package of tough new laws and programs designed to reduce the number of drunk driving deaths. The program was well-funded and included a number of different ways to stop drunk driving deaths. More patrol cars were put out on the roads. Friday night and Saturday night roadblocks were put into place in major problem areas. Stiffer sentences were imposed for drunk driving offenses, including a mandatory overnight jail stay for all individuals convicted of drunk driving. The drinking age was raised to 21 and health programs in all high schools included a mandatory unit on the serious consequences of drunk driving. That unit included showing films on the consequences of being in traffic accidents. Dramatic public service announcements about the dangers of drunk driving and about the new programs were aired on television stations and radio programs.

Table 6-1. Judgments of Actual Trend Change.

	No intervention	Intervention
Low variability	6.68_{bc}	7.87_c
High variability	3.87_a	6.04_b

Note: The higher the mean, the greater the perceived change.
Means sharing the same subscript do not differ at the 0.5 level.

In sum, participants received information about different degrees of variability, and were either apprised or not apprised of an intervention. Finally, everyone learned that in the year 1984 the total number of alcohol-related fatalities was 19. After reading the case-study materials, subjects were asked to answer questions related to the supposed purpose of the study and also to answer a number of questions about their impressions of change.

Before examining the results on the change measures, it should first be noted that the manipulations were effective. Participants in the high-variability condition judged the variability in the 10-year baseline period to be greater than did participants in the low-variability condition ($Ms = 7.15$ and 5.30, respectively), $F(1,87) = 23.26, p < .001$, and the variability manipulation did not inadvertently influence perceptions of the prior average, as participants across all conditions rated the average number of fatalities similarly for the 10 background years ($M = 37.10$).

The purpose of the study was to see whether judgments of change would be different when subjects knew of an intervention than when they did not, and, further, whether the availability of program information would lead people to ignore the degree of past variability. On all of the change questions a similar pattern of results emerged whereby participants readily inferred more change when they knew an intervention had been introduced than when they did not, but remained attentive to prior variability even when program information was available. Participants were first asked how likely it was that the low number reflected an actual trend change in the drunk driving death rate. Here both a main effect for program information, $F(1,87) = 14.60, p < .001$, and a main effect for variability information, $F(1,87) = 27.79, p < .001$, were found (see Table 6-1 for means). In both the presence and absence of intervention information, participants in the low-variability condition were more likely to infer change than those in the high-variability condition, but, overall, the judgments were higher with the intervention information than without it. This same tendency for perceivers to be influenced by knowledge of an intervention, but to still take prior variability into account, was also exhibited on the other questions. For example, when participants were asked how likely it was that the drunk driving fatality rate in 1985 would remain as low as it was in 1984, subjects in the high-variability/no-intervention condition saw it as least likely to remain low

(M = 4.70); subjects in the low-variability/intervention condition saw it as most likely to remain low (M = 7.39), and subjects in the high-variability/intervention condition and low-variability/no-intervention condition were intermediate in their responses, which were indistinguishable from one another (Ms = 5.87 and 5.95), main effect for variability $F(1,87) = 10.57, p < .003$, main effect for cause $F(1,87) = 9.31, p < .004$. Similar effects were found when subjects were asked whether the 1984 death rate represented a true decrease or just one more fluctuation, main effect for variability $F(1,87) = 39.54, p < .001$, main effect for cause $F(1,87) = 12.52, p < .001$, and when they were asked how much of a genuine change there had been in the problem of deaths due to driving under the influence of alcohol, main effect for variability $F(1,87) = 32.58, p < .001$, main effect for cause $F(1,87) = 14.39, p < .001$.

As these results show, perceivers were sensitive to the implications of background variability in assigning meaning to a particular low value. At the same time, knowing that a change-related program had been introduced shaped how readily the low number was interpreted as evidence of change. Indeed, knowing of the program's existence was sufficiently impactful that subjects who had been given information about a highly variable past but knew of the intervention made change judgments that were indistinguishable from those made by people who had information about a more stable past but who were unaware of the intervention.

It has sometimes been noted that corrective or ameliorative programs tend to be introduced just after an extreme point in a data series, for example, when the incidence of some social problem is at an all-time high (Cook & Campbell, 1979). When program introduction is confounded in this way with peaks in a series, opportunities are created for fluctuations that may be due to regression toward the mean to be interpreted as genuine changes. One possible consequence of such confounding could be that high-variability series could support intuitive change inferences more readily than low-variability series because in the former the peaks away from the mean are considerably more extreme. At the same time an extreme high point underscores the difference between the high- and low-variability conditions (illustrating that the high variability is naturally more unstable and hence that differences are more readily obtained by chance and are perhaps less meaningful), the extreme point paradoxically provides more opportunity for the kind of dramatic decline that could be interpreted as indicating greater program-induced change. Some experimental analyses of how perceivers interpret fluctuating series have focused on the relationship between two sets of values, the values immediately before the program was introduced and the values immediately following the program's introduction. The sifting of data for evidence of change can be highly focused in such cases, with earlier variability in the series being less impactful when perceivers analyze short time spans to decide whether or not a change has occurred.

The extent to which intuitive change judgments in high- and low-variability series are shaped by problematic differences in extreme values just prior to a program intervention was not a concern in the study just summarized. Participants in the two variability conditions received identical fatality values for the year preceding the introduction of the program (a number that was set at the mean) and the drop in

Table 6-2. Judgments of Actual Trend Change.

	No intervention	Intervention
Low variability	6.19$_b$	7.21$_b$
High variability	4.07$_a$	6.47$_b$

Note: The higher the mean, the greater the perceived change.
Means sharing the same subscript do not differ at the .05 level.

fatalities was then away from the mean rather than toward it. The mean value was used in order to unconfound peaks with causal information and allow for the assessment of the impact of overall prior variability. Whether the same pattern of change impressions would be found when a higher-than-average fatality value was placed just prior to the intervention was investigated in a second study. In each variability condition, the high value in the series (63 in the high-variability conditions and 49 in the low-variability conditions) occurred in the year just prior to the program's introduction. The overall amount of prior variability remained the same as in the previous study.

Once again, participants in the high-variability conditions judged the variability in the first 10 years to be greater than did participants in the low-variability conditions ($Ms = 7.3$ and 5.6, respectively), $F(1,57) = 12.88, p < .002$. The overall pattern of responses to the change questions in this version of the study was somewhat different. As before, it was found that in the absence of intervention information, high-variability participants were less prepared to interpret a numeric drop as evidence of change than were their low-variability counterparts. But in the intervention conditions, the difference between the high- and low-variability conditions was eliminated (see Table 6-2). Participants in the high-variability condition who had intervention information just as readily interpreted the drop as an indication of change as did participants in the low-variability condition who had intervention information, main effect for cause $F(1,57) = 4.66, p < .04$, interaction $F(1,57) = 4.35, p < .04$. A similar pattern of results was found on the other change questions. When asked how likely it was that drunk driving fatalities would remain low, subjects in the high-variability/no-intervention condition least expected that the fatalities would remain low ($M = 4.21$); subjects in the other three conditions had significantly higher expectations that the fatalities would remain low, and did not differ across the three conditions ($M = 6.29$ high-variability/intervention; $M = 5.75$ low-variability/no-intervention; $M = 5.79$ low-variability/intervention).

In sum, extreme preprogram values did have an effect on impressions of change in this study. The results suggest that when high- and low-variability baselines fail to lead to differing change conclusions, it may be due not to an inevitable failure of judgers to attend to differences in variability or their implications for judging program-induced change, but rather to the fact that baselines with different degrees of variability sometimes provide different comparison points for the period just before the program begins.

Thus far, variability and ostensible change-relevant causes have been treated as easily separated and as independent; however, in many everyday cases they are not so readily separable. This is because the factor that is seen as a putative cause of change can also figure in why the past has been highly variable. When this lack of separation exists, it is unclear whether differences in prior variability will still be taken into account in making intuitive judgments of change. The studies to be described next—studies dealing with inferences of change in family interactions—were designed to illustrate this more complicated situation where the change-related cause is not necessarily independent of prior variability.

Common to all the following studies was a basic procedure and a cover story drawn from a social work context. Participants were told that they would be reading a case study of a troubled family's interactions over a 10- week period. During those 10 weeks, the interactions were said to have been rated each week by a court-appointed social worker using a scale ranging from 0 to 100 (with 100 representing a family with interactions that are ideal for the psychological health of all its members). Each week's rating was said to be primarily based on a weekly visit by the social worker, and subjects were told that the value could be affected positively or negatively by any single event in the family. Relevant evidence that might be obtained directly from the actual visit included verbal abuse, tension, hostility, lack of concern, disruptive behaviors, marital conflict, positive remarks about other family members, cooperation, praise, and planned family activities. Indirect diagnostic information might be drawn from police or school reports for that week.

Participants received 10 interaction scores. The mean value was 37 but the background variability was manipulated so that it was either high or low. The range was from 11 to 63 in the high-variability condition and 25 to 49 in the low-variability condition. The mean and range for each half of the baseline were held constant and the last value in both high- and low-variability conditions was at the mean. In each of the replications, participants also learned of a follow-up score said to be based on a single visit to the family six months after the baseline period. That follow-up value was 53.

The putative cause information in this case concerned a family member who had been present during the baseline period (and hence could have contributed to prior variability) and who had left the family well before the six-month follow-up point. Prior to receiving the putative cause information, participants in all conditions were given background information about the family, which was provided in the form of descriptions of the six members of the family (parents, grandparent, daughter, three sons). Together, the descriptions were designed to convey the impression of a troubled family having multiple problems, with each family member contributing to the family dynamics: children in trouble with the law and having school difficulties, parents with poor parenting skills, limited education and job skills, problems with the family finances, and so forth. In the case of the father, the description noted that he had a sporadic employment history in low-paying jobs, as well as a history of drinking, being physically abusive, and being easily angered. Although not directly

Table 6-3. Judgments of Change.

	No cause	Cause
Low variability	17.8_b	16.4_b
High variability	9.4_a	16.2_b

Note: The higher the mean, the greater the perceived change.
Means sharing the same subscript do not differ at the .05 level.

stated, the father's behavior could have been one factor contributing to prior variability in the family interactions.

All subjects were given the same follow-up interaction score for a point six months after the baseline period. Some subjects, in addition, were given information about a putative causal event, namely, that the father had permanently left the family shortly after the baseline period ended. On a variety of scales, the participants were asked to judge the extent to which the family interactions had changed by the six-month follow-up point. All questions were answered on 31-point scales, with lower numbers representing less change. Of interest was whether the degree of prior variability in interactions would be taken into account in judging change at the six-month follow-up point, in conditions where perceivers had knowledge of a putative cause and in conditions where they did not.

The manipulation of variability was found to be effective. Subjects in the high variability condition perceived the variability ($M = 26.7$) to be greater than did subjects in the low variability condition ($M = 13.9$), $F(1,36) = 83.82, p < .001$. There were no differences across conditions in ratings of average level of prior interaction ($M = 36.3$), in poorness of the family's interactions during the baseline period ($M = 20.9$), or in the perceived responsibility of the father for the quality of the family's interactions ($M = 19.6$). Participants were then asked whether they thought a change had occurred in the family's interactions. Here a significant Variability × Cause interaction was found, $F(1,36) = 4.22, p < .05$, such that, without the causal information, responses in the low- and high-variability conditions differed but with the causal information they did not (see Table 6-3). Only the subjects in the high-variability/no-cause condition differed from any of the others in their judgments of change. A similar pattern of results was found on all related questions, including those asking how likely it was that the family's interactions would remain at the six-month follow-up level, how much the family's interactions had improved how permanent the improvement was, and how confident subjects were that any observed change based on the follow-up score was permanent.

To assess the generality of this effect and its robustness against various procedural alterations, the study was repeated several times with variations in the family information provided and in the specifics of the causal information. To see whether the detailed family descriptions might be leading to the differences in results between the foregoing study and the traffic fatalities study, subjects in these versions of the family-interaction study were not given the impressionistic summaries of family members' characteristics. The only family details that were included concerned the age and gender of the family members (and, in the case of the father, the brief descriptions specified below). Subjects were provided with variability values, a description of the scale on which the values were based, and some version of the causal information. Slight variations in the putative cause information were introduced in the different versions to assess their impact. In one case, subjects in the cause condition were given information that the father had been troubled (in unspecific ways) and had permanently left the family; in another, they learned that the father had been physically abusive and had permanently left the family; and in a third, they learned that the father had been chronically alcoholic and had permanently left the family. The subjects without putative cause information did not learn any details about the father's behavior.

Subjects in the replication in which the father was said to been troubled before leaving the family responded similarly to subjects in the original version of the study on the majority of the change questions. For example, when asked how likely it was that the family's interactions would remain at the six-month follow-up level, high-variability subjects without putative cause information judged the change to be less ($M = 6.83$ than low-variability subjects without putative cause information ($M = 13.5$), but in the cause conditions, the responses of the high-variability subjects ($M = 15.15$) were indistinguishable from the responses of low-variability subjects ($M = 14.65$), main effect for cause, $F(1,77) = 7.99, p < .007$, interaction, $F(1,77) = 4.58, p < .04$. Slightly different results were found on the first change question (i.e., whether subjects thought a change had occurred in the family's interactions). Although the pattern of means was very close to that for both the six-month follow-up question and the first change question in the original version of the study, both variability and causal information produced main effects on the dependent measure, main effect for variability, $F(1,77) = 10.10, p < .01$, main effect for cause, $F(1,77) = 6.40, p < .02$ ($Ms = 8.88$ high-variability/no-cause, 15.75 low-variability/no-cause, 14.6 high-variability/cause, 19.0 low-variability/cause).

In the version in which subjects learned that the father had been physically abusive before leaving the family, the pattern of responses on the change questions was again similar. When subjects were asked whether a change had occurred in the family's interactions, subjects in the high-variability condition without causal information ($M = 7.6$) differed from subjects in the low-variability condition without causal information ($M = 15.7$); but with the causal information, responses of subjects in the high-variability condition ($M = 16.0$) did not differ from responses of subjects in the low-variability condition ($M = 15.7$), main effect for cause, $F(1,56) = 6.58$, $p < .03$, and a nearly significant interaction, $F(1,56) = 3.76, p < .06$. A similar pattern of results was found on the other questions concerning change.

Finally, in the replication where the father was said to have been chronically alcoholic before leaving the family, subjects who had knowledge of the causal event saw more change than those who did not, and even with the causal information they remained sensitive to the degree of prior variability. On the question asking whether change had occurred in the family's interactions, the means for the various conditions were 6.77 for high-variability/no-cause, 11.92 for low-variability/no-cause, 16.21 for high-variability/cause, and 21.18 for low-variability/cause, main effect for variability $F(1,42) = 6.29, p < .03$, main effect for cause $F(1,42) = 21.49, p < .01$. A similar pattern of results was found on the other change questions. This pattern differs somewhat from the pattern of results in other versions of this study in that the change-related causal information and the variability information acted independently in their effects on inferences of change (as found in the original study on alcohol-related traffic fatalities).

Despite some differences across the variability studies reported in this chapter, there are important commonalities to be noted. Most notably, subjects who did not have causal information were found to be quite sensitive to differences in prior variability in drawing intuitive change conclusions, and in particular, those who had highly unstable baselines remained very cautious about inferring change across all the different studies. Furthermore, in all studies the putative cause information had an impact on change inferences, at least in the high-variability condition where evidence of change based on past-present differences in data was less clear-cut. It appears that whether causal information will eliminate differences between high- and low-variability conditions cannot be predicted simply on the basis of whether subjects have knowledge of a potentially powerful cause. Sometimes the impact of causal information was such that the responses of subjects in the high- and low-variability conditions became indistinguishable; in other cases, subjects continued to see change differently as a function of the degree of prior variability. In general, in those cases where the cause could be seen as related to prior variability, subjects in the cause conditions were more likely to fail to differentiate between degrees of prior variability, as might be expected if high prior variability were discounted in light of the removal of its possible cause. Whether this failure to differentiate degrees of variability was due to the intertwined nature of the cause and variability or to some other characteristic of the stimulus situation cannot be determined from the present results, but the findings do suggest that use of prior variability information may be self-limiting under certain circumstances.

The present results are interesting not only for their implications concerning how people infer change when they are given information about high and low variability, but also for what they suggest for cases where prior variability is poorly remembered or information about it is simply unavailable. From the findings presented here it appears that exposure to high variability baselines does inhibit subjects' tendencies to infer that change has occurred. In the absence of such exposure or after exposure to highly variable series that are not remembered as such, perceivers may produce responses like those seen following exposure to the low-variability series used in the present studies. It is likely that, for the intuitive perceiver, past variability is generally not a salient property of the information used in making informal judgments, and unless information about high variability is actively attended to and recalled, the absence of such information will be treated by default as equivalent to the absence of variability itself (see Nisbett et al., 1983, for additional discussion of variability default assumptions). In such cases, the resulting change judgments will in all likelihood be elevated over what they would be in those cases where perceivers do bring to the change judgment task full knowledge of prior variability.

In terms of mathematical properties and issues of measurement, only the simplest of variability situations have been illustrated here. No shifts in the mean over time occurred and there were no shifts in degree of variability through the series. Variation in measurement techniques across time, an added difficulty not uncommon in real-world situations, did not figure in the information provided to participants. Also, the subjects were simply given numerical data rather than being required to make the relevant observations themselves and then score those observations in a way that would make degrees of variability discernible (see Kunda & Nisbett, 1986, for a general discussion of the issue of data codability and its implications). In the foregoing studies, the situation was simplified in order to illustrate how causal information can shape the use of information about the past. Yet factors such as those just mentioned would normally make the change judgment task an even more formidable one for the intuitive perceiver. The relatively complicated conditions found in the everyday world are likely to make actual change judgments considerably more complex and variable across the wide range of situations in which they occur.

Looking for Change in Other Contexts

This chapter has considered some examples of change judgments that arise in the context of a change-related causal event, where an ostensible cause may both evoke the perceiver's interest in change and serve an evidential role in the assessment of change. It remains to be noted that change judgments, and the originating interest in change, will not always be linked to causal events. In this concluding section, several other contexts likely to generate an interest in change will be discussed.

Among the contexts in which something other than a putative cause is associated with an interest in change, an important class consists of the "milestone" points that occur in a continuing series. That is, an interest in change can arise at certain conventional (though often arbitrary) breaking points in ongoing experience. At the close of a decade, for example, people often begin to reflect on the amount of change that occurred over the previous ten years. On a birthday, a person might look back to see how much he or she has changed over the previous year. At a 10th wedding anniversary, a couple might reflect back on the ways their marriage has changed over the decade. An event such as the occasion of a 25th class reunion will often serve as an opportunity to look for change in old friends and in oneself. These occasions are not ones that the perceiver is likely to view as causing a change; rather they are taken to be appropriate times to pause and examine how much change has taken place.*

---

*Although the class of milestone change judgments will generally differ from those that are linked to causal events, the two types will not always be independent and will sometimes overlap. The 65th birthday is a good example of such an overlap. Not only does this birthday represent a conventional milestone point (in the sense of a time to look back and assess change), but it is also often seen as a causal event, a time that many might be expected to change because of retirement.

Milestone-induced change judgments may be understood in part through investigating how people think about periods and the influence such thinking has on intuitive change conclusions. Categorization of continuous sequences into discrete time periods appears to provide perceivers with an impetus for analyzing the past for change through the imposition of stopping points. If this is the case, one would expect that those series having salient stopping points will be more likely to produce distinct change judgments than those without such points. Change judgments would be expected to occur most frequently around these stopping points, and more change should be seen on either side of the arbitrary point of division than in the middle of the sequence. The act of categorization may exaggerate differences between periods — a result that would be consistent with findings in other areas (e.g., Wilder, 1986) — and thus would have important implications for change judgments. The case of judging change across decades illustrates the possible effects of periodization. As a result of periodization, each decade may come to be seen as having a separate and distinct character that makes it unique relative to surrounding decades (e.g., the turbulent '60s, the narcissistic '70s). Seeing decades as having distinctive characters might lead people to look back to see how much change has taken place from one decade to the next, and it may lead them to perceive greater change across decade boundaries than between consecutive years within decades.

Breaks in continuity need not always be shared, traditional milestones. Any hiatus in experience may have the same effect of breaking the continuity and prompting an interest in change. For example, a relatively continuous series of experiences may, in effect, be broken by not being around someone or something for a long period of time. The occasion of unexpectedly seeing an old friend after a number of years could serve as an opportunity for stepping back and examining how much change has taken place. Again, it is not that the seeing of the friend is expected to cause the change; rather seeing the friend may arouse an interest in finding out whether change has occurred during the hiatus. Both in the more limited individual case of the hiatus and in the broader case of milestone points, certain occasions in the perceiver's life can produce an interest in looking for change although the occasions are not, in themselves, likely causes of change. Identifying these occasions and developing a sense of their importance to intuitive perceivers will no doubt enhance our understanding of change judgments.

Developmental change is a yet another important area where the concern for change probably does not emerge directly out of an interest in any particular cause. Here the interest may be prompted by concerns with what has happened over the course of time as part of a natural developmental progression. Such judgments are not entirely divorced from causal concerns, but most judgments of developmental change probably are not directed as ascertaining the extent to which a specific preceding event has resulted in change. These change judgments may grow out of relatively global beliefs about how various entities develop over time and where change is to be expected as a part of the pattern. The concept of developmental change is perhaps most often associated with an individual, but the developing entity could also be a group, a business, a community, a nation, a political movement, and so forth. In any of these areas, an understanding of developmentally related change judgments is likely to come from closer scrutiny of the conditions under which intuitive theories of developmental change come into play and from the analysis of schemas that people bring to the task of judging developmental change in different kinds of entities.

Finally, it is important not to overlook the fact that change judgments will sometimes arise simply in response to compelling differences in information. Past-present informational differences will sometimes be powerful enough in themselves that they engage the perceiver's interest in the possibility that things have changed. At times the past will appear so different from the present that perceivers will perceive change regardless of whether or not other factors related to change exist. Such judgments will be best understood by continuing to investigate the kinds of past and present information people are confronted with on a day-to-day basis.

Chapter 7

Judgments of Person Change: A Closer Look

In an intriguing cartoon, the cartoonist and social commentator Feiffer (1982) focuses on two lovers and their concerns with the possibility that the other will change, or fail to change, at various points during their relationship. In the cartoon, one of the lovers says that in the year they were together they changed a lot about change. Initially they begged each other not to change. At various points they said to each other "Why won't you change?" and "You'll never change!" and, later, an accusing "You have changed!" when the other behaved in some undesirable way. The sequence ends with the lovers encountering each other on the street a year after they broke up and barely recognizing each other because they had changed so much. This dialogue in which people are preoccupied with change strikes us as amusing, but also as familiar in certain respects.

The humorous juxtaposition of these conflicting pieces of dialogue raises intriguing questions about judgments of person change and the nature of the assumptions and concerns that underlie them. Do we assume and perhaps even fear that those we are close to are likely to change? Or do we assume that they cannot change and will not change even when we believe they should? Underlying these questions are several intricate issues in need of elucidation if we are to understand the complexities and ambiguities in person change judgments. The first part of this chapter is therefore devoted to setting out these issues and detailing their implications for the analysis of person change judgments.

Ambiguities in What Constitutes Person Change

Person change judgments are marked by crucial ambiguities in what constitutes person change—ambiguities both in the data that may serve as evidence of person change and in the meaning of change to the intuitive perceiver. These ambiguities are important to the analysis of person change judgments for two reasons: first, because these ambiguities fundamentally complicate the relationship between change-related data and the inference of change, and second, because these ambiguities lead to a situation wherein a claim of person change can take on quite different meanings depending on the depth of change being referred to. As we shall see, these ambiguities also point to larger issues about whether data about persons are ever capable of signifying change except with reference to a particular theory of what constitutes change.

The first source of ambiguity that will be of interest to us here concerns life events and their ambiguity as data in relation to change. To illustrate the nature of this problem, consider the following cases and their ambiguity with respect to change. Suppose a child was a class bully in early grades but became a class leader in later grades: should such a transformation be regarded as a genuine change? Or, suppose a perceiver knew someone who was a cheerleader in high school and subsequently became a college professor. From the perceiver's perspective is such a shift appropriately termed a change? Suppose one is attempting to decide whether a child has changed in level of social maturity and has knowledge concerning how well that child dealt with meeting new children in grade school and how well that child adapts to junior high dating experiences. How does the perceiver decide in this case what constitutes change, given that the behaviors that would commonly be taken as valid indicators of social maturity in the two contexts may be quite different? Perceivers of change often confront markedly different sets of behaviors for different comparison periods. Thus, person change impressions can often be arrived at only through comparing the behavioral equivalent of "apples and oranges." In each case the perceiver confronts the problem that the information for different periods is incommensurable at the concrete level. In many cases, different activities are available for comparison only from different life periods, for different roles, for different ages — for childhood and adulthood, for adolescence and midlife years, for college and later in the business world, for before and after marriage, for before and after retirement, and so forth. Only rarely can one look to life-events data that are commensurable on the face of it, such as would be the case in having information about the number of pounds lost or the number of inches grown. It is more common to face ambiguity such as that encountered in deciding whether something like a switch from being the class bully to being the class leader represents stability or change. The upshot is that information is frequently ambiguous relative to the change inference task, and thus there can be no unequivocal answer in terms of the data themselves as to whether a person can rightfully be said to have changed.

The second ambiguity in the meaning of change claims results not so much from ambiguity in the data themselves as from the fact that person change can be construed as having occurred at different levels. Quite different meaning could be intended by an assertion that a person has changed. A claim that someone has changed could represent a judgment that a person has changed at a surface level, or that the person has changed at some deep level, or that the person has changed at several different levels. Moreover, it is possible for deep change to be accompanied by very little surface change, and for considerable surface change to be accompanied by little or no deep change. In terms of deep-seated change, a person could have undergone a major religious transformation that is only weakly or indirectly reflected in behavior. Or, a person could be seen as changing behaviorally but as showing little change in deeper respects such as underlying values or core personality. Consider a child who formerly started fights and is now the popular class clown: although the child's behavior appears to have changed, it is possible to construe both behaviors as arising from the same underlying characteristic of attention seeking. Often the same set of facts could support an interpretation of either superficial or deep change (or even an interpretation that there has been no change at all).

In a fundamental way, the twin ambiguities of change-related data and the concept of change reflect the absence of any inherent link between what is seen in the person and the conclusions about person change that can be drawn from the information. Such ambiguities allow for a variety of views about change to be supported by the same set of life events. What these ambiguities mean for the everyday perceiver facing the task of judging change is explored in what follows. Why the absence of an inherent link is significant for understanding the process of judging change becomes apparent if we consider the perspective of the personologist. The personologist's chosen task of redefining in stability terms all that is seen in people is made easy by this ambiguity. Given the lack of an inherent link between the behavioral data and an appropriate conclusion regarding stability or change, the personologist is free to postulate a link such that surface flux can be translated into deeper stability. In effect, change can be defined away as a surface phenomenon by being recast as something that at a deep level never really occurs. Consider the following interpretation of a well-known individual who went from being a college professor to being a mystic:

> Most people look at Richard Alpert, the hard-driving psychology professor of the early 1960s and Ram Dass, the bearded free-floating guru of the 1970s, and see that totally different persons are here now. But Harvard psychologist David McClelland who knew Alpert well spent time with the Indian holy man and said to himself, "It's the same old Dick—still as charming, as concerned with inner experience, as power oriented as ever." (Rubin, 1981, p. 27)

In a case like this, which perception is veridical—the one of change or the one of stability? It is probably an unanswerable question. The question of person change is not answerable solely in terms of the facts of the case, but instead must take into account the perceiver's way of deciding, first, what constitutes person change and, second, which patterns of data are to be regarded as indications of change. As we will see in the studies to be described in this chapter, questions that are central to understanding person change judgments inevitably involve how people make these judgments in the face of considerable ambiguity.

Ambiguity of Life Events and Evidence of Change

As psychologists, we often teach students how to recognize the underlying traits and stability that are assumed to be at the root of individual behavior. For example, it is traditional for students to learn about personality, and sometimes abnormal psychology, through case studies designed to teach them to discern enduring traits beneath the diversity in life events. Such emphasis on stability is evident in one form or another in most major personality texts but is especially clear in the case-study anthologies that are often used in conjunction with texts in personality or abnormal psychology (e.g., White's, 1985, *Lives in Progress* or McNeil's, 1967, *The Quiet Furies*). With the express purpose of showing students how to identify the continuity of personality, students are commonly given opportunities to practice these skills by providing them with several events—some from early life and some from later in life—and then asking them to explain how the early events foreshadowed what was to come. Such training reinforces the impression that the stability lies in the events themselves, thereby allowing psychologists to view the training task as simply one of teaching students a neutral, higher-order skill that prepares them to recognize factual patterns.

As Kagan (1984) and Gergen (1977) have noted, any view that treats stability as unambiguously in the data themselves is problematic. In writing about developmental psychology, Kagan has pointed out that claims that stability is inherent in the data are no more than theory-driven attempts to tie together diverse life events from different ages. Considering developmental progressions, he notes the marked differences between the events and acts that occur during infancy and those that occur during youth, and holds that it is impossible to find preservation of sameness at the level of actual behavior. For the links to be observed, one must bring to the case study a theory-guided belief in the connectedness of diverse behaviors:

> Because the profile of manifest characteristics changes dramatically over the first dozen years, all psychologists agree on the impossibility of finding preservation at the level of the phenotype. If it is present, it must be found in hidden essences that undergo transformation at the surface. Thus, it is assumed that the insecurely attached infant who becomes a delinquent twelve-year-old has done so because fear and hostility to parents have remained as deep qualities from infancy to adolescence. (p. 81)

Whether we are speaking of children, youth, or adults, the diverse life events from which a pattern is extracted are highly complex, capable of being organized in many ways, and subject to differing interpretations. These points bear directly on understanding change claims about persons. The contradictory change statements that are sometimes heard may be intimately bound up with this equivocality of life events and the possibilities for differing interpretation.

To the extent that change is less an attribute of the event sequences themselves than a consequence of perspective, it follows that the same life events could provide the basis for differing—perhaps even opposing—statements about stability and about change. The first study to be reported in this chapter was intended to demonstrate this point and to highlight its implications for understanding the variability in perceptions of change. Subjects were provided with a case study that, on the surface at least, involved diverse life events and significant life change. The case involved a detailed description of a young woman named Lany Tyler who was a cheerleader in high school and, after failing to be accepted into college, later completed a Ph.D. and became a feminist and a professor of history at Princeton. The case study, an abridged version of an actual life history, was taken from Medved and Wallechinsky's *What Really Happened to the Class of '65?* (1976, pp. 303–318), and included observations about Lany from eight of her former classmates as well as Lany's comments about herself.

The traditional personality approach orients students to look for stability in diverse life events, often by giving explicit instructions in how to discern the stability and how to interpret specific sequences of events in stability terms. To recreate this instructional set, some participants were asked to read the case study looking for how the facts indicated an underlying sameness and how the target person remained basically the same. Their instructions read as follows:

> As you read over Lany's life history, it is important that you try to identify the signs of Lany's underlying sameness. Think about these questions as you read over the life history: In what ways did Lany remain essentially the same? What are some examples that show this underlying sameness? How would you explain the stability? In other words, why do you think she remained the same in the ways she did?

Others were given just the opposite instructions. They were asked to read the same case study but with an eye for ways the facts showed that Lany had changed:

> As you read over Lany's life history, it is important that you try to identify the signs that Lany is changing. Think about these questions as you read over the life history: In what ways did Lany change? What are some examples that show this change? How would you explain the changes she went through? In other words, why do you think she changed in the ways she did?

After reading the case study, subjects were asked to reflect on two core episodes in the progression of Lany's life story—her having been a cheerleader and her becoming a college professor. Those in the stability condition were asked to explain how going from being a cheerleader to being a professor could be an indication of Lany's underlying sameness, whereas subjects in the change condition were asked to explain how going from being a cheerleader to being a professor could be an indication of the changes Lany underwent.

In personality classes, we often ask students to extract stability from life stories, to show, as Kagan puts it, that "each life is an unbroken trail on which one can trace a psychological quality from a point back to its beginning" (Kagan, 1984, p. 11). But under parallel instructions to do the opposite, will students confronted with the same life story be able to perform the opposite task of extracting and explaining change? In a case like Lany's, is the equivocality of events such that students are equally capable of finding an unbroken trail or of finding its opposite?

So it seems. The results showed that the very same progression could be interpreted as evidence of stability in the stability condition and as evidence of change in the change condition. Twenty of the 21 subjects in the stability condition were able to construct a stability explanation and all 21 in the change condition were able to construct a change explanation. Those immersed in the stability framework found an underlying sameness in the roles of cheerleader and Ivy League professor. Consider some typical examples of their analyses:

> A cheerleader and an Ivy League professor are two very different but both prestigious positions. I think this reveals Lany's need to feel as if she has achieved and even over time her need to be held in esteem by others never changed.

She liked what was envied by her peers. In high school the boys love the cheerleaders and the girls want to be them. As you grow older the Ivy League schools tend to have snobbish prestige. She thought it was important to belong to the snobbishly prestigious groups.

Both of these positions are sought after by many people. To a high school girl being a cheerleader is the best. To a student being a professor at an Ivy League school is the best. Attaining two goals that she wanted shows that sameness in her desire to achieve the highest.

She has always been ambitious. In high school she wanted to be popular and set out to obtain her goal by being a cheerleader. I also believe that her attaining her teaching position at Princeton is the sign of an ambitious woman.

In the change condition, participants found ways to interpret the progression from cheerleader to Ivy League professor as reflecting change in Lany.

I feel that Lany grew up from an outer-oriented person to an inner-oriented person. She had to work to become a professor, yet to be a cheerleader she did not. She went through emotional, intellectual, and self changes.

This example shows that she has changed in being a more intellectual individual which is a major change .... This showed a change of values, what she considers important. Cheerleaders are looked on as pretty girls with no minds, a terrible case of stereotyping but true. Ivy League professors are looked upon as prudes, not very outgoing. In no way would it be expected that a high school cheerleader would turn out to be an Ivy League professor.

This shows her changing from the stereotyped "social butterfly" to an intellectually geared individual. She decided to use her intelligence to benefit rather than use her social charm.

Kagan (1984, p. 85) has noted that "the biases of the observer determine the details for the story that is told." This is no doubt true: the details of a life story that are selected as significant will surely depend on the observer's theoretical prescriptions. But what is interesting about the study just described is that—selection of details aside—the core episodes of a particular life story are capable of supporting different stories about that life—stories differing drastically in the roles that stability and change play in them.

The exercises described above, involving the interpretation of a transition from one particular life event to another, is one kind of analysis that students are commonly encouraged to engage in when dealing with case studies. Another, more challenging kind of analysis, involves interpreting the case as a whole, without having students' attention explicitly drawn to particular episodes. To examine overall interpretations, a second group of 45 subjects read the case study, some under the stability instructions, some under the change instructions, and some with no instructions as to set. After reading the case study, participants were asked to judge on two 9-point scales the degree of Lany's stability and change: "Overall, how much do you think Lany's personality and characteristics changed?" and "Overall, how much do you think Lany's personality and characteristics stayed essentially the same?" (endpoints "To a very little extent" "To a great extent"). Order of questions was counterbalanced.

The results once again showed that the same series of life events could give rise to differing interpretations of how much Lany had changed. Subjects in the change and no-set conditions were more likely than the subjects in the stability condition to see Lany's personality and characteristics as having changed (Ms = 6.8, 7.0, 5.4), $F(2,42)$ = 3.80, p < .05, and subjects in the change and no-set conditions were less likely to see Lany's personality and characteristics as having stayed essentially the same (Ms = 3.2, 3.6, 5.2), $F(2,42)$ = 4.87, p < .05, than were subjects in the stability condition. Several features of these results are of interest. These results do not reflect completely opposing views of Lany, but they do indicate overall differences in interpretation of the relative amounts of change and stability in personality and characteristics. The subjects in the change condition saw change but very little stability, whereas the subjects in the stability condition saw both more stability and less change than the other subjects. These results also show that in the absence of direct instructions to look for change, people do not automatically revert to a stability interpretation. At least in a case like the present one, change was readily seen in the absence of explicit instructions.

These results are also instructive in suggesting the importance of including both stability and change conditions in the study of the conclusions people draw from ambiguous life-events data. In a study comparable in certain respects to the stability condition in the present study, Tversky and Kahneman (1982) provided participants with a personality description together with an inconsistent vocational choice made at a later time, and asked participants to account for the relationship between the two. According to Tversky and Kahneman, the participants were adept at finding a stability link between an unexpected vocational choice and underlying personality. The authors concluded:

> In our view, the subjects' responses illustrate both the reluctance to revise a rich and coherent model, however uncertain, and the ease with which such a model can be used to explain new facts, however unexpected . . . . (p. 128)

Treating their results as an indication of the robustness of stability views, they went on to argue that: "highly developed explanatory skills probably contribute to the proverbial robustness and stability of impressions, models, conceptions and paradigms in the face of incompatible evidence" (Tversky & Kahneman, 1982, p. 128). The present results suggest that the incompatibility in the data may provide opportunities for interpretations of the data that are themselves incompatible. Indeed, Gergen, Hepburn, and Fisher (1986) have made a similar point with regard to specific behaviors and the extent to which they are capable of providing support for different trait labels. Gergen et al. showed that a single behavior can be construed as an indication of any of various traits, with the result that perceivers can come away with very different conclusions from observing the same actions. The results here demonstrate an equivocality of life events with regard to the constructs of person stability and person change. The findings highlight the problematic nature of the question of which view—that of stability or of change—is the correct one. When one is dealing with diverse life events, the data may be fully capable of supporting different but equally plausible and "correct" views.

Unanswered by this study is the question of the extent to which participants in the different conditions may have been differentially focused on deep versus superficial features. Even though the wording of the dependent measure included the terms both of characteristics and of personality, it remains possible that change is still a term reserved for the more superficial aspects, whereas at the deeper levels the person is always regarded as having remained the same. The study to be described next bears on this issue of whether people ever see change as deep-seated.

Depth and Direction of Expected Change: The Patty Hearst Case

In the early 1970s, Patty Hearst—young, apolitical, and a member of the wealthy Hearst family—was taken hostage by a revolutionary group in a series of events that made daily headlines across the country. Held hostage for several months, Hearst publicly renounced her family at the time of her expected release and chose to remain with her captors, claiming to have become a leftist revolutionary. This turn of events was the focus of countless newspaper stories where the idea that someone would change so significantly was met with widespread skepticism.

This case is an intriguing one in relation to the question of whether perceivers see genuine and significant change in others. Indeed, the apparent disbelief that so radical a change could take place in such circumstances would seem to be a natural demonstration of the general inability of perceivers to see people as truly changing in significant ways. The Hearst case has often been regarded as providing just such evidence. Widespread incredulity about the facts of the case has itself been a focus of analysis in social psychology textbooks (e.g., Myers, 1987; Zimbardo, Ebbesen, & Maslach, 1977), where responses to the case have been treated as indicators of the nature of intuitive beliefs about the limited likelihood of deep-seated change. Yet, despite its seeming to be an instructive natural experiment on intuitive expectations of person stability, disbelief about the facts of the case potentially provides us with a far different message about the nature of intuitive beliefs about person change: namely, that perceivers strongly expect significant change in others under certain circumstances, but that such expectations are delimited to certain kinds of change. Responses to the Patty Hearst case may represent the effects of violations of strong expectations of certain types of change rather than violations of expectations of no change. Perhaps perceivers would be just as surprised to find a person was not changed deeply as a consequence of such an experience as to learn that he or she changed in an unexpected direction.

To examine these possibilities, participants in three studies were provided with a summary of the events in the Patty Hearst case. The summary was an abridged version of the Zimbardo et al. (1977, pp. 4–8) description of the case. In several different ways across the three studies, expectations for person change were explored. In the first study, participants (general psychology students) simply read Zimbardo's account of the abduction and of the demands made by the captors. Participants learned that Patty Hearst was released after being held for two months, but participants were not given any additional details as to the sequence of events beyond that point. After reading the case description, 15 subjects responded to an open-ended question that asked them to describe their expectations as to whether Patty Hearst would be the same or different afterwards. The question read: "Would Patty be different afterwards or have stayed the same?" All 15 respondents felt that the hostage would be different afterwards. Examples of subjects' comments indicate the extent to which they believed the experience would have significantly changed the hostage.

> I think that Patty would be a different person after two months. Her personality would have changed for the worse . . . . I think she would be different. It's possible that she could recover mentally, but she'll always remember it. Being kidnapped has to be a traumatic experience. I can't imagine anyone coming out of it in the same state of mind they were before . . . . I think Patty would always carry this horrible episode along with her the rest of her life . . . . I think Patty would be changed by this incident. Patty would realize that there were all sorts of different people with different needs. Any traumatic experience would change a person. They would have different insights and different feelings. I think her attitude toward life would change.

It is of interest to note that the changes mentioned by subjects included changes of personality.

In a second study, participants were provided with the case study, again describing the events just to the point of Patty's announced release, and were asked to answer a series of questions about person change. Subjects in the experimental conditions were asked to answer questions about change in Patty that occurred during the two-month period as a consequence of her being held hostage; subjects in the control conditions were asked to answer the same set of questions but to answer them under the assumption that the kidnapping had not happened and that Patty had remained a typical college student during the two-month period. The interest was in seeing how much change was expected, how deep that change was expected to be, and the specific nature of the expected change.

Subjects were first asked, "To what extent would Patty be changed during this two month period?" (9-point scale, endpoints "Not at all" and "Very much"). Subjects said that the hostage would change considerably during the two-month period ($M = 7.16$), whereas subjects in the non-hostage condition expected much less change to occur ($M = 3.44$), $t(35) = 6.12, p < .001$. Subjects were then asked, "Would this two-month period be likely to affect her deeply or superficially?" (9-point scale, endpoints "Would be likely to affect her at most superficially" and "Would be likely to affect her deeply"). Again, subjects in the hostage condition were very likely to see her as affected deeply ($M = 7.32$), whereas subjects asked to make the judgment in the non-hostage condition saw the change as more likely to be superficial ($M = 3.39$), $t(35) = 7.43, p < .001$.

To further examine change expectations, subjects were then provided with a set of possible outcomes and were asked to select the outcome that best represented their opinion of what Patty would be like at the end of the two-month period. Four options were provided: "She changed by becoming a leftist revolutionary," "She changed by becoming a more fearful person," "She stayed the same," and "Other." In the hostage condition, 13 of 19 participants selected the "more fearful person" option as the most likely outcome, whereas only two of 18 in the non-hostage condition selected this choice, $\chi^2(1, N = 37) = 12.59$, p < .001. In contrast, the option that described Patty as staying the same was selected by 11 of the 18 subjects in the non-hostage condition, whereas only one of 19 subjects in the hostage condition selected this option, $\chi^2(1, N = 37) = 13.16, p < .001$. The actual outcome of the Hearst case — choosing to become a leftist revolutionary—was selected by only one subject, a participant in the hostage condition. Thus, not only did subjects in the hostage condition hold change expectations, but those expectations tended to both include certain types of outcomes and strongly exclude others (including the outcome that actually occurred).

In a third version of the study, participants received a more detailed description of the case. Subjects learned of events following the hostage's expected release, as described in one of three endings. In the original-ending conditions, subjects learned in detail about Patty joining her captors. These participants were given the full account of Patty working with her captors, as taken from the Zimbardo et al. chapter (1977, pp. 4–8). In the abbreviated original-ending condition, subjects merely learned that she had joined her captors, but were provided with few details as to the nature and extent of her collaboration with her captors:

> Scheduled to be released to return home to her parents, Patty announced on April 3 that she had decided to join the SLA, and had renounced her former lifestyle, denounced her parents, and taken the name Tania after a revolutionary who fought beside Che Guevara.

Finally, in the fear-ending condition, subjects learned:

> Scheduled to be released to return home to her parents, Patty did return home but was a changed person. She was fearful, unable to trust people, and unable to concentrate or do well in school. She dropped out of school and rarely went out in public.

After reading the case, subjects were asked, "How likely is it that someone would change in this way as a consequence of being kidnapped?" (9-point scale, endpoints "Not at all likely" and "Very likely"). Once again there was a significant effect whereby subjects judged the fear ending to be a more probable change outcome than the changes described in either the abbreviated original ending or the extended original ending ($Ms = 7.25, 3.53, 1.82$, fear ending, abbreviated ending, original ending), $F(2,33) = 36.54, p < .001$.

Across the different versions of the study, subjects were given opportunities to write various open-ended comments. A number of their responses raised interesting issues about personality change. One subject mentioned that perhaps Patty would have been brainwashed by her captors. A few other subjects mentioned the possibility that as a result of her experiences as a hostage she would perhaps be more sympathetic to the plight of poor people— that is, she would have come to sympathize with the position espoused by her captors. Both of these possibilities are interesting in terms of the issue of person change, although they are interesting for somewhat different reasons. Some years ago, Worchel and Byrne (1964) published a volume entitled *Personality Change*, in which they addressed a number of questions about the processes by which personality change takes place, including personality change through forcible indoctrination. They noted there that forcible indoctrination stands in an odd relation to personality change. A perceiver cannot be fully certain whether the change in such cases is real change or whether it is something that merely mimics genuine change in response to coercion. It may be the case that change that violates perceiver expectations is especially likely to be labeled as an instance of brainwashing. But what consequences follow in terms of beliefs about change? Use of the concept of brainwashing may indicate something about the perception of the cause alone, or it may also indicate something about the perceived nature of the change or its degree of genuineness.

Second, the comment about a hostage coming to sympathize with the political stance of his or her captor is interesting in that such a shift in sympathies is not unknown in real cases where hostages have been exposed to information about political motives while being held hostage. Hostetler (1987) has argued that in the past people have often not expected change of this sort, with the result that families and former associates of the hostage were ill-prepared for the kinds of change the victims may have undergone. Yet expectations may be shifting as public awareness about the possibility of this effect has grown. The argument has even been made that interventions that involve teaching about the possibility of this sort of change may be helpful in preparing families for what to expect with the return of hostages. These considerations are interesting in their suggestion (a) that intuitive change expectations tend to be strong and directional, (b) that change falling outside these expectations generates difficulties for perceivers, and most important, (c) that expectations for change may undergo modification over time through encounters with additional information or forceful example.

Being held a political hostage is far from a common experience, yet it is part of a much larger class of powerful and traumatic life events, any one of which perceivers may view as having the potential to bring about deep change. Powerful and traumatic life events have been the focus of much research devoted to assessing their actual impact on the individual. In an edited volume on nonnormative life events (Callahan & McCluskey, 1983), various authors discussed the consequences to the person of undergoing nonnormative life events—consequences frequently believed to involve substantial change (e.g., Veronen & Kilpatrick, 1983). In Chapter 6 of the present volume we also saw that heightened expectations for person change were the norm after a variety of causal events. The present studies add to that work by indicating that the expectations for change created by significant experiences can be quite definite in terms of the anticipated direction of change, and that they can involve deep-seated, rather than merely superficial, change.

The present findings may help us better understand results described in earlier chapters wherein participants were willing to judge change in the absence of past information. The specific nature of the change expectations may be such that perceivers have a very clear picture of what people should be like following a putative causal event; if the behavior observed after a cause is consistent with that profile, then perceivers most likely have what they need to be confident that the behavior indeed represents a change. The fit between their rather definite expectations of change and the observed behavior may be so impressive to them that it overshadows the fact that the observed behavior may have a high likelihood of occurrence independent of change-related causal events.

In the following section, we turn to studies on the perception of change in individuals actually known to perceivers. In previous work reported here, hypothetical cases have generally been employed in order to facilitate experimental analysis of issues about expectations and information use. Yet it remains to be seen whether change is also perceived in cases where the perceiver is personally acquainted with the target. Because sequences of life events are simultaneously complex and equivocal, there are opportunities for change in real people to be perceived in many ways, ranging from nonexistent to superficial to deep. In particular, with the rich data sets that perceivers have about those who are well known to them, it would presumably be possible for them to find abundant evidence of stability without seeing change or, conversely, to see widespread evidence of change in those they are close to.

Concern with Change in Personal Acquaintances

One of the ways to gauge whether change in actual acquaintances is perceived as a real possibility is to see if perceivers spend time thinking about the possibility of change, worrying about change, or trying to bring about change. If person change is thought to be substantial enough that it could alter relationships, then perceivers would be expected to worry about the possibility of change in those they care about. If, on the other hand, perceivers believe people do not change, or if whatever change is believed possible is thought to be of minor importance, then worries about person change should be relatively rare or relatively insignificant. To examine beliefs about change in people actually known to them, participants were asked several questions about their concerns with change in themselves and in others who were important in their lives.

The participants (25 females and 24 males, average age 19.2 years) were first asked whether they ever worried about person change and, if they answered in the affirmative, to describe those concerns. In response to the first question, "Do you ever find yourself worrying about how change in yourself or others might affect your relationships?," 39 of the subjects reported worrying about the possibility of change, whereas 10 participants reported not having worried about it. Perusal of participants' narratives revealed that the possibility of change in those actually known in indeed of substantial concern. The following examples reflect participants' concerns about person change and its possible effects on relationships:

> When September came, I found myself worrying about if my friends were going to change when they went off to school. And if so, in what ways? I also worried if I would change.

> Sometimes changes can end relationships so I'm concerned about ending relationships that were once meaningful.

> I sometimes worry that if I change it might alter the relationship, most likely for worse, or if the other person changes I might not understand and thus hurt the relationship.

Over the past few years, since I entered college, I have not seen a few of my high school friends as much as I would have liked. Now, if I happen to be with them, I feel like I've missed out on things they've done and they've missed out on things I've done. We've changed so much in a year or two that there is a sort of awkwardness about being together.

It is also of interest to note that even the responses of those reporting the absence of worry suggested in some cases that it is not so much that they viewed change as a remote possibility as that they had decided that to worry about what they consider inevitable would be of little value.

I don't really worry about changes in myself because I know that any change will be for the better. I also realize that change is necessary in order to grow. Sometimes it is upsetting to know that a change in another may cause a relationship to end but in the long run if both cannot change together and grow from the experience it is better to be apart.

Beliefs about change were then investigated by looking at whether it is believed possible to bring about change in friends and self. Of interest was the question of whether people are viewed as capable of changing and whether change is viewed as important enough that attempts are commonly made to bring it about in the interest of relationships. To assess these issues, participants were asked several questions about attempts to effect person change in the context of an important relationship. Participants were first asked about trying to change themselves for a relationship: "Have you ever tried to change something about yourself or thought about changing something about yourself because of the relationship?" Forty-one participants reported having tried to create such changes and eight reported having not. To assess the perceived importance of these changes, the participants who reported having tried to bring about changes were then asked to rate the importance of them to the relationship: "In your opinion, how important was the change you tried to bring about or thought about bringing about?" (9-point scale, endpoints "Not at all important to the relationship" and "Very important to the relationship"). The changes were rated as quite important to the relationship ($M = 6.8$, $SD = 1.91$), with 18 of the participants selecting one of the top two scale points in importance and only two of the participants selecting one of the bottom two scale points.

When participants were asked about attempts to bring about change in others, they were equally likely to report that change had been attempted or considered, with 40 of 49 describing themselves thus. The changes were once again viewed as having substantial importance. When asked how important this change was to the relationship, participants rated the importance as quite high ($M = 6.76$, $SD = 1.67$), with 15 of them selecting one of the top two scale points and none selecting either of the bottom two. When asked to describe the areas of behavior and personality that were the focus of their change attempts, subjects' responses were quite varied. The targets of attempted change ranged from habits to values, interests, and interactional styles. These target areas did not differ appreciably as a function of whether the attempted change was in the self or in others.

The above results suggest that person change does enter into everyday concerns and also has a place in the personal politics of relationships. Although the investigation was not intended to examine perceptions of actual change, it would be of interest to consider how perceivers know when those changes that are feared or anticipated have taken place. Do informational factors such as focusing on frequency rather than rate, for example, or use of variability information influence perceptions of actual change? Do social perceivers' own efforts to effect change in others some- times serve as causal information that makes them more likely to perceive change? Beyond the particular concerns of college students, the wider range of worries about person change that occur would also be of interest to examine.

The role of person change in everyday life and personal politics is further evinced in the popular press, where the issue of person change and its possible consequences for relationships across various ages are common topics of discussion. Consider, for example, Goodman's (1979) discussion of change and its central place in altering long-term relationships. She focuses on divorce: "Every divorce is a story of change . . . . How many divorced people have we heard say, 'We grew away from each other . . . . We didn't have anything in common any more . . . . We both changed" (p. 168). Standard fare in advice columns includes numerous inquiries about how to change loved ones, how to cope with a changed loved one, or how to deal with fears that the other might change.

Perceptions of Change in Those Known Well

Given that person change looms as a real possibility in the lives of social perceivers, it was next of interest to examine participants' perceptions of change in persons with whom they were well acquainted. In a series of studies, subjects were asked whether they had perceived change in different types of target persons, and if so, to describe those changes. The type of target person was varied across studies, with subjects being asked about change (a) in any friend they felt had changed, (b) in someone who had previously been but was no longer a friend, (c) in their best friend, (d) in themselves, (e) in their parents, or (f) in their grandparents. The results of these studies are discussed in this section.

In the first study, 85 participants (43 males, 42 females, average age 19.2 years) were asked to describe a friend that they believed had changed in recent years. All 85 were able to describe someone whom they felt had changed in some way. Several aspects of the descriptions of change in these essays are of interest. When enhancers were examined (statements in which the subjects used phrases like "changed com- pletely," "changed totally," "is the opposite of what he/she was like," "changed whole outlook," "changed greatly," "changed quite a bit"), 31 of the 85 (36%) narratives about people who had changed included strong enhancers. Representative of the comments in which enhancers were used are the following:

> I have seen a dramatic change in a friend after he had finished one year in college. He was always quiet and reserved, now he is very arrogant, pushy, and even obnoxious.

> I have a friend who I think has changed quite a bit in recent years. She used to be very immature. She often would do things that she knew were wrong but she would continue to do them. Now, because she is off at college, she has matured greatly. She now knows

what she is going to do with her life. Her personality has changed also. She used to have a negative attitude about herself. Now she is very confident.

My friend has changed greatly within the past two years. The reason is due to the death of her father in a car accident. She has changed in the sense that she no longer is a reserved person. She doesn't keep it in. She holds grudges and can stay mad for a long time.

When asked to do so, participants were also able to describe ways that the person has remained the same. For example, one student wrote of a friend, "Although she had changed and is now more of a social butterfly she still kept her old trustworthy friends very close to her because she values their friendship very much." Another wrote of his friend, "He is still pretty religious. He's still morally straight but has become very fun-loving also."

An indication of the concerns engendered by the perceived changes in the other is that 21% of the essays described the consequences of the changes for some aspect of relationships, even though participants were not asked to comment on that subject. Consider the following example:

My friend Gail has changed in many ways in the past year. She has changed especially since her 20th birthday. She is two years older than I am. Before she turned 20 we did everything together. But the day she turned 20 she changed. She never calls me, we never go out. She is always out with older friends at clubs or out drinking. She not only changed in that way but her whole personality has changed since before her birthday. She talks like she is better than I am and that she has a better time going out to clubs than she did going out with me. That's how Gail has changed and I don't understand why.

In much of the above, reference to change occurs in conjunction with deteriorating relationships, which might lead to the conclusion that person change judgments emerge at the dissolution of relationships. A possible difficulty with looking simply at faltering relationships and the degree of change perception found there is that the base rate of change perception may itself be fairly high, particularly in lives in which transitions and upheaval are fairly commonplace. As another way to examine the generality of perceptions of change in those actually known and at the same time to see if change perception is typically associated with the breakdown of friendships, participants were randomly assigned to rate change and stability in one of two sorts of individuals: either in someone they were good friends with in high school and were still good friends with or in someone they were good friends with in high school and still knew but with whom they were no longer friends.

The participants (20 males, 8 females, average age 19.1 years) were first asked to describe in their own words the nature of the stability and change in this person, and then were asked "To what extent did the person described in the essay change since high school?" (9-point scale, endpoints "Has not changed at all" and "Has changed a great deal"), and "To what extent did the person described in the essay stay the same since high school?" (9-point scale, endpoints "Has not stayed the same at all" and "Has stayed the same"). In response to the change question, the change rating in the "no longer friends" condition ($M = 6.21$) was higher than the mean response in the "still friends" condition ($M = 4.79$), but only marginally so, $t(26) = 1.82$,

$p < .10$. No differences between the conditions were found when the question was phrased in terms of sameness, with the mean response in the "no longer friends" condition being 4.21 and the mean response in the "still friends" condition being 5.07. Thus, there was only marginal evidence to suggest that change was seen as more common in those with whom participants were no longer friends than in those with whom they were still friends. In both cases the tendency to rate high school friends as having changed somewhat could be said to provide a fairly high base rate. To see if participants regarded change as a factor in the breakdown of friendships, they were also asked in a separate essay question to describe what they thought accounted for the fact that the relationship had maintained itself (in the "still friends" condition) or what accounted for the breakup of the friendship (in the "no longer friends" condition). In both cases participants wrote fairly detailed statements, but change was no more common as a theme in describing a relationship that had deteriorated than in describing a relationship that had maintained itself.

From the present findings it appears that judgments of person change are not limited to relationships that have faltered, although change judgments may be slightly more common in such relationships. With regard to person change and issues of friendship, a separate but unexamined question is whether the perception that change has failed to occur is also a factor in whether relationships maintain themselves or deteriorate. The present study does not address this intriguing question, but the question suggests that the links among perceptions of change, perceptions of stability, and friendship maintenance may be highly complex. Such complexity is suggested by recent research on patterns of dissolution in friendships and other relationships (Duck, 1982, 1984; see also McFarland & Ross, 1987 for an analysis of intact relationships and whether change is perceived in dating partners and in the self).

To further examine the prevalence of perceptions of change in others, 120 participants were asked to describe in their own words areas of change and stability in their best friends and in themselves. Each participant wrote two essays about his or her best friend, one about the ways in which the friend had changed in the last few years and one about the ways in which the friend had stayed much the same in the last few years. Each subject also wrote two essays about the self, one, an essay about change, and the other, an essay about stability. The order in which essays were written was varied. To control for order effects, only the first essay written by each subject was included in the subsequent analysis, which focused on the frequency of comments about change and stability. The interest was in whether participants would be able to generate change inferences about their best friends and themselves, or whether comments about stability would largely predominate.

In all, 493 statements were made, 238 describing areas of change and 255 describing areas of constancy. The way the language of change was applied to individuals was quite varied. The aspects of self and other to which the term "change" was applied included goals and maturity, feelings for others, interests, physical characteristics, intellectual skills and abilities, attitudes and values, and trait attributes. An overall average of 4.1 comments were made per essay, with the number ranging from one to eleven. On average, 3.8 comments about other-change and 4.5 comments about other-stability were made. For the self, an average of 4.1 comments were made about change and 4.0 comments were made about stability. A test for significance showed that participants were no more likely to make stability comments than change comments, and there was no interaction between type of statement (change or stability) and whether the target of the statements was self or other.

Germane to points made earlier about friendship, several of the narratives spontaneously mentioned the effects of change on relationships. These narratives also revealed the emotion aroused by person change in friendships. One student remarked, "My best friend has changed in so many ways and I'm finding it hard to deal with." Another student expressed his puzzlement and concern over the changes he saw and their effects on the friendship:

> My best friend has just come back from a three-year stay in Germany as a helicopter mechanic for the army. And in this time we have both grown up quite a bit, both physically and mentally. Though I can't put my finger on any specific item, he and I seem to have changed. I no longer feel comfortable with him. I don't know if it's me or him. I first thought it was the army that changed him, but I'm not so sure now. I think we've both developed into individuals and that we each have specific values and goals, where when we were growing up we had a common goal of just having fun. We have our own unique responsibility. My best friend is a stranger to me and I do not wish to know him.

These comments are interesting not only in terms of their focus on change, but also in raising the question of whether people sometimes sense change in others or self without being able to articulate the nature of the change that has taken place. In particular, the subject's pondering over whether "it's me or him" raises an interesting issue regarding attributions for change in cases where neither the target nor the observer can be assumed to have remained stationary. In this case, the subject clearly feels an attributional dilemma. How people resolve attributional ambiguities is of general interest in those cases where the question is not one of whether change has occurred but rather one of where it can be located.

The present findings showing that people make judgments of change as well as of stability are consistent with other recent findings. Adopting a phenomenological perspective for examining perceptions of self-change, Ryff (1984) asked participants to fill out personality scales describing their personality in the past, in the present, and what they expected their personality to be like in the future. Ryff was able to show that people perceived change as well as stability in themselves over time, with the self-descriptions for the different periods showing patterns of shift in some areas and stability in others. Applying a social constructionist perspective, Gergen and Gergen (1984) have also presented evidence of perceivers' tendencies to refer to both change and stability in themselves as a part of strategies of self-presentations. Their work has emphasized the directional aspects of self-narratives about change —the tendency of such narratives to contain progressive or regressive themes— which Gergen and Gergen see as intertwining with stability themes to create narratives that are intended to maintain relationships: "Functioning viably in a relationship may depend on one's ability to show that one has always been the same, and will continue to be so, and yet contrapuntally, to show how one is continuing to improve. One must be reliable but demonstrate progress; one must be changing but maintain a stable character" (p. 18). Although the present work also finds the language of change being used to describe others and the self, it suggests that change judgments go beyond simple concerns with improvement and decline to encompass more generalized concerns with shifts in characteristics.

In the previously discussed studies, the examination of references to change focused on individuals of approximately the same age as the participants. The data to be discussed next bear on the question of whether change perception is limited to young target persons. In the first study, 42 participants were asked to describe in their own words any changes they saw in either a grandparent (if still living) or a parent. Fourteen wrote about a grandparent and 28 wrote about a parent. The average age of the parent described was 53.06 years ($SD = 8.51$) and the average age of the grandparent was 77.85 years ($SD = 7.39$). The participants described changes of many sorts: physical changes, changes in relationships, religious changes, changes due to retirement, interactional changes. The statements were scored for use of enhancers (e.g., "really changed," "changed a lot," "changed in many ways") and for the use of diminishers (e.g., "didn't really change," "not much at all," "very little"). In all, eight of 28 parent essays employed change enhancers and three of the 28 employed change diminishers. Similarly, four of 14 grandparent essays included enhancers and three of 14 included diminishers. Representative of the essays are the following:

> My dad has become much more mellow in the last few years. He loses his temper less often, and he's even able to laugh at himself now sometimes when he does. He has also become much more open. He has learned to be physically affectionate. He has also learned how to show his family that he cares, something he could never do before. My dad allows himself more leisure time now. He takes time out to pursue his favorite activities like reading and gardening. In general, my dad has become a much more sociable and pleasant person to live with.

> My father has changed in the past few years by becoming more talkative. My father has always been a quiet man. It is sometimes hard to have a conversation with him. Recently however he seems much easier to talk to and much more willing to start a conversation.

> My grandmother has undergone several significant changes. I have noticed that she has not kept in touch with a lot of people she used to. She seems to be enclosed in a little shell. She rarely goes out for a social evening unless it's to come to our house. I have noticed she is not as sharp mentally. At times she calls me the wrong name or seems confused when I tell her something.

Although change statements about parents were generated by participants in the preceding study, other results suggest that participants see themselves as having changed more than their parents—at least with regard to change that is directly related to their relationship with their parents. Participants (13 males, 11 females) were first asked to describe in their own words any changes they perceived in their relationship with their parents (average age of participants 19.8 years, average age of parents 48.5 years). Following this, participants were asked to gauge the relative roles of parental changes and self changes in the changes seen in the relationship with their parents, "Please assess the relative contributions to the changes you see in your relationship with your parents" (10-point scale, endpoints "Completely due

Table 7-1. Change Expectancies by Age of Target Person.

Age	25	35	45	55	65
Change expectancies	2.83_a	2.05_b	1.87_b	2.08_b	2.88_a

Note: Means reported in inches. The higher the mean, the greater the expected change. Means sharing the same subscript do not differ at the .05 level.

to changes in my parents" and "Completely due to changes I have gone through"). Participant responses were skewed in the direction of seeing changes in themselves as most responsible ($M = 6.8$, $SD = 1.8$) for the changes that had taken place in their relationship with their parents.

Age of Target Person and Change Expectations

Change expectations for persons as a function of the target's age were examined directly in a pair of studies. In the first study, participants were asked to quantitatively show the amount of change expected using length vectors rather than to describe their age-related change expectations in words. Forty-one participants were asked to draw arrows representing the relative degree of change they expected to occur in the average person at various ages. After being told that zero inches represented no change, they were asked to draw arrows whose lengths would represent amount of expected change for ages 25, 35, 45, 55, and 65. As Table 7-1 shows, there were significant differences in expectations for the various ages, with the youngest and oldest being subject to the greatest change expectations, $F(4,160) = 6.83$, $p < .001$.

The second study was designed to investigate the role of age in conjunction with several other variables. Participants were provided with 25 areas of functioning and were asked to judge the extent to which the average person would stay the same or change in these areas over time. The areas of functioning were taken directly from Block's (1971) "lives through time" research, where they were the basis for a longitudinal research program directed at assessing the degree of stability of people within cohorts over time. Three variables were manipulated in the present study: age of the target person (20, 40, or 60 years); period of time over which change being judged was to occur (1 year or 20 years); and whether the 25 areas of functioning were to be thought of as traits or as behaviors when making the judgments. Using 9-point scales, each subject rated the expected change in each of the 25 areas of functioning. Among the topic areas were the following: dependability/responsibility, breadth of range of interests, talkativeness, fastidiousness, and generosity. Ratings on the individual questions were averaged and a $3 \times 2 \times 2$ between-groups ANOVA was performed on the mean ratings.

In terms of overall expectations for change, a marginal effect was found for age, $F(2,96) = 2.41$, $p < .09$, whereby 40-year-olds were expected to show the least change in these areas of functioning. A strong effect for time was found, $F(1,96) = 15.71, p < .001$, with people expecting much less stability with the longer passage of time. No effects were found for whether the ratings were said to be about behavior or about personality. There were no interactions.

In Chapter 6, an extensive study on change expectations was reported in which subjects were asked to rate the amount of change they expected in people's traits versus in their behavior. In that study, unlike the present one, subjects' expectations for change in behavior were much stronger than their expectations for change in traits. The procedures of the two studies were different in a number of respects, but one notable difference is that subjects in the earlier study were asked about change in the abstract whereas subjects in the present study were provided with specific areas of functioning and were asked to make judgments abut change in traits or behavior in those specific areas. Thus, although subjects were instructed to think about those areas in terms or behavior or traits, the areas themselves may have carried implicit connotations that readily overrode any differences in instructions.

What Do Change Expectancies Represent?

With respect to the foregoing study's focus on age as a cue for change expectations, the results of the earlier study are of interest because they indicated that change expectations are directly tied to the perceived impact of particular life events. By focusing on age, the studies of the preceding section implicitly framed the issue of change expectations in terms of an underlying developmental perspective, that is, in terms of what participants expect in the way of patterns of growth and decline. But a developmental interpretation of change expectancies may not fully capture the reasons that perceivers expect change at different ages. Age-related expectations could very well represent event expectations, where change at a particular age is expected in part because of the impact of particular age-specific events—going to college, starting a first full-time job, entering retirement, and so forth. A large number of such events could be sufficiently confounded with age that asking about changes at various ages becomes, in effect, a way of asking about the impact of those events. Stated differently, if major life events (e.g., divorce, life-threatening illness, going to college) were distributed with equal probability across the years of adulthood, expectations for change might well be highly similar across different ages. Attempts have been made to investigate the relationship between events in the family life cycle and perceptions of change at least for the self (Brim & Ryff, 1980; Reinke et al., 1985), but the suggestion here is that a range of events broader than those involved in the family cycle may contribute importantly to age-related expectancies.

The idea that external age-related events are potentially important determinants of change over and above developmental progressions is an idea that has received considerable attention in recent years. As a result, the question of whether such factors prompt intuitive change expectancies takes on all the more interest. Higgins and

Parsons (1983), for example, have suggested that some of the changes in childhood that have been attributed entirely to developmental stages might better be understood as changes brought about by shifts in the external environment. In a similar vein, Baer (1970) and Fisher and O'Donohue (in press) have argued that the factor of age may be of limited explanatory value in psychology because many of the effects normally attributed to aging are due to factors that covary with age but are not caused by it. Once those other factors are taken into account, there may be little left to be explained in terms of aging per se. This may also be the case with change expectations. Once expectations for change due to particular events are fully considered, there may be little in the way of purely age-related change expectations that remain to be accounted for.

This issue of whether intuitive change perceptions are related to events, age, or some other factor brings us back to the question of whether intuitive views of change can be expected to coincide with findings from the systematic study of change. Much of the work measuring actual change in individuals over the life span (including Block's 1971 research) has adopted the strategy of evaluating the degree of change in the individual by examining changes in rank within the person's age cohort over time. As a measure of relative change or stability that attempts to control for general developmental and age-related trends, such a technique serves its intended purpose. Yet evidence based on maintenance of ranks may be at odds with the intuitive assessments of change where the intuitive concerns are age-related or event-related. As was shown in Chapter 6, event-related causes can be powerful determinants of perceivers' expectations for change. Where ordinary perceivers depart from researchers in their interpretation of change, this may often be the result of intuitive perceivers making their judgments on bases other than rank.

A final question raised by the foregoing discussion is that of whether change expectancies, whether based on age or events, undergo broad, systematic shifts over time. Certain events are specific to particular demographic cohorts (e.g., the Great Depression, World War II experiences); similarly, the pervasiveness of certain classes of change-related events may shift over time (e.g., prevalence of divorce, frequency of household moves, incidence of job loss). Are such differences—what Elder (1979) has identified as unique cohort effects—reflected in widely altered change expectancies? Stated differently, to the extent that there is a perceived accumulation of greater numbers of change-related events now than in the past, person change may be seen as more of a possibility and more of a worry now than in the past. Although it is intriguing to speculate that people may be more concerned with person change now than ever before (see Zurcher, 1972, 1973, for an interesting analysis of this possibility), it would be difficult to know to what extent such conjectures are correct. Certainly people are currently experiencing a variety of events that perceivers are apt to see as change-inducing, but the claim that person change judgments occur more frequently now than in the past is itself a change judgment and as such is subject to many of the same problems that arise in assessing the veridicality of other change judgments. In any event, it is probably safe to conclude that person change judgments are not unique to our time.

In the next chapter it is argued that judgments of social change are far from unique to our time despite the fact that they are often viewed as such. Just as we have seen in this chapter that there are certain issues that are especially important for understanding person change judgments, so in the next chapter we will find that there are certain issues that are especially important to the understanding of judgments of social change.

Chapter 8

Judgments of Social Change: A Closer Look

Judgments of social change—the type of change judgments that will be the topic of this chapter—are frequently regarded as distinctively contemporary, and thus as saying something unique about our times. Yet despite appearances, they are far from unique. Consider change judgments about the institution of the family. As historians of the family have noted, the perception that the once-perfect institution of the family has suddenly undergone a decline has been a perennial fixture in American culture (Caplow et al., 1983; Scott & Wishy, 1982; Seward, 1978; Tufte & Myerhoff, 1979). Each generation seems to believe that theirs is the first to experience the family as a deeply troubled institution. Thus, in 1983 we heard it said that "thirty years ago the American family was still happy and spirited and intact" (Ager, 1983, p. 47). Yet, more than half a century before the time of that statement, family life was also viewed as very much in jeopardy. At that time, the Lynds, authors of a classic study of American life (Lynd & Lynd, 1929), "feared for the future of the community and its institutions. They were especially apprehensive about the family, which, it seemed to them, had lost the emotional harmony that prevailed in earlier generations and was being riven in one place by a generation gap and in another by marital instability" (Caplow et al., 1983, p. 15). In their book, the Lynds noted that the theme of the decline of the family was common to many inspirational Chautauqua speeches of the time. In the words of one such speaker: "We seem to be drifting away from the fundamentals in our home life. The home was once a sacred institution where the family spent most of its time. Now it is physical service station" (Lynd & Lynd, 1929, pp. 178–179). Even earlier, at the beginning of this century, the same theme of family decline was commonplace: "What in family life by 1900 was not in question? In the remotest communities, country newspapers and family religious magazines repeated the national sense of family disruption" (Scott & Wishy, 1983, p. 175). Still earlier, in 1859: "The family in its old sense is disappearing from our land, and not only our free institutions are threatened, but the very existence of our society is endangered" (*Boston Quarterly Review*, 1859). And in the 17th century, commentators often attributed the problem behavior of individuals, criminal conduct, and general social disorder to the alleged disintegration of the family. It is reported that "the public sermons of colonial divines . . . invariably contained dire warnings about the evil consequences of the decline of family order" (Scott & Wishy, 1983, p. 137). Summing up the recurrent nature of these views, at a recent conference on the crisis in the family, the head of the federal agency HEW expressed the belief that "concern over the possible disintegration of the family has been present in every society throughout the history of civilization" (Harris, 1982, p. 670)

The perennial appeal of certain social change judgments to the popular mind is apparent in other areas as well. Over half a century ago, parents were claiming that teenagers had changed: "Girls are far more aggressive today. They call the boys up and try to make dates with them as they never would have when I was a girl" (quoted in Lynd & Lynd, 1929, p. 140). Parents today seem to think of their generation as the first to experience such a sizable generation gap but researchers who have investigated such matters have concluded otherwise: "the generation gap, although perceived by today's parents to be widening, seems, on the evidence, to have narrowed slightly from 1924 to 1977" (Caplow et al., 1983, p. 321). Over a quarter of a century ago, it was being said that people were once helpful but that this was no longer true: "we no longer care about the fate of our neighbors" and "compassion is disappearing, the old moralities are crumbling" (reported in Latane & Darley, 1970, pp. 1–2). In the 1980s, the same change conclusions about declines in helpfulness were being drawn: "I can tell you that the callousness and indifference toward human suffering and misery seems to have hit a new low. We have become an insensitive, me-first society and no longer feel an obligation to help others" (Landers, 1982, p. 38). In each generation, questionable business dealings and governmental practices are seen as a sign that ethics and values have undergone a dramatic deterioration from earlier times. The shady activities come as a surprise and are viewed as representing a change from the level of conduct typical of business practices in the past (see, e.g., Lupo, 1987). In donating millions of dollars to support programs on ethics at a prominent business school, the head of the Securities and Exchange Commission stated: "I've been very disturbed by the great number of leading business and law school graduates becoming felons. It's symptomatic of a change in moral attitude in America since the end of World War II" (Lupo, 1987, p. 94). Similar assertions of declines in morality were made in response to unethical dealings throughout the 1900s and before. Yet, as has been noted by those working in the field of business ethics (Wickman & Dailey, 1982), no one is certain to what extent business ethics may have changed from the past because, despite a wealth of FBI statistics on larceny, rape, assault, and murder, no single agency gathers and records statistics specifically on white-collar crime.

Despite the ubiquity of social change claims, they cannot be said to always mirror actual changes. Where relevant data exist, they often do not fully support the intuitive impressions. Again, if we look to the family literature, we find indications that change claims may be overstated. Basing their remarks on a careful longitudinal study of family life, Caplow et al. (1983) assessed the situation as follows: "Tracing the changes from the 1920s to the 1970s, we discovered increased family solidarity, a smaller generation gap, closer marital communication, more religion, and less mobility. With respect to the major features of family life, the trend of the past two generations has run in the opposite direction from the trend that nearly everyone perceives and talks about" (p. 321; see also Seward, 1978). There is a similar lack of support in the data for many other familiar change conclusions. Evidence concerning childhood in the past suggests that childhood was not invariably a time of great innocence untroubled by parental neglect and abuse (Bybee, 1979; Radbill, 1980). With regard to sexual mores, the available evidence suggests that sexual behavior in this century has not undergone any great change until recent years despite common change beliefs to the contrary. As noted by Bell and Chaskes (1970), "there have been no striking changes in the probabilities of having premarital coitus . . . . There is no evidence to suggest that when women born after 1900 are compared by decades of birth, there are any significant differences in their rates of premarital coitus" (p. 81). With regard to political change, the intuitive view that the majority of Americans keep dramatically changing political views from one decade to the next is not supported by the data. For example, the perceived turn to the right in recent years is not consistent with the extant data for most political issues (see Ferguson & Rogers, 1986; Pomper, 1981).

Many intuitive change conclusions fail to be supported by the available data; other change conclusions exist despite the paucity of reliable formal data. As many scholars have noted, no one knows for certain how family life in the distant past compares to that in the present because statistical records comparable to today's were not kept (Demos, 1986; Scott & Wishy, 1982; Seward, 1978; Tufte & Myerhoff, 1979). To assess change in families from earlier centuries one would have to reconstruct evidence from fragmentary records of what family life must have been like at different times (Scott & Wishy, 1982). To infer change in the incidence of sexual practices in the distant past would be difficult because no large-scale systematic studies of sexual behavior were conducted until well into this century when Kinsey first reported findings from his surveys. It is uncertain as to whether people have become more or less helpful because records on levels of helpfulness have not been kept. To make any inferences about change in helpfulness requires the use of highly indirect information — for example, information about how willing people were to be interviewed by a stranger (House & Wolf, 1978) — and, even so, such information may or may not be indicative of typical helpfulness-related practices. The incidence of child abuse in the past cannot be known with any authority because records similar to those available today were simply not kept. To make any reasonable case for change one would have to piece together records from the Humane Society and various other informal sources — an undertaking beset with problems that have been described at length by Pleck (1987). As Bauer (1966) has commented, "for many of the important topics on which social critics blithely pass judgment, and on which policies are made, there are no data by which to know if things are getting better or worse" (p. 20).

If there are, at best, fragmentary data for the past and often very little substantiating data in the present, why have change judgments been so commonplace and so similar across time in content and form? In other words, how do we account for change judgments given the fact that the relevant data are often either lacking entirely or are pointing in the opposite direction? Ideas as to the underlying basis for social change judgments have often focused on intuitive perceivers as myth makers and believers in myths, with the claim being made that people have a propensity both to believe in myths and to generate them because myths are in some way consoling. Thus, it has been said that "the dominant myths of complex society obsessed with social change are likely to be either myths of inevitable progress or inevitable decadence" (Caplow et al., 1983, p. 323). Caplow et al. argue that the myth of the declining family has some value for its believers: "When Middletown people compare their own families with the 'average' or the 'typical' family, nearly all of them discover with pleasure that their own families are better than other people's" (p. 326). Other historians of the family have asserted that people are motivated to believe in a kind of Garden of Eden myth about the family (Demos, 1979, 1986). Goodman (1982) argues that "we all carry around inside us some primal scene of a family Eden, an ideal of family life. Among the strongest yearnings we take out of childhood is the desire to create this perfect family" (p. 15). It is from that yearning that our intuitive judgments of change presumably come into being.

Intriguing as such ideas are, they leave us with little actual understanding of the workings of intuitive change considerations. Although they highlight the widespread fascination with social change in American culture, they do little else. They leave the impression that intuitive change conclusions represent nothing more than a wish on the part of perceivers to believe in a certain state of affairs. Yet, as has been argued throughout this book, change judgments—even those that might appear flawed from some other perspective—are likely to represent predictable and systematic interpretations of the information available to the intuitive perceiver.

The present chapter concerns exactly this question of how everyday information and its use might account for the confidently held social change conclusions that are so much a part of American life. In this chapter we look again at the findings described in earlier chapters and show how they might apply to social change judgments in particular. After suggesting how these previous findings might shed light on the character of social change judgments, we go on to report a number of additional studies concerned with the question of how perceivers come to see social change so readily under what would appear to be difficult informational circumstances.

The Case of Confident Change Judgments: Relevance of Earlier Studies

The studies of change judgments already described—some of which have been on social change judgments and others of which have not—have pointed to a number of factors likely to shape social change impressions. These include (1) the tendency to think about change in terms of simple concepts like frequency rather than more complex concepts such as rate, (2) the tendency to contrast complex knowledge of the present with simplified, variability-reducing versions of the past, and (3) the readiness to infer change in the absence of specific information about the past.

In previous studies we saw that perceivers often use facts about sheer frequency in making rate-change judgments. They do so in part because population information is not always included in everyday accounts and in part because such information is not given much emphasis in the information contexts in which these intuitive judgments arise. We found that in the illustrative cases of judging rates of teenage pregnancy and child abuse, the consequences of relying on frequency information alone were considerable; where population shifts were not highly visible, people inferred change in the incidence of the problem whether such a change had occurred or not.

In earlier chapters emphasis was placed on the misleading character of change impressions that can result from reliance on frequency data. Here it is worth noting that reliance on frequency facts in isolation is also likely to increase the ease with which social change judgments are made. By simplifying the available information and making it less complex, frequency facts may give the intuitive change data the appearance of being self-evident and even indisputable.

Reliance on frequency data alone is not inevitable—nor is it always problematic —but it is of special concern in cases where population sizes are shifting. With regard to social change judgments, a basic fact of life is the increase in the total U.S. population. Bauer (1966) has commented that virtually every trend series pertaining to social problems has a built-in inflationary bias as a result of the population expansion. To cite one example, he notes that "the average citizen listening to and reading about the cataclysmic holiday weekends would conclude that driving has become increasingly dangerous especially on holiday weekends. The figures invariably cited are uncorrected for volume of traffic. Overall figures on annual fatalities are usually uncorrected for increases in population" (p. 27). Taking population fluctuations into account will be important to many cases of social change and failure to do so is likely to make increases in rare events such as those in the tail of a distribution seem indicative of a change even when the increases result from the growth of a larger, but otherwise unchanged, distribution.

Another set of findings from earlier studies that have direct relevance for the class of social change judgments consists of those having to do with variability information and its use. Several studies illustrated that the limits on how variability information is represented and used will sometimes influence the change judgments that are made. In particular, the fact that prior variability information if often not readily available, or is often less available for the past than for the present, was shown to influence intuitive change judgments of various sorts. Poor recall of past variability led to seeing changes in present environmental quality. Also, when present variability was compared to a variability-reducing summary for the past people judged variability in the weather to have increased. In cases of judging changes in rates of drunk driving and similar series with variable baselines, prior causal information was found to influence the interpretation of change and to sometimes affect the use of prior variability information. Because many social change judgments—those in the present as well as those in the past—are made in the context of variable series, these findings may have serious implications for social change judgments. Only further work will show the extent to which previous results generalize across a variety of circumstances, but the results are intriguing in their suggestion that people may readily see social change and find it easy to make social change judgments both because the everyday information they use has been simplified in terms of prior variability and because these judgments using variability information are made under conditions where change is anticipated on the basis of causal information.

Other earlier studies also uncovered findings potentially relevant to understanding the general character of social change judgments. For example, people showed relatively little concern about the quality of the data they received when they had reason to believe that change would occur. Thus, when they expected child abuse to occur, they were not especially concerned that the statistics for the present came from a more inclusive source than did the statistics for the past. Similarly, in several other studies (the content of which was not directly concerned with social change), participants were found to draw change conclusions in the absence of explicit information about the past. For example, they inferred change in an individual even though they knew little about the person's past. If people show a similar alacrity in judging social change with minimal knowledge of the past, then the opportunities for perceiving social change at an intuitive level would be broadened considerably. People may not require explicit past information to judge the amount of change that has taken place. Although intuitive perceivers appear to be open to using information of many sorts, not all of this information meets traditional formal standards for the quality and appropriateness of data.

In sum, several of the factors that were the focus of earlier studies are germane to social change judgments. In the area of social change, these factors may act to enhance the clarity with which change is perceived by reducing the "messiness" — the incompleteness and complexity—of comparison information. The likely result is that social change will often appear considerably more unambiguous than it actually is. These informational factors may also help account for the recurrent nature of social change judgments because the past and present informational differences from which such judgments appear to arise recur from one present and past comparison to the next. To the extent that social perceivers of each era, generation, or decade are confronted with these asymmetries of past and present information, they will be likely to see social change as readily as those who come before and after them. Moreover, if the problematic asymmetries of information are not ordinarily salient to perceivers of social change, one would expect their judgments of change to be held with more confidence than would be warranted by the ordinary standards of formal change assessment.

Studies of Social Change Judgments: Selected Topics

In the remainder of the chapter we turn to studies directly concerned with judgments of social change. Focusing on some of the areas where confidently held, recurrent social change assertions arise, we look more closely at those assertions and at the information base that may support such recurrent impressions. For each topic area, the studies to be reported focus on only a limited set of the phenomena of information use that seem particularly likely to play a role in shaping judgments in that area; but it should not be assumed that the factors analyzed would be unique to change judgments in that area alone. Taken together, these studies add detail to our emerging picture of how information is used in judging social change. As we shall see, the findings of many of these studies also contribute to understanding the important phenomenon of the nostalgic fallacy, that is, the tendency for recurrent social change judgments to concern themselves with declines over time rather than improvements. We begin with perceptions of changes in helping behavior.

Perceptions of Change in Helping Behavior

As noted earlier, certain problems are commonly regarded as unique to our times. The seemingly pervasive unwillingness to get involved—to help one's neighbors—is probably prototypic of the kind of problem taken to be distinctively contemporary. We hear it said that the lack of helpfulness is a sign of our times, an indication of how apathetic and uncaring people have become. We are told that this kind of apathy was simply unheard of in the past. Not surprisingly, such commentary on the lack of helping often follows some vivid instance of failure to help. Consider the public outcry following the 1964 murder of Kitty Genovese. The failure of any of Genovese's 38 neighbors to become involved in warding off Genovese's attacker or even summon help led to much impassioned commentary about what our society had become. The incident was treated as a sign that things had changed and that people no longer helped their neighbors in the way that was once expected and even automatic (see discussion in Latane & Darley, 1970; Rosenthal, 1964). In large part, the point of the subsequent social psychological studies on bystander intervention was to suggest that the explanation for the failure to help lies in something other than large-scale changes in levels of helpfulness.

It has been almost a quarter of a century since the Genovese incident occurred and as an example of failures to help, it is no longer contemporary—indeed, it happened before many of the current cohort of college students were born. Yet it remains a fixture in college-level social psychology textbooks. These textbooks (e.g., Baum, Fisher, & Singer, 1985; Deaux & Wrightsman, 1984; Freedman, Sears, & Carlsmith, 1981; Schneider, 1988; Worchel & Cooper, 1979) routinely use the case as a way of highlighting questions about why bystanders fail to help, although they often do so in the context of referring to the absence of helping behavior as if it were a problem somehow peculiar to very recent times. In social psychology texts and classes, the "contemporizing" of this event and of the problem it represents has remained a standard way of treating the incident.

In reaction to similar cases today we hear responses very reminiscent of those evoked years ago by the Genovese case. In the wake of some current failure to help, we hear it said that the absence of helpfulness is something that could not have happened in the past. It is seen as a sign—as some put it—of the "moral sickness of our times." The irony here is obvious. How could it be that the past we are now referring to—the past in which everybody presumably helped—is the time when the neighbors were failing to help in the Genovese case and when people were talking about the incident as a sign that people were no longer helpful?

The question of whether people view failures to help as somehow unique to today was the basis for the study to be described next. To look at this question, study participants were given a description of the Genovese case but without information about when it occurred. The subjects (32 general psychology students) were provided with a description of the case taken directly from a social psychology textbook (Williamson, Swingle, & Sargent, 1982, p. 390), but with the victim's name changed. In order to better examine people's beliefs about helping behavior, the information was varied such that the neighbors were said to have either helped or not. Thus, half of the participants received the original details in which the neighbors heard the attack but none helped and the other participants were provided with details of the same incident but were told that all of the neighbors helped. No identifying information was given as to when the incident actually took place. The intent was to see how people think about this incident in conjunction with their perceptions of helping behavior at different points in time.

After reading about the incident and the neighbors' response, participants in both conditions were asked how likely the neighbors' responses (helping or not helping) were to have occurred at various times: 20 years ago (around the time of the Genovese case), 10 years ago, 5 years ago, and within the last year. Each of these questions included a 9-point response scale with endpoints "Not at all likely" and "Very likely" and the order of these questions was reversed for half the subjects in each condition. As Figure 8.1 shows, over the last 20 years students perceive a dramatic change in helpfulness. The lack of helpfulness is viewed as something that would have happened in the last few years rather than at the time that it actually did. In judging life 20 years ago, subjects believed that the lack of helping was somewhat unlikely ($M = 4.20$), but that helping by all of the neighbors was very likely ($M = 7.13$), $t(30) = 3.57, p < .01$. Just the opposite was found for recent years. Subjects believed that the total failure to help was very likely ($M = 7.63$), but that helping by all of the neighbors was very unlikely ($M = 3.44$), $t(30) = 4.95, p < .001$.

Another way to capture people's views of helping behavior at different points in time is to ask about the typicality of the neighbors' reaction. Subjects were asked how typical the neighbors' behaviors would have been of the kind of reaction one would have seen in the past and in the present to a situation like that described (9-point scale, with endpoints "Not at all typical" and "Very typical"). In judging what was typical in the past, subjects thought that having all of the neighbors help was typical ($M = 6.38$), but that having all of the neighbors fail to help was much less so ($M = 4.13$), $t(30) = 2.89, p < .01$. Again, just the reverse was found for the present. Subjects thought that having every one of the neighbors fail to help was very typical ($M = 7.13$), but that having all of the neighbors help was much less so ($M = 4.56$), $t(30) = 2.77, p < .01$.

Subjects were also asked directly about what had happened to people's willingness to help others over the last 20 years (9-point scale, endpoints and midpoint "These days people don't help as much as they used to," "Has not changed," and "These days people help more than they used to"). Regardless of condition, participants believed that people had become less helpful in the last 20 years, with a mean response of 2.84 (2.88 No helping, 2.81 Helping, $SD = 2.13$). That impression is also con-

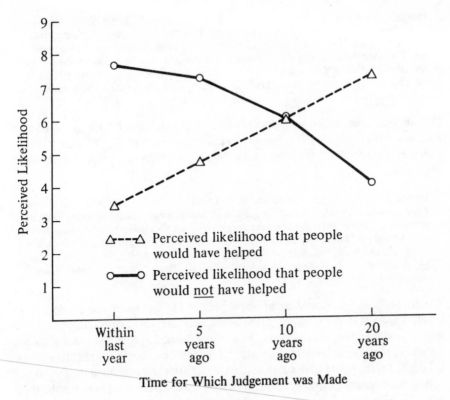

Figure 8-1.

firmed when subjects were asked how helpful they thought people are these days and how helpful they were in the past. In both conditions subjects rated people as not very helpful in the present ($M = 4.10$; 3.75 No Helping, 4.44 Helping), and as very helpful in the past ($M = 6.91$; 6.63 No Helping, 7.19 Helping), and the judgments for past and present differed significantly from one another, repeated measures $F(1,30) = 35.03, p < .00002$.

The extent to which students were convinced that there has been a dramatic decline in the levels of helping in the last 20 years is underscored by the kinds of comments made in response to two open-ended questions, the first asking participants to describe what they thought was the typical person's reaction 20 years ago to a helping situation and the second asking them to describe the typical reaction these days to a helping situation. Twenty-six of the 32 subjects (81%) believed that 20 years ago the usual response was to get involved in any helping situation that presented itself. Their responses indicate that they view helping behavior in a way as to suggest that the Kitty Genovese sort of event could not have happened 20 years ago. The following sample responses represent the kinds of views of past helping behavior held by the subjects:

People did not have to think about helping—it seemed to be just a natural instinct .... People would go out of their way to comfort another person, even if it meant risking their lives. Like the heros of the olden days .... I think 20 years ago that if a person saw someone needing help, they would reach out and help them before they even thought about possible consequences .... I think 20 years ago everybody worked together as a community, all neighbors knew each other and would stick up for them in any situation.

The subjects' open-ended responses about typical helping behavior in the present were markedly different. The majority of participants (25 of 32, 78%) said that the typical response today is for people not to help others. Consider some representative responses:

Basically people are much more selfish than they used to be .... Today I think the basic view is each man for himself .... Most people nowadays are so wrapped up in themselves they would rather see a person get killed without helping in case they themselves might get hurt in trying to help .... People these days are not as likely to get involved in a helping situation as they were years ago. They don't have the time or simply don't want to be bothered by helping someone. People's attitudes have changed quite drastically over the years.

Twenty years ago one could count on people helping, but today one cannot—or so it seems to most of our students. In many respects, 20 years ago is quite recent, yet for our students it apparently is not. To many of them, 20 years ago was a distinctly different time. As one student remarked: "If the same incident occurred 20 years ago I think someone would have come to her aid just after she screamed the first time."

Are these results surprising? Perhaps not, if we consider what is heard about the past. Usually what is heard is not about single instances involving the acts (or failures to act) of ordinary people. Furthermore, when we reflect back on the 1960s, we probably do not immediately think of cases like that of Kitty Genovese as the indication of what times were like then, just as in thinking back on the 1980s at some future time we probably will not immediately think of these times as characterized by behaviors of someone like Bernhard Goetz (the so-called subway vigilante) even though that incident was seen as a sign of the times when it happened. Single incidents—salient as they are at the time—do not seem to become linked to our view of what those times were like nor do they seem to be included in what gets reported to younger people about those times. There would seem to be a kind of asymmetry in the availability of certain sorts of events. In the present, single instances are available to be freely generalized from, but once they become a part of the past, we less often hear about them and they may rapidly lose their symbolic implications.

What happens when people *do* hear about single instances that occurred in the past and that violate expectations? Are these incidents incorporated into the view of the past in ways that influence change impressions? Hearing now about the failure in the past to help in the Genovese case, would people use the information about a single incident of this sort to revise their opinions about helping in the past and hence about changes in helping? The study described next examines this question.

Participants (70 general psychology students) were provided with information about the Genovese case. In a 2×2 design, subjects learned either that the neighbors helped or that they did not, and that the event took place in the past (1964) or in the present (1984). The question of interest was whether single-incident information would lead students to revise their opinions. If people use single-instance information, we should find that participants who learn of a failure to help in the past will revise downward their impressions of how helpful people used to be. Subjects were found to do exactly that. After reading about the incident, subjects were asked how helpful people were in the past (9-point scale, endpoints "Not at all helpful" and "Very helpful"). People who learned about an actual instance of a past failure to help were significantly less likely to view people as helpful in the past ($M = 5.44$) than were those who heard about a similar incident occurring in the present ($M = 7.12$) or those who heard about an instance where helping rather than nonhelping took place ($M = 6.89$ Past and $M = 6.82$ Present). A Duncan's Multiple Range Test showed that the latter three conditions differed significantly from the first but not from each other; a main effect was found for year, $F(1,66) = 4.89, p < .03$; and there was an interaction, $F(1,66) = 5.72, p < .02$. When asked about the present, subjects did not differ across conditions in how helpful they viewed people as these days (mean across conditions = 4.0). Thus, even those who received a case that violated expectations for the present (where every one of the neighbors in the present helped) did not revise their estimates upward relative to the subjects in the other conditions ($M = 4.0$).

Subjects were also asked how typical the neighbors' behavior (helping for some subjects and nonhelping for others) would have been of reactions in the past. A pattern similar to that for the first question was found. Those who read that the neighbors had helped viewed this as quite typical of the past regardless of whether the helping they read about occurred in the present or in the past ($M = 6.06$ Past; $M = 6.82$ Present). In contrast, the year information had an effect for people who read about a failure to help. People who read about a recent instance of nonhelping saw the failure to help as atypical in the past ($M = 3.35$), whereas people who read about the same incident as taking place in 1964 were much less likely to see this as atypical in the past ($M = 5.22$), $F(1,66) = 19.48, p < .0002$, Helping; $F(1,66) = 7.31, p < .009$, Interaction. A Duncan's Multiple Range Test showed that the two No-Help conditions differed significantly from each other and from the two Help conditions.

The effect of reading about the incident on perceptions of changes in helpfulness was considered next. Subjects were asked "What has happened to people's willingness to help others over the last 20 years?" (9-point scale, endpoints and midpoint "These days people don't help as much as they used to," "Has not changed," "These days people help more than they used to"). Here a nearly significant effect was found, $F(1,66) = 3.18, p < .075$, whereby people who received the nonhelping incident for 1964 were less likely to perceive a decline in helpfulness ($M = 4.50$) than those in any of the other three conditions ($Ms = 3.00$ No Helping Present, 3.28 Helping Past, 3.12 Helping Present; Duncan's Test significant at the .10 level).

Ordinary perceivers would seem to significantly alter their impressions of change on the basis of a single incident. Why might this be the case? One possibility is that people hold the view that failures to help could *never* have occurred in the past.

Thus, even a single instance could serve to disconfirm that view and hence could be informative. If this were the case, it would also suggest that one reason people failed to revise their prior beliefs about changes in helpfulness when they learned of an instance of all neighbors helping in the present was that they had not assumed a complete absence of helping in the present, and thus a single case was not as disconfirming or as informative.

The Genovese case embodies the sort of vividness and impactfulness that previous work suggests would lead to a single case being used as a basis for revising beliefs as well as for discounting potentially more reliable information (see Hamill, Wilson, & Nisbett 1980; Nisbett et al., 1976). Less vivid cases might have a more limited effect. Furthermore, the incident's impact on views of what the past was like may also be tied to the fact that the time of the incident was clearly specified. Simply hearing about an event that happened to have occurred in the past may not be similarly impactful. Consider the fact that when we hear the parable of the Good Samaritan, in which all but one potential helper refused to help, we do not conclude that people used to help infrequently. The fact that the incident occurred in the past is not taken to be the central feature of the incident. The story is not constructed in such a way that people will draw the conclusion that insufficient helping was also a problem in the past. Darley and Batson (1973) showed that hearing the parable had limited effects on subsequent helping, and it may be that such stories about past behavior are likewise not used to revise beliefs about such matters as how helpful people were in the past.

As we have seen, intuitive judgments are routinely made about broad cultural shifts such as changes in levels of helpfulness now relative to the past, despite the fact that little is systematically known about actual day-to-day levels, present or past, of the characteristics or behavior being judged. The fact that judgments occur where systematic evidence is lacking could indicate a possible blurring of distinctions in kinds of past knowledge when change is being intuitively considered. Perceiving evidence of change does not always depend on identifying what one has as reliable numeric information and perhaps, as the next study suggests, does not even depend on having knowledge specific to actual past events. Perhaps all that is necessary for comparisons to occur is that there be a guiding impression of some sort about the past.

One of the characteristics of commentary on helping (and on other culturally valued behaviors) is that we frequently encounter normative prescriptions. In discussions of helpfulness and its importance, we hear not merely whether people have helped in particular cases, but also about what people *should* do in such situations. Perhaps thinking about these "shoulds" somehow influences change impressions. Could the mere experience of being reminded of the cultural norm that people should help others (with the implication that people never quite do as much of it as they should) be sufficient to increase the likelihood of judging that there has been a decline in levels of helpfulness? To investigate this issue, a guest lecture was given in an introductory psychology class on the topic of helping behavior. All members of the class knew at the outset that the lecture would be on this topic. Before the actual lecture began, the class was told that the concept of a norm would be important to the lecture and that a written definition of the concept would be handed out to all class members. The students then received the definition (e.g., "In social psychology we are finding out that people hold general beliefs about what constitutes appropriate behavior. These beliefs are called norms.") with either an example that concerned helping behavior or without an example. The example stated, "An example of a norm is the following: People should help others." Soon after receiving the definition (and example), class members were asked to respond to a short questionnaire about their perceptions of various kinds of social behavior (e.g., helping behavior, sexual behavior). Included in that questionnaire was an item intended to assess their beliefs about the extent to which people were less likely to help now than in the past. The statement read "People are less likely to help other people these days" (responses were made on a 31-point scale, endpoints "I strongly agree" and "I strongly disagree"). As predicted, class members who had just been exposed to the norm for helping were more likely to agree that people were less helpful these days ($M = 10.67$) than were members who had not been exposed to a norm about helping behavior ($M = 14.30$), $t(36) = 2.73$, $p < .05$.

Being reminded of a relevant helping norm might have this effect for any number of reasons. It might make one think more about helping in general, which perhaps automatically calls forth one's view that helping has declined. It is also possible that this effect reflects a tendency to regard what "should be" as "what was": by having one's attention drawn to normative expectations one has, in effect, been provided with a reminder of what things supposedly were once like. In this case, people would be operating with a vague guiding impression of the past, without distinguishing between normative and descriptive sources of that impression. Another possibility is that salient norms act as a kind of memory prime and produce their effect by leading people to recall specific incidents of helping or nonhelping from the present and past. If so, the norm is an interesting sort of prime in that it would seem to prime different sorts of information about the present and the past given that the perceived differences between the two periods widen when thinking in normative terms. Finally, it is also possible that norms direct thinking entirely toward the present and toward thinking about the ways people are currently failing to live up to expectations. Comparisons of present failures with norms may be sufficient to induce generalized conclusions about declines in helpfulness.

In any event, the fact that norms seem to influence beliefs about change is significant in that normatively toned cues and comments permeate many aspects of public dialogue about helping behavior in our society. Comments about how people ought to have behaved often appear in response to notable failures to help. As a consequence, our ordinary view of changes in helpfulness might be affected considerably by a reliance on available normative information.

Helping behavior represents one kind of positive social behavior that is widely viewed as being in decline; family life is another. The next section reports a study on perceptions of declines in family life that are designed to shed light on the impact of perceptions of average families and ideal families on views of family decline.

Perceptions of Change in Families: Viewing the Average Past Family as Ideal

Judging by frequently heard comments, many people seem convinced that a dramatic decline has taken place in the quality of family life, a conviction by no means limited to such obvious factors as the increase in divorce rates. According to this widespread view, families have shown a marked deterioration from what they once were along a broad array of dimensions ranging from familial cohesiveness to parental authority and involvement in children's education. Yet families in the past were not without the problems experienced by today's families. Child and spouse abuse, alcoholism, and serious conflict were hardly absent from the families of the past (see Straus et al., 1980). The problems of children disobeying their parents and of parents being at a loss as to how to raise their children have long been matters of much concern. Such family problems were the staple of syndicated advice columns in the past (see Lynd & Lynd, 1929) and were the basis of popular books with contemporary-sounding titles like *Broken Homes* (Colcord, 1919). Why then do people today so readily view such problems as distinctively contemporary and as evidence of family values being in decline?

It might be contended that the reason for perceiving a decline is that perceivers think of the ideal case when they imagine the family of the past, and then use this salient ideal of the past as their point of comparison. Although this may sometimes occur, one difficulty with this explanation is that it seems puzzling that people would generalize so easily from an ideal case in the past to a decline in the present when there may also be ideal cases in the present (even if these are relatively rare). Perhaps other phenomena involving ideals play a role in judgments of decline. It may be that in making comparisons, people do use the average family in the past for comparison purposes, but that they also construe the average family as being close to the ideal. If people already think of the past average as ideal this would help account for why they so readily make judgments of deterioration. They are not generalizing from some rare-case ideal but rather from what they perceive to be typical of the past, in which case they can acknowledge the existence of some ideal cases in the present without abandoning their judgments of decline.

To examine views of the average and ideal family in the present and the past, subjects (64 general psychology students) were provided with a set of 60 adjectives (30 positive and 30 negative). These adjectives were drawn from a larger pool and had been pretested to select only those that were viewed as clearly negative or positive and that were believed to be applicable to the category of families. From the list provided, subjects in separate conditions were asked to select the 10 adjectives that best described either the average family or the ideal family and they did so for one kind of family in the past (ideal or average) and one kind of family in the present (ideal or average). Of interest was the number of negative adjectives that would be selected for each of the four family types and, in particular, whether the average and the ideal for the present and the past would be different.

Only those subjects who were asked to describe the average family in the present selected a considerable number of negative adjectives ($M = 4.94$); subjects who described the ideal family in the present selected few negative adjectives ($M =

1.00). When people were asked to describe the average family in the past, they selected few negative adjectives ($M = 0.50$), as they did for the ideal ($M = 0.38$). A significant main effect was found for past versus present, $F(1,60) = 29.19, p < .001$, as well as for average versus ideal, $F(1,60) = 18.80, p < .001$, and there was an interaction, $F(1,60) = 16.56, p < .001$. A Duncan's Multiple Range Test showed that only the Average/Present condition differed from the others. Examples of the negative descriptors frequently chosen included: quarrelsome, not close, conflict-filled, argumentative, fragmented, resentful. Examples of positive descriptors frequently chosen included: strong, supportive, dependable, loving, involved with their children, loyal, and respectful.

After subjects selected descriptors, they were asked to describe their views of family change. Using a 9-point scale, they were asked whether, "Compared to family life in the past, family life these days is greatly improved (1), is unchanged (5), is greatly deteriorated (9)." With nearly universal agreement, subjects viewed the family as having declined. The vast majority of the subjects (88%) marked above the midpoint, with the modal response being 7 on the 9-point scale.

At the close of the study, subjects were also asked to write an essay describing either the average or ideal family in the present or the past. From these essays we get yet another view of the blending of the perceptions of the ideal and average for the past. One subject wrote of the ideal family in the past:

> In the past, the whole family functioned together as one, depending upon and loving each other. Such a family rarely engaged in arguments or heated discussions, and when a member of the family had a problem the rest of the family was sure to try to understand and help. In the past, the head of the family, usually the father, was looked up to with much respect, yet the father was not someone to be feared as many fathers are today. Finally, families rarely separated, and every member was happy simply to spend time with other members. For example, brothers and sisters were far closer to one another and to their parents.

Another wrote:

> I think that an ideal family of the past would be very similar to the family portrayed on the T.V. show, "The Waltons." Supportive grandparents would provide a solid base for the family. The parents would be fiercely stubborn but also loyal and loving. The children would squabble among themselves, but not to the point where the arguments would tear the family apart. Most importantly, the parents and grandparents would exercise strict discipline over the children so that they would grow up with a solid moral framework.

In describing the average family of the past, students wrote essays that were largely indistinguishable from the essays describing the ideal past family. Two examples:

> I believe the average family in the past was more united. They showed a lot of respect for each member of their family. They supported one another. The average family in the past would go out and do things together as a unit. They were affectionate, caring, loyal to the family name. They were more involved with each other and were interested in what the family and parents had to say concerning different subjects.

In my opinion, the average family of the past was a group that was well-organized and strict. The father was the head of the household and the only bread-winner. The mother played the single role of housewife and took care of the children. In the families of the past, children were very obedient and acted much like they were expected to. The traditional family worked together as a unit and were able to solve all problems and conflicts within. Whenever one member was in trouble, the other members joined together to solve the problem.

One intriguing feature of the commentary in these essays is the tendency for family change to be described at a remove—that is, subjects seemed to perceive the descent from the perfect family in the past to the highly imperfect family in the present as something occurring in anonymous families seen only in the abstract rather than something readily observed across generations of families actually known to the subjects. The present study was not designed to probe subjects' perceptions of decline in families that were highly familiar; but one might suspect that if subjects were asked to make judgments about the decline of families in the abstract versus the decline of families actually known to them, the perception of decline would be most apparent for families in the abstract. Reliance on knowledge of actual families may draw subjects back toward concrete cases and away from the abstract or idealized views of the past. Such a finding would be consistent with the point made throughout this section that judgments of decline are especially likely to arise when emphasis is placed on normative information for the past.

Perceptions of Change in Crime: Another Use of Simplifying Information

Thus far in this chapter we have considered several factors that could contribute to the readiness with which social change is perceived. As has been noted, certain kinds of information create a simplified yet compelling image of the events at a particular time, an image that can then be picked up by the perceiver and used in arriving at a confidently help impression of change. Here this point will be illustrated in another way, in this case by looking at simplifying information that is available for drawing inferences about changes in levels of crime.

Crime is a topic of great interest to ordinary social perceivers. As a consequence, many sorts of informal data are available that speak to the issue of crime and its prevalence in the present and in the past. The mass media often present us with statistics of one sort or another, perhaps about how many people were mugged last year, how many children were abducted by strangers or disappeared from their neighborhoods, and the like. News reports commonly feature crimes that are taken to be newsworthy, often those of a particularly bizarre, horrifying, or vicious nature. Neighbors and friends comment on crimes that have happened to them or to people they know. Listening to commercials, we learn that robberies and muggings can befall the unwary traveler. Often these everyday reports have a kind of presentist focus, emphasizing present crimes rather than crimes of a similar sort in the past. Informal views of crime—as shaped by television and similar sources—have been examined in numerous studies (e.g., Sheley & Ashkins, 1981; Skogan, 1986; Tyler,

1984), but typically the concern has been with perceptions of the crime rate at one point in time rather than perceptions of changes across time.

One type of everyday information that *is* closely associated with change statements is that of the time-referenced statistic, in which the perceiver is provided with an impression of crime in some area by being told how often a crime (child abduction, rape, assault, etc.) occurs in the United States each day (or hour or minute). Often these statistics are used to underscore some point about change, that is, about how much more often these sorts of events are happening in the present than in the past. The intriguing characteristic of this index is that it provides a ready base for making such comparisons but one that fails to capture essential population information. Whenever the population increases — as it regularly does in the United States — the impression will be conveyed that problems have worsened when time-referenced statistics are the basis for comparison, even if the actual rate has remained the same. In other words, such statistics have a built-in inflationary bias (Bauer, 1966). The study to be described next investigated the responses of perceivers to simplifying time-referenced statistics.

In order to examine how statistics of this sort affect change judgments, participants were provided with time-referenced information of a sort similar to that typically encountered in everyday sources. Thus, the subjects (68 general psychology students) were told how often each day a certain kind of crime was occurring in the present (1980) and in the past (1900). The choice of the year 1900 was dictated by the fact that it was long enough ago that the United States population had undergone a substantial increase since that time (having approximately tripled, *World Almanac & Book of Facts*, 1985), a fact that the participants themselves may or may not have been aware of given that the index fails to include this information. The specific numbers provided were designed so that half of the subjects learned that in 1900 an assault occurred somewhere in the United States about every 12 minutes, whereas in 1980 an assault occurred about every 6 minutes. The other subjects learned that the incidence of assaults in 1900 was about one in every 18 minutes, and that in 1980 one assault occurred about every 6 minutes. Thus, for the second group of subjects, the increase was simply on a par with what would be expected given the population increase alone, whereas for the first group the increase was less than that expected on the basis of population growth. The specific crime to which the statistics referred could be any of four types (assault, child abuse, murder, rape), with equal numbers of each type being included in each condition. The inclusion of several types of crimes was intended to insure greater generality of the results.

Of primary interest is the question of whether people find these statistics to be informative and whether the index is seen as a useful tool for inferring change. Several different questions were used to address these issues. First, participants were asked to evaluate the usefulness of these statistics for judging crime at a single point in time. They were asked, "In your estimate, how informative is this index of reporting a crime by how often one such crime occurs in a particular amount of time?" (9-point scale, with endpoints "Not at all useful for getting an idea of how often an event happens" and "Very useful for getting an idea of how often an event

happens"). The majority of subjects in both conditions found the index to be informative, with 53 of 68 subjects marking at or above the midpoint for estimates of usefulness (for these favorable subjects, $M = 7.03$ in the triple condition and 7.15 in the
double condition). A number of the subjects (8 of 68) indicated clear reservations
about the index, marking one of the two most extreme points at the "Not at all useful"
end of the scale. Subjects were next asked to evaluate the informativeness of this
index for comparing different years (9-point scale, with endpoints "Not at all useful"
and "Very useful"). The majority of subjects in both conditions found this index to
be useful, not only for evaluating a particular year but also for making comparisons
across years. In all, 43 of the 68 subjects were at or above the midpoint in their judgments of usefulness (for these favorable subjects, $M = 6.88$ triple condition and
$M = 6.72$ double condition). Sixteen subjects reported clear reservations about the
use of this indexing method for comparison purposes by selecting one of the two
extreme values at the "Not at all useful" end of the scale. For the majority of the subjects, then, time-referenced statistics appear to represent a useful kind of information for either single-point or comparison purposes.

The actual use of the index in judging change was then considered. The intent was
to see whether judgments would differ in the two conditions and also whether use
would show a sensitivity to population change (i.e., whether people would shift their
estimates downward to control for population increases or make judgments based on
the index information alone). Subjects were asked to judge the actual change in the
United States crime rate from 1900 to 1980 on a scale with nine choices ranging
from "The rate now is 5 times higher than it used to be" to "The rate is ⅕ of what
it used to be." The responses in the two conditions differed significantly, $t(66) =$
$3.19, p < .01$, and these responses mirrored the time-referenced statistics without
adjustment for population change. In the condition in which the time-referenced
statistics made crimes appear to have tripled, the mean response was 2.62, with 27
or 34 subjects selecting the choice, "The crime rate is 3 times higher." In the condition where the time-referenced statistic made crimes appear to have doubled, the
mean response was 1.88, with 26 of the 34 selecting the choice, "The rate is 2 times
higher." The responses of 16 participants did not mirror the index, and of these, 10
were given by people who had indicated earlier that they were highly dissatisfied
with the index.

A question about population size was also included. Although most people failed
to incorporate population information into their judgments, it was found that they
did estimate the population to have increased between 1900 and 1980, and in these
judgments the degree of population change tended to be overestimated. On a scale
with nine response choices ranging from "The current population is 5 times the 1900
population" to "The current population is ⅕ the 1900 population," all but five of the
subjects reported the current population of the United States to be higher than the
population in 1900. The mean estimate was that the population had increased 3.27
times in the triple condition and 3.29 times in the double condition. No subject said
that the population size had remained the same.

At the end of the study, several open-ended questions were included to see if people could be prompted to think about problems with the index. Participants were

first asked, "Do you see any problems with using this index for comparisons across years?" and then were asked more directly, "Do you see any problems with using this index for comparisons across different population sizes?" In response to the first question, 44 participants expressed some reservations about the index, yet of these reservations, only 18 dealt with the issue of population change. Most of the objections concerned the limited nature of the information about crime and surrounding circumstances (e.g., "it [the information] is too vague to really make comparisons —what types of crimes?"). In response to the second question, 48 of the 68 expressed reservations, and of these, 27 concerned the problem of changes in population not being represented in the index. Examples of these comments include:

> The information is misleading because the population has increased .... It doesn't take population change into account .... If the population changes, the index does not give a true indication of the murder rate .... You need more facts, for example, the population in both years so that the ratio of abuse to population could be figured out.

Yet many other subjects continued to find the index quite informative. In response to the question of whether there were any problems, a number of students remarked that there were none. For example:

> No. I believe it is a good way of seeing how much something increases or declines over the years.... No, it informs a person about how much the rate of a person being raped has gone up.... There is no problem in using this index in comparing different population sizes.

The foregoing study exemplifies the use of simplifying information that is made available to social perceivers on an everyday basis; it provides one example of the use of informal information in judging crime and its occurrence. We should not assume, however, that people will invariably use time-referenced information. Use may well depend on the extent to which the direction of the change conforms with previous views. The fact that time-referenced statistics commonly occur in reference to increases in social problems and not declines may be an indication of their tendency to be introduced in belief-confirming contexts. Bauer (1966) has noted:

> Many an indicator favored for revealing key conditions of the society derives this favor precisely from the fact that it confirms and reinforces existing conceptions rather than augments or alters them. The indicator serves as a short-hand certifier of beliefs, rather than as a shaper of them. In the cases where it lacks this resonance with everyday, qualitative, global, or spatial impressions, the indicator is likely to be rejected. (p. 126)

The study to be described next illustrates in another way the potential effects of simplified crime-related information on change judgments, in this case the effects of information that fails to make change-relevant demographic shifts salient to perceivers.

Many aspects of social change are affected by demographic shifts, that is, by changes not in the population as a whole but in the relative size of birth cohorts and in the proportion of the population falling into certain age groups. In countries with stable demographic profiles, the structure of age cohorts varies little from one decade to the next. In contrast, the demographic profile of the United States has undergone considerable flux over the recent decades (Robey, 1985). In recent years we have experienced what has been termed the "graying" of America; that is, the proportion of the population made up of older Americans has grown substantially. Similarly, two decades ago, there was a very large teenage population made up of the so-called baby boom generation. At present, a smaller proportion of the population is composed of teenagers, and the large cohort of baby boomers has moved into their midlife high-earning years and is, in turn, creating its own baby boomlet. These demographic fluctuations are not without an impact on the character of American life. As America "grays," more resources go into the lifestyles and needs of older persons. As baby boomers move into childbearing years, their uses of money and resources shift, with a resulting characteristic impact on American life.

It is important to note that in many cases social changes that are taken to be substantive arise in whole or in part from these same demographic trends. Thus, even though changes in something like the crime rate may be viewed as solely the result of, say, substantive changes in the law, they are frequently a consequence of growth or diminution in the portion of the population that commits a disproportionate share of crimes (O'Brien, 1985). This point about demographics and social change is of general importance because demographic shifts cut across many areas and their impact on how often certain events are occurring may go unrecognized, both in everyday reporting and in the intuitive explanations that are offered for shifts in certain kinds of behavior. If such shifts are ignored, the emphasis in explaining such changes may be placed entirely on substantive causes—people may decide that fewer crimes occur not because there are fewer teenagers (who commit a disproportionate share of crimes) but because there must have been some improvement in how effective we are at fighting crime. The absence of attention to demographic factors would be consistent both with the results of our earlier studies and with current theorizing about the kinds of causes that are given emphasis in intuitive theories. In discussing the limited use of base-rate information, Azjen (1977) has noted that people prefer meaningful "causal" information. The difficulty with demographic shifts is that they are unsatisfying as explanations for exactly the sorts of reasons outlined by Azjen for base-rate information. Like the other kinds of population details discussed previously, demographic accounts are essentially abstract and statistical in nature, and consequently may be neglected in ordinary accounts and interpretations of change (but see also Ginosar & Trope, 1980; Nisbett et al., 1983).*

As noted above, teenagers commit a disproportionate share of crimes (Hindelang, 1981). According to the Bureau of Justice Statistics, the decline in teen numbers in

---

*People's preference for attributing perceived changes to "meaningful" causes over attributing them to abstract demographic factors is sometimes the source of political controversy. For an instructive example of political controversy in connection with the preference for meaningful causes over demographic ones, see Wirtz's (1977) discussion of interpretations offered for the Scholastic Aptitude Test score decline. One suspects that politicians who are successful are those who are skilled at inducing people to attribute favorable social changes to the politician's own initiatives and unfavorable social changes to the workings of the political opposition.

recent years has had a significant impact on the crime rate. The recent drop in the crime rate is partially a result of a drop in the size of the population of teens and young adults. However, this decline in teen numbers is typically not emphasized in the information that social perceivers receive about the crime rate. Even more rarely is the link between the two actually spelled out in popular accounts. What makes this crime-rate case especially interesting is that meaningful putative causes (changes in what we do about crime) are highly salient—even if those meaningful causes are of uneven effectiveness. In recent years there has been much talk of "getting tough on crime," and in many parts of the country, laws have been toughened and sentences made more severe at the very same time that the teen population has been declining. A tendency to emphasize one sort of cause versus the other will likely have different policy implications.

In the following study these points about the importance of demographic shifts are illustrated by looking at people's understanding and use of demographic explanations in accounting for declines in crime. Specifically, we examined people's tendency to see the decrease in the number of teenagers as a contributing factor to the drop in crime, both where there is an absence of information linking the two and where the link between the two is made explicit. To examine responses to demographic shifts, people were provided with information about the crime drop and various other changes in American life. This information, much of it taken directly from an almanac (*World Almanac & Book of Facts*, 1985, p. 790), was part of a statistical portrait of the United States during the years 1980 to 1983. Included in the information were statistics about the drop in crime, about teen numbers going down, and about criminal laws being toughened. Participants read paragraphs on each of these various topics. Under the heading "U.S. Crime Rate Down," subjects learned that the number of serious crimes reported to the police in the United States fell 7% in 1983 and 3% in 1982 according to the FBI Uniform Crime Reports and that there were drops in all seven major categories of crime, in every region, and in communities of all sizes. Under the heading "U.S. Population," they learned that the population continued to increase in average age between 1980 and 1983, the median age rising by 0.9 years to 30.9; that the trend was expected to continue as members of the baby boom generation head toward middle age, and that while the under-5 age group increased, the next three age groups decreased—the 5-to 13-year-olds by 3.3%, the 14- to 17-year-olds by 9.9%, and the 18- to 24-year-olds by 5%. Under the heading "New Laws Instituted Around the Country," they learned that in the early 1980s America was in a "get tough" law period; that tougher laws were passed to increase sentence lengths, introduce mandatory sentences for certain crimes, and provide increased support for additional law-enforcement personnel. Subjects also received various other sorts of information taken from the almanac's statistical portrait, including information about changes in migration patterns, changes in family composition, and the like.

For half of the subjects, this was the full extent of the information they received. Others also received information not normally included in such sources, information that made the connection between teen demographics and crime. These subjects were told, "Generally the years 14 to 24 are high crime tendency years. Teenagers commit more than their share of crimes." This demographic cue was included immediately after the information about the decline in teen numbers. Thus, some subjects received help in drawing the connection between teens and crime whereas others did not. After reading the statistical portrait, participants were asked to provide a general description of the period and then to state in their own words what factor or factors were responsible for the drop in crime during the period. Using 9-point scales with endpoints "Probably not at all responsible" and "Probably very responsible," they then responded to a series of questions about how responsible each of four factors was in causing the drop in crime. The second of the four question concerned the decline in population in the 14 to 24 age group and the third of the four questions concerned "the new stricter laws and tougher sentencing." Two other questions were included as fillers so that none of the major factors included in the description would be neglected (regardless of whether changes in the factor had coincided with the direction of the change in crime).

In response to the scaled questions, people who received the demographic-link cue were more likely to conclude that teen demographics were responsible ($M = 7.38$) than were those subjects who did not receive the cue ($M = 5.79$), $t(46) = 2.98, p < .01$. Yet, at the same time, these cued subjects were not significantly less likely than the noncued subjects to rely on the law explanation ($M = 7.33$ Noncued and 6.71 Cued), $t(46) = 1.30$, n.s. The relative weighting given to law and population explanations by subjects in the two conditions was such that the noncued subjects weighted the law explanation significantly more heavily than the population explanation, whereas the two were equally weighted by the cued subjects, yielding a significant interaction, repeated measures $F(1,46) = 8.65, p < .01$. Neither of the factors tapped by the filler questions received much weighting by subjects.

Without the cue, subjects relied heavily on the law interpretation, and with the cue subjects used demographic explanations but without reducing their reliance on the law explanations to any appreciable extent. Although the responses on the scaled questions indicate that the cue was effective, an examination of how people responded when asked to state in their own words what was responsible for the drop in crime provides a somewhat more limited picture of its impact. Subjects' written responses were coded both for the factor mentioned first and for the factors mentioned among their first two explanations. Looking at first nominations, most cued and noncued subjects failed to mention anything related to the drop in teen population. Only 2 of 24 subjects in the noncue condition invoked the teen decline as their first explanation, and only 6 of 24 in the cue condition brought it up as their first explanation $\chi^2(1, N = 48) = 2.4$, n.s. Looking at joint first and second nominations, 7 in the noncue condition included the teen drop in their first two explanations, and that number increased to 14 of the 24 in the cued condition, a difference that was significant, $\chi^2(1, N = 48) = 4.2, p < .05$. An examination of nominations for the law made it clear that both groups tended to see the drop in crime as a consequence of changes in the law. In the noncue condition 16 of the 24 relied on changes in the law as their first explanation and 20 of 24 in this condition mentioned it among either their first or second explanations. Of the 24 subjects in the cue condition, 11 selected the changes in the law as their first explanation and 17 included changes in the law in their first two explanations. The tendency to see changes in the law as the cause of the drop did not differ significantly between conditions for either first or joint nominations.

At the close of the study, participants were also asked an open-ended question regarding what they felt should be done about the problem of crime. Of interest was whether subjects would mention interventions or policies targeted at teenagers. Analysis of the answers showed that relatively few subjects incorporated any reference to the demographic factor in their suggestions for addressing the problem of crime. Only eight participants in the noncue condition and seven in the cue condition mentioned taking some action related to teenagers. An example of the kind of suggestion made by those subjects who did target teenagers was: "Teach teenagers that they should not resort to crime." Most subjects instead elaborated on a "get tough" theme, sometimes doing so in emphatic language:

> Build more prisons . . . . I feel that the main problem with crime and criminals is that the laws are still too lenient . . . . The death penalty should be used more . . . . I firmly believe in capital punishment as a deterrent. I believe rapists and child abusers should go through exactly what their victims did . . . . Capital punishment should be reinstated throughout the U.S., also hard labor, and longer sentences . . . . They should make prison a sort of living hell for the inmates.

All in all, the results of this study support the thesis that people prefer explanations of social phenomena, including social change, that are couched in terms of causes with familiar meaning rather than ones couched in terms of factors that are abstract, statistical, or demographic. Further studies that model the way in which the structure of ordinary environmental information promotes this sort of preference may help to determine the extent to which the preference reflects a cognitive bias at the individual level or a bias in the cultural transmission of information. In the meanwhile, it is clear that the typical failure of everyday information sources to cite relevant demographic data can have important implications not only for how social change is intuitively judged but also for how society deals with that change.

Confidence in Perceiving Change: The Effect of Vague Language

Having explored social change judgments in a number of different areas in this chapter, we have seen that perceivers frequently construe things as having changed and use various kinds of information in doing so. In this section, ambiguity in language is considered as a factor contributing to the confidence with which these judgments are made.

An underlying theme throughout this chapter has been that people are often ambiguous as to the specifics of change at the very same time that they are confident that change has occurred. When people converse about change they often do so in highly vague terms. Rather than speaking of concrete behaviors, they comment on "the erosion of moral fiber" or they assert that "America is standing tall again." Instead of referring to a specific amount of change, they speak broadly of an "epidemic" of teenage pregnancies or runaway children. Without giving any indication as to the specific comparison period in the past, people confidently assert that "it used to be that life was simpler" or that "you can't count on things any more." The specifics of what has changed, how much it has changed, and the period over which it has changed are often left open-ended in the confident assertions of change that are so much a part of American life.

This vagueness may be a phenomenon of more than incidental interest. Indeed, it may be a key to why informal change judgments occur with such regularity and great confidence. Vagueness and the tendency to frame issues of social change in the most general terms may well induce people to feel confident in making assertions of change in the absence of specific information. The typically vague language may encourage people's inattention to their own lack of information of a numeric sort, and the generalized nature of their self-queries may even make specific information appear irrelevant or unnecessary. The possibility that vagueness in language helps to maintain confidence in change impressions in the absence of relevant specific knowledge, and that it does so in a number of different areas, is considered in the final study to be described.

In the study, participants (68 general psychology students) were asked a set of 10 questions concerning their confidence in their knowledge about change in several areas in which change assertions are commonly made. For some subjects the questions were phrased at a very general level (sometimes in clichés), whereas others received questions on the same topics that were stated at a more specific level. The generality/specificity of questions was varied in several different ways across the questions. Sometimes the clichéd quality of the language used to refer to the change was varied. For example, in one case the subjects in the general condition were asked about their confidence in their knowledge of an epidemic of "children having children," whereas those in the specific condition were asked about their confidence in their knowledge of a change in the teenage birthrate (number of teenagers having children). In other cases, the questions were made less vague by making the comparison period more explicit. Thus, in the general condition, participants were asked about their confidence in their knowledge of the erosion in moral fiber in recent years, whereas in the specific condition they were asked about their confidence in their knowledge about the erosion in moral fiber over the last 20 years. In still other cases, the query was made more explicit by taking a question about confidence in whether they knew how much things had changed (general condition) and asking about confidence in whether they knew what degree of change in terms of percentage had taken place (specific condition). In all, questions on 10 different topics were included. In the language of the general condition, these topics (in the order given) were: an epidemic of children having children, a loss in childhood innocence, an epidemic of child sexual abuse, crime being out of control, the family unit being in trouble, people not helping each other any more, moral fiber eroding, schools not being as effective, an epidemic of drug abuse, and life being simpler in the past. Each participant received either all specific questions or all general questions, and each question was answered on a 9-point scale, with endpoints "Not at all confident" and "Very confident."

The results confirmed the expectations. Across the questions as a whole, participants were significantly more willing to express confidence in their own knowledge when the queries were vague and clichéd than when the queries on the same topics were made more explicit, $t(66) = 4.08, p < .001$. As long as the assertions remained general (even if that generality entailed a strong claim such as that there had been an epidemic), people felt confident about what they knew about the changes ($M = 5.91$). It was when the assertions about those same topics became more concrete that confidence declined ($M = 4.64$). This decline in confidence held not only for the questions as a whole, but also for the individual questions. With the exception of the question on the topic of drug abuse, all others were significantly different ($p < .05$) in the two conditions. In sum, people were more ready to assert that they knew that there had been a change when they were asked about that change in general language, even if the general language referred to a very large change.

There are various reasons why these results might have been obtained. Perhaps the general questions are simply more familiar questions. Being phrased in a familiar way, they could perhaps be answered with less hesitation than could the more explicit questions. Possibly the time frames or other characteristics included in the specific questions simply failed to capture the kinds of implicit questions people ask themselves. More likely, though, what we see here is a demonstration of the effects of the clichéd quality of many change assertions and of the limited nature of the knowledge they represent. The results, though perhaps not surprising, are telling as to why people may so readily make assertions about change. People are confident as long as they are not required to look closely at what they do and do not know. Whatever the interpretation of these results, the fact that people are more comfortable with their knowledge in response to general questions would suggest that when people encounter change queries in this form, they may feel little need to seek out explicit numbers or information. This conclusion would square with what was found in earlier studies and would also help explain why in those studies people were willing to rely on nonnumeric information sources in making their inferences of change.

Concluding Comments

Taken together, the studies in this chapter suggest a number of reasons why intuitive judgments are made so confidently and why they occur so readily in the absence of appropriate statistical information. Intuitive perceivers can look to a host of other sorts of information that can be used to arrive at an impression of change, perhaps especially so when perceivers are asked (or ask themselves) open-ended, nonspecific questions about change. Furthermore, these studies suggest that the kinds of events that are salient for the present may not always be salient in our information for the past, with the result that change judgments at times arise more readily than we might expect. These asymmetries of information no doubt contribute also to the fact that change conclusions of a similar sort arise repeatedly across time as the recurrent differences in past and present information present themselves over and over again.

Central to much of this chapter has been a focus on the nostalgic fallacy, that is, on the apparent asymmetry in impressions of change whereby social change judgments concern declines more often than improvements. Several factors have been suggested that could contribute to this tendency: the impact of highly visible negative cases in the present, the reliance on norms as a baseline for the past, and the blurring of the distinction between the ideal and the average for the past. Important as these factors may be, they by no means exhaust the factors that could be contributing to the nostalgic fallacy. Future work should help not only to expand our understanding of these factors but also to determine other factors that may serve to support and maintain the fallacy. The thrust of this work might best be devoted to a deeper analysis of the accepted views of the past and their impact. The past may look more coherent and simpler—and hence better—than the present because for the past we have already constructed a story line with a beginning, middle, and end to explain what happened and why. As Florovsky (1969) has noted: "In retrospect, we seem to perceive the logic of events which unfold themselves in a regular or linear fashion according to a recognizable pattern with an alleged inner necessity so that we get the impression that it could not have happened otherwise" (p. 369). Thus, we know the outcome of the Great Depression and that it did not go on forever, so it has come to be treated as something like a national exercise in character building. Knowing how World War II ended, we can view it as the "Good War," as a time not when the outcome was in doubt, but rather when the country was brought together around a common cause with a foregone conclusion. The past looks innocent because we can look back at people's hopes for it and see the naivete of those hopes in light of what came after. The demonstrations and riots of the 1960s may have led some people at that time to fear that the country would be torn apart or led others to hope that a revolution would take place; now those times, the riots, and the rhetoric appear to many as merely quaint, as topics to be treated with the sense of irony that retrospection affords. A kind of hindsight bias on a grand scale, what Fischhoff (1975) refers to as "creeping determinism," may figure in the recurrent change judgments we see.

Somehow the richness of past times is lost, as in the reality of the fears and uncertainties that existed. In his novel, *The Incredible Lightness of Being* (1984), the Czech writer Milan Kundera provides in stark terms an image of this inability to recreate a true sense of the past. Kundera's protagonist talks of the puzzling impact of seeing photographs of Hitler now, many years after the war: "Recently I experienced the most incredible sensation. As I was leafing through a book on Hitler, I was touched by many of the portraits of Hitler. I grew up during the war; some of my family perished in Hitler's concentration camps." But instead of bringing back a sense of the evil of the times, the pictures brought back longing for a lost time in his life, a period he could never live again. Elements of the nostalgic fallacy may be bound up with a complicated nostalgia for one's own lost past.

Chapter 9

Past and Future Directions for the Study of Change Judgments

We are now ready in this chapter to assess the ground that has been gained thus far in understanding intuitive change judgments and to survey the ground that lies ahead. The studies presented in the foregoing chapters by no means provide a comprehensive assessment of even the limited set of theses proposed here, but they do provide a systematic, if incomplete, guide to an important and otherwise unexplored topic. In the first part of the present chapter, our current understanding of change judgments will be summarized and laid out in systematic fashion. The second part of the chapter, which is devoted to outlining directions for future research, will describe a sampling of important problems that remain for investigation.

The Emerging Picture of Intuitive Change Judgments

Our investigation of change judgments began with the articulation of four general themes. These concerned information from the environment, information in the individual, the types of change judgments that occur, and the meaning of change for the intuitive perceiver. Consideration of these themes gave rise to sets of questions that could then be investigated empirically. The resulting collection of studies has captured different facets of what goes on when change is intuitively judged. However, up to now, no attempt has been made to fit the findings of these studies into a systematic theoretical formulation concerning change judgments. In this section such a formulation will be presented. It is intended to make explicit the shared implications of the studies, to lay out the general factors that underlie change judgments, and to account for the differences observed among the various change judgments studied. The following theoretical formulation, which focuses on the nature and use of comparison data in everyday judgments of change, consists of five propositions derived from the research presented in the foregoing chapters.

Change Judgments and Perceived Differences

Change judgments arise for *perceived* differences between the past and present. The perceived differences, in turn, arise from differences between the information the perceiver has about the present and the information the perceiver has about the past. The informational differences contributing to the perception of change can arise in a large variety of ways, not all of which reflect actual differences between the past and the present, and change judgments cannot be understood without an understanding of the sources of these informational differences.

Usable Information

In making change judgments on an everyday basis people will use the information they have at hand. This usable information can be in the form of personal knowledge, largely held in memory but also gained through ongoing experience, or it can be information presented by the environment in a variety of forms where it is already highly structured in certain respects. Perceivers tend to be opportunistic in their use of information, drawing on readily available information regardless of source, rather than seeking out less accessible (but perhaps better quality) information from remote sources.

Everyday Information as Problematic

Because the information used in making intuitive change judgments is largely that which is most readily available, it typically falls far short of the usual normative standards for comparison information (i.e., for comparison information used by professional assessors of change). As a consequence, intuitive change impressions can be rendered problematic by the nature of what is available in the way of informal information. As compared against normative standards, everyday information is subject to a number of potential problems that directly affect the extent to which what is informally known is appropriate for comparison. These problems are as follows:

Incommensurability. Information that is available for judging change will sometimes be incommensurable, that is, the information from the present and the information from the past are incapable of being compared in a way that meets normative standards. This situation arises in cases where information has not been obtained in the same way over time or has not been generated under the same conditions. Several different forms of incommensurability were examined in the studies described above. For example, in a study in which child abuse statistics were presented, the problem of incommensurability arose when comparison information was drawn from differentially inclusive sources—police reports at one point in time and physician reports at another. In a study of attributions for an elderly person's behavior, the potential problems with incommensurability were raised because observations were made in different situations at the two points in time. Incommensurability was also involved in cases where frequency information was compared without controlling for population size. Such problems of incommensurability can be especially acute when perceivers are unaware of them, as is often the case (see discussion of the opaqueness of problems below). The problem of incommensurability is usually associated with one or more of the following problematic features of the available comparison information.

Incompleteness. The information at hand will sometimes be incomplete. Facts regarding certain kinds of events may be wholly unavailable or certain dimensions of events may be neglected in the summaries that are available. When the information is highly incomplete, the perceiver may be without the kind of information that would normatively constitute a baseline for the past. Although incompleteness does not in itself necessarily entail incommensurability, it will produce incommensurability whenever the incompleteness is different, in degree or kind, for the two time periods being compared. Incompleteness was illustrated here by cases where components of baseline information were missing—as in the absence of population information in the day-care abuse studies and in one of the teen pregnancies studies—and by cases where individual baseline information was wholly missing—as in the assault victim study.

Asymmetry. Often the amount of information available for the two time periods will be substantially different, producing an informational asymmetry. What is known for one period—typically the present—will be more detailed and extensive than what is know for another. The asymmetry problem thus involves an incommensurability based on relative fullness of information. These informational differences can arise from simple differences in completeness of the records of events or from differences in the form in which events are represented. Asymmetry was illustrated in the studies in which weather information for the present was made up of many items, but the corresponding information for the past was in the form of a single summary statistic.

Inappropriateness. Much of what is available in the way of information will, by normative standards, be inappropriate for use in judging how often events occurred in the present and the past. Instead of concerning actual events or frequencies thereof, what is known may be in the form of symbolic expectations based on social norms and the like. Despite its inappropriateness, such information is then brought to bear in judging the extent to which things have changed. Reliance on symbolic or normative information was exemplified in the studies on declines in the family and declines in helpfulness.

Ambiguity. The information that is available will sometimes be sufficiently ambiguous and open-ended that it can support either a stability or change interpretation. In the "Lany study" we saw one example of the way the same information—in this case, a pattern of life events—can be used to support opposite views of whether a person has remained the same or changed. Only active interpretation on the part of the perceiver, not the information itself, can dictate whether being a Princeton professor and a high school cheerleader are more alike or different, that is, whether they constitute evidence of stability or change. Ambiguity of information, although not necessarily absent in cases where the change-relevant information is quantitative in form, is generally a serious problem only in cases involving qualitative information whose meaning is indeterminant without a major interpretative contribution on the part of the perceiver.

Each of these factors could be manifested in a multitude of ways beyond those illustrated in the particular studies reported in this monograph. The foregoing problems involving the comparability of data can occur either separately or in combination; but given that the problems are interrelated, they will frequently occur together. Thus, information that is highly incomplete will likely (though not necessarily) be asymmetric. Similarly, situations characterized by incompleteness of the available information are also likely to be the situations in which perceivers will rely on inappropriate, sometimes even nonfactual, sources of comparisons. The particular problem or combination of problems results in patterns of data that clearly have important implications for the kind of change impressions that will be fostered.

The above problems in the data can arise for reasons that are either internal to the perceiver or external to the perceiver. That is to say, the problems can occur either because of the perceiver's own processing and experiences or because of the way the information comes to the judger from the social environment. In the former case, the perceiver might incompletely remember aspects of the past that are relevant to the comparison, or because of differences in the perceiver's roles in the present and the past, the perceiver may have incommensurable information for the two comparison periods. Similarly, the information that comes to the perceiver from the social environment can be incomplete, incommensurable, asymmetric, and in other ways problematic. In general, there will be strong parallels between the two cases: for example, the loss of information about the past from individual memory is paralleled by the loss of past information from the social vehicles of information transmission, storage, and retrieval in the environment; likewise, the incommensurability of comparison data arising from differences in an individual's roles at different times is paralleled by incommensurabilities in data from the environment that arise from differences in cultural context and social awareness at different times (e.g., judging changes in the danger of toxic wastes will be complicated by the fact that adequate records of their effects will be kept only after the problem of toxic wastes is socially constructed as a problem to be monitored). Although the problematic data for the past and the present can convey the appearance of change for reasons either internal or external to the perceiver, the present studies to a large extent have focused on factors that are external to the perceiver. That focus was deliberate, inasmuch as problems in change-related information are often not byproducts of processing by the individual perceiver but rather an outgrowth of shared ways that information for the past is socially constructed and stored.

Problems with everyday information have the potential to shape intuitive change judgments in large measure because of two additional factors:

The problem of opaqueness. The foregoing problems with the data are such that they will typically be opaque to the intuitive judger. The incommensurability of comparison data does not come written on its face. Problems in the data are made inconspicuous by the social vehicles of information transmission in the environment, and perceivers' intuitive reasoning habits typically include few resources for discerning and correcting the problems. At the point at which the judgment is made—which is often well beyond the baseline period—it will generally not be apparent to the perceiver that the quality of the comparison data, especially from the past, has been compromised.

The problem of underdetermination of inference by data. In the world of the social perceiver, information that is highly inconclusive is nonetheless often sufficient to support a strong impression of change; perceivers do not (and in fact cannot) wait until fully adequate kinds and amounts of relevant information are in hand before making judgments. As a result, conclusions about change tend to overreach the data that evoke them. An important consequence of the underdetermination of conclusions by data is that the drawing of plausible alternative conclusions from the same set of (necessarily inconclusive) data is always possible, although perceivers may not be aware of it. Thus, although information can sustain a particular view of change, typically that view is by no means the only one that plausibly can be supported by the events.

What is meant by this underdetermination problem can be illustrated by considering the consequences of the separateness of information in the environment. The information relevant to making a change judgment typically does not come as a package or as a unit that must be used as a whole or not at all (e.g., frequency facts can be used without population information; central tendency information can be used without information about variability). Instead, pieces of information that are sufficient in and of themselves to prompt some kind of change judgments can come independently of and separate from other relevant or normatively important information. Separately presented simple information can sustain its own change inferences, with the resultant change impressions likely to be just as confidently held as are those evoked by more complex information. An important consequence of this property of separateness is that contradictory change views can arise regarding the same set of events depending on how relevant information is presented (e.g., whether frequency alone is made salient or whether both frequency and population are made salient). Because these contradictions arise from separate information cases, however, they will have little impact on perceivers' confidence in their change judgments made with the information that is at their disposal.

Contexts for Seeing Change

Because perceivers tend to be rather unselective and opportunistic in using the at-hand information in judging change and because such information is generally plentiful, one might expect change judgments to occur in the full array of situations in which data to support them exist. However, perceived differences in information about the past and present tend to be picked up and made the basis of change judgments only under certain conditions. Even though change judgments can be understood largely in terms of informational differences, the judgments still may not occur unless an interest in change is occasioned by appropriate circumstances. Such an interest—either of a temporary or chronic sort—will occur under the following conditions:

Occurrence of events believed to cause change. A concern with change can be activated by the occurrence of specific events that are viewed intuitively as being likely to produce change. Change-relevant causal events can be of many sorts and of differential perceived potency, both in terms of their likelihood of producing change and in terms of the magnitude of change that is viewed as likely to result from them. As we have seen, what constitutes a change-relevant cause can be identified by appropriate questioning of intuitive judgers. When such an event has occurred, the stage is set for using whatever information is available in making judgments.

Belief in intuitive and socially constructed theories of change. Judgers also hold intuitive theories of developmental change, life-span change, and of the kind and amount of change expected with the passage of time. These theories—whether of individual origin or socially constructed—provide a basis for expecting change of a particular sort and provide a context in which incomplete, ambiguous, or inappropriate or otherwise problematic information is especially apt to be interpreted as evidence of change.

Preexisting background expectations. Relevant background expectations can set the occasion for the evaluation of specific sets of comparison data as indicating change. Perceivers might have an underlying belief that social change in general is likely, or the expectation might be for a particular kind of social change. In the context of these broad expectations, the perceivers will be prone to accept incommensurable or otherwise problematic information as meaningful indicator of change.

The foregoing conditions for an interest in change can occur either alone or together, but in cases where these interest factors are absent, the perception of change will occur both with less readiness and with less frequency. By themselves, differences in the data for the past and present will only rarely constitute a sufficient cause for seeing change.

Minimal-Effort Processing: Interest Factors as Potentiators of Superficial Data Comparisons

When perceivers become interested in change, for any of the above reasons, the processing required to compare past and present data in order to arrive at a change impression will often be carried out in a superficial way that involves a minimum of cognitive effort. That is to say, perceivers may well depend on a kind of cursory and immediate yes/no reaction about whether the appearance of differences has been detected and hence whether a conclusion of change is warranted. The immediate feeling that change has occurred can be an accurate reflection of change that has actually occurred or it can be a direct outgrowth of any and all of the problems in the information array. As a consequence of opaqueness and underdetermination, the processing that leads to a change judgment will *not* typically involve a search for alternative explanations to see if the change might be more apparent than real. Rather, the kind of processing that occurs will be a minimal sort, with the perceiver unsystematically inspecting the available information for signs of sameness of difference, and the resulting judgments often having a superficial quality.

The theoretical formulation presented above provides a first-approximation account of how and when change judgments are made by intuitive perceivers. The account helps us to understand change judgments of the sort studied in this book, to know the conditions under which they are to be expected, to know the type of judgment that is likely to occur, and to explain the commonalities across change judgments as well as the differences among them. As a way of displaying the implications of the account for furthering our understanding of change judgments, a series of questions is presented below, along with the answers suggested by the foregoing formulation.

1. *When can change judgments be expected to be pervasive and why?* Intuitive change judgments can be expected to be pervasive when there is a large number of factors in the available informational array that contribute to the perception of apparent differences between past and present and when the problematic quality of the apparent differences remains opaque to the perceiver. The number of change judgments occurring will generally increase rather than decrease with an increase in incommensurability-generating problems so long as the problems are opaque.

2. *Why are change judgments made with such alacrity?* Where there is the conjunction of the opaqueness problems, interest-generating conditions, and a plethora of perceived differences, a marked readiness to make change judgments will be observed. The problems that exist will be difficult to see, but at the same time those problems will form the basis of differences that suggest the occurrence of change.

3. *Why are change judgments frequently made even when relevant information is lacking?* Even without a full complement of information, change judgments will be made when there are background expectations that predispose the perceiver to make judgments about change and when fall-back information, such as nonfactual norms, can be invoked to serve the role of baseline data. Because judgments are generally underdetermined by their supporting evidence, there is room for considerable flexibility in drawing on a variety of nonnormative support for judgments.

4. *Why is a multiplicity of change judgments so commonly seen?* A variety of change judgments—some of which may contradict others—will be seen because the appearance of differences fostered by the data will vary as a function of the nature of the data constellation that is available to each judger of change. This fact, along with the opportunities for differential interpretation of information due to the underdetermination problem, makes it natural that different conclusions about change will be drawn by different perceivers.

5. *When might perceivers be expected to be skilled at judging change?* Perceivers' judgments will be most accurate when the informational array poses fewest problems and when the perceiver is made aware of and controls for incommensurabilities. In cases where the information array poses problems, the perceivers' willingness to use the information will be a function of opaqueness. As forces operate to decrease the opaqueness of the problems, we should find increased reluctance to made change judgments. Perceivers should most acutely experience the incommensurability in the data and become more circumspect in judging change in exactly those situations where the perceivers' expectations for change are lowest. In the absence of any marked interest in change, search for and openness to potential problems of incommensurability should be more common.

As can be seen from the above discussion, the theoretical formulation offered here gives rise to a set of general expectations about the nature and content of change judgments as well as the contexts in which they are expected to occur. In its present form, the formulation does not permit detailed predictions of the judgments that will be made in any particular case. However, the account provided here does provide useful guidance for how individual cases can be approached. In specific cases, one can analyze the information available, its possible problems, and the relative opaqueness of those problems for the perceiver. Those factors, in combination with the interest factors, will give a rough indication of the change impression that is likely to be formed.

Directions for Future Research

Filling in the gaps in this model and further testing its overall usefulness will be valuable directions for future research to take. The model can be used to identify interesting avenues of study, such as the examination of other types of incommensurability and of interactions among various factors. Future studies could be devoted to the detailed investigation of the forms of incompleteness, the ambiguities of information, and the like, as well as the effects they have on judgments of change. But future work need not focus on just the factors that have been emphasized here. Valuable as the present approach may be, it is important in an emerging area that we not limit ourselves to a single model or use any one model as the sole source of ideas. Future research would doubtless benefit from the adoption of a broadened focus — both in terms of methodology and in terms of content. The remainder of the chapter is intended to suggest just what such a broadened focus might include.

Expanding the Methodologies Used to Study Change Judgments

Some who will become interested in change judgments will ultimately find other methodological approaches to the study of change judgments more appealing than the approach taken here. The laboratory approach and related level of analysis adopted here focus our attention on certain questions while directing our attention away from other, equally important questions. The emphasis here has been on a kind of micro-analysis that involves examining the extent to which particular kinds of information operate to determine change judgments in a patterned way. The approach begins with an analysis of the information available to perceivers in real-world situations in order to provide hypotheses about the informational factors that may be operating in the formation of change judgments. Through this preliminary analysis, those factors that are believed to be critical are abstracted and their impact is then tested in the laboratory. Certainly the laboratory approach facilitates the test-ing of an analysis that focuses on combining information in different ways and con-sidering the consequences. The potential disadvantage of this approach is that it encourages the dividing up of problems into subcomponents that may be artificial, with the result that some of the elusive flavor of the original problem may be lost. In particular, approaches of this sort are always in danger of failing to capture the skill that perceivers may exhibit in handling information in highly familiar, cue-rich, or cue-redundant contexts. Exactly what kinds of richness of information are charac-teristic remains uncertain, however. It might be argued that too little information was presented to subjects in the present studies to reflect the natural situation; or it might be argued that just the reverse is true, that sometimes too much information (e.g., variability information) was provided to be realistically comparable to the usual information situation perceivers face. The difficulty, of course, is that only a thorough understanding of which information in real-world situations is actually used by perceivers can tell us how realistic our laboratory analogues are; but we are unlikely to gain such an understanding without the aid of experimental studies to begin with.

Concerns with mundane realism are important, and the view that a problem may be more than the sum of its parts is equally important—especially to the extent that such views encourage pluralism in approaches to the study of change judgments. Consider, for example, the interesting questions that could be addressed by conduct-ing longitudinal studies of the change judgment process. How does the processing of change-related information vary as a function of developmental stage through the life span? How does information acquired at one age come to serve as a baseline for change judgments made at a later age? Do comparison data derived from experi-ences at different age levels always involve serious incommensurabilities, and where such incommensurabilities occur, are they taken into account by perceivers? Con-sider, also, the approaches that might be useful for studying how perceivers make change judgments about those for whom they have extensive information and for whom the various informational features are confounded and not easily separated. The voluminous change-related information that perceivers have about significant others might be analyzed through extended case studies or other investigative tools that would place such ongoing processes of social perception in an integrative con-text (e.g., family-systems analysis). Or consider how a language analysis of real-world change judgments as they occur in context might be useful. Do differences in the language used by perceivers to report their change perceptions systematically reflect differences in the underlying judgments, their informational origins, or the degree of confidence with which they are held? In sum, a range of methodologies can be deployed in the effort to understand the rich domain of change judgments.

Expanding by Examining More Complex Uses of Information

Even without going beyond the thematic orientations employed here, there remain many aspects of information use yet to be explored. These involve, among other things, questions about the judgments made when people have available not just one kind of information but many different kinds of information, and about how perceivers use information that is redundant or information that is contradictory. Understanding how perceivers approach the task of making cascaded or multistage inferences in judging change would be important for knowing how information is integrated across time and sources in real-world cases. Accounting for other types of change judgments will be of interest, including judgments having to do with specific rates of increase or decline, with exponential growth, and with cyclical change.

In terms of information use, factors that have been considered separately could be looked at together. For example, person change judgments and social change judgments could be looked at jointly. Do perceivers' views that there has been rapid social change affect their willingness to see change in individual persons? For example, do beliefs in the decline of helpfulness extend to views of individual helpfulness over the same time period? Or, conversely, do beliefs about individual change affect willingness to draw inferences of social change? Do individuals appear less stable or more stable during times of rapid social change? In a recent book on social change, Marris (1974) describes how Charles Dickens used stability in his characters to make the social change even more apparent:

> This sense of the power of survival of intransigent identities pervades the comedy of Charles Dickens, whose novels — perhaps more than any others in the English language — express a brooding awareness of profound social change. "It is a world of change," exclaims the absurd Mrs. Chick in *Dombey and Son*. "Anyone would surprise me very much ... and would greatly alter my opinion of their understanding, if they attempt to contradict or evade what is so perfectly evident. Change! Even the silkworm, who I am sure might be supposed not to trouble itself about such subjects, changes into all sorts of unexpected things continually." But, characteristically, the lady herself does not change. Like Dickens's comic figures, she remains indestructibly herself .... The structure of *Dombey and Son* represents an allegory of social change where, against the background of a London whose familiar landmarks are being torn apart in confusion and squalor, only those who cling intransigently to their prejudices survive. (Marris, 1974, p. 13)

Intriguing questions are suggested here. When dealing with person change and social change together, do perceivers sometimes locate the change in one rather than the other, or do they see change as permeating both? Do they see social change as reflected in individuals they know, or perhaps see less social change at those times that they are focused on change in persons?

Notwithstanding the importance of continued explication of information use, change impressions represent more than the perceiver's dispassionate reasoning from the available information. In all likelihood, change judgments are also influenced by a host of other factors not explored here — for example, the motivation underlying the interest in change, the broader social context in which the judgments are made, and the characteristics of the individual judger. Although these factors have not been crucial to the major themes laid out here, their investigation may eventually provide important additional evidence as to why change judgments take on their distinctive features. These factors are briefly discussed in the following sections.

Motivation as a Determinant of Change Impressions

As was noted in Chapter 1, it has been commonplace to view change judgments, particularly those concerning social change, as having motivational underpinnings. The explanations brought to bear on this topic have frequently been motivational: "Intellectual fashions and individual preferences play a large part in the choice between myths of progress and myths of declines . . . . Myths of progress are commonly associated with acceptance of the status quo, and myths of decadence are associated with social activism of all kinds—revolutionary, reactionary, and reforming" (Caplow et al., 1983, p. 323). Such explanations that tie change judgments to a motivational base appear straightforward, but the issues are elusive. Social psychologists have long struggled with the issue of motivation and questions of the relative contributions of motivation and cognition (Clark & Fiske, 1982; Sorrentino & Higgins, 1985), but as yet no full resolution has been reached as to how to characterize the separate and joint influences of cognition and motivation. As has been argued throughout this monograph, much of what appears to represent the force of motivational factors may well be a function of information conditions. Without controverting this basic point, it can still be said that motivation almost certainly plays some role in the making of change judgments. The empirical exploration of motivational issues in some more direct way than has been done here is likely to add to what has been learned.

At the simplest level, one might begin by varying motivation in order to see how such variation affects the selection of information and shapes the interpretation given to ambiguous events. Although this has been done in a limited way here by varying expectations, when done on a broader scale it may provide important information on motivation. More generally, in pursuing the question of how motivation might figure in change judgments, it may be useful to make contact with literatures that have considered the place of motivation in cognition. A case in point is the work on need for control. Many social psychologists have regarded the need for control as a basic motivational factor shaping the search for information (Harvey & Weary, 1981; Wegner & Vallacher, 1977; Weiner, 1986), and in accounting for people's attributions and the like, attempts have been made to analyze them in terms of need for control. Such analyses have been useful in illuminating certain characteristics of information use, such as when people are motivated to make attributions. An attempt to construct a motivational account of change judgments might pursue the question of how change judgments are fostered by the need for control. Consider the case of change judgments about deterioration. Could seeing things as having deteriorated—in other words, as having been better in the past and being problematic only now—serve to satisfy a need for control? Rather than construing problems as insurmountable—because they have to one degree or another always been around—one sees them as surmountable by seeing them as new. Rather than new solutions, what is needed is a return to what worked in the past. Although examples such as this can only suggest the potentially important questions to be addressed within a motivational framework, they do indicate the value of undertaking a systematic program of research that takes into account factors that typically fall within a motivational account by examining the effects of emotions, predispositions, motivational biases, and so on.

Change Judgments in Broader Social Contexts: The Case of Persuasion

Examining change inferences as they occur within particular social contexts is another important direction for future research. As we see below in the illustrative case of persuasion contexts—where questions arise as to how change impressions are created and managed—this focus on the context is likely to be useful both for getting at the importance attached to particular views of change and for suggesting how change judgments are linked to particular courses of action.

Persuasion represents one of the intriguing contexts where change is talked about and change judgments are made. Change-related comments often appear as a part of efforts at persuasions, especially when those attempts are political in nature. Facts might be given to an audience in such a way as to show a decline in the country's competitiveness or an increase in the level of poverty. Often change is not only emphasized but also used to mobilize political action, as when we are told that steps must be taken to stop the decline in our international competitiveness, or that something must be done to stem the rise in rates of poverty. We are urged to vote for political candidates in part on grounds of their alleged ability to end changes of one sort or to bring about changes of another sort.

The rhetorical use of change impressions has not been treated in the foregoing chapters; we have yet to consider how the persuasive context may affect the use of change information, how it might influence the willingness of perceivers to subscribe to a particular view of change, or how the persuasion context may account for the origin of particular themes of perceived change. And, although existing work on persuasion has been wide-ranging in its investigation of the content and impact of persuasive appeals (Cialdini, Petty, & Cacioppo, 1981; McGuire, 1985; Roberts & Maccoby, 1985), little of that work has directly concerned the question of why change is so often the topic of politically persuasive communications or how people interpret change-related information when it does arise as a part of such a rhetorical strategy.

Linking the study of change impressions with particular contexts such as the rhetorical context is likely to be useful both as a way to draw on what has been learned here and as a way to identify aspects of the change-judgment process that have been neglected thus far. Were one to begin investigating the change impressions that arise in rhetorical contexts, for example, several points made earlier about the data base might once again prove instructive. Throughout the analysis presented in the foregoing chapters, it has been suggested that the facts about change can be at one and the same time both ambiguous and complex. Information about change may be especially malleable and thus capable of providing support for quite different and even conflicting images of what has taken place. Change-related facts can be presented in different ways and can be given different shadings depending on persuasive intent. As just one example, when there are declines in the rate of increase, the focus can be placed on the fact that there has been an increase or alternatively on the fact that there has been a decline in the increase. Similarly, there is often a choice of baselines, with many different periods plausibly serving as comparison periods depending on one's purpose.

The fact that the topic of change arises in persuasion contexts also leads directly to interesting questions framed in terms of persuasion research. For example, in persuasion contexts, do audiences ever grasp the extent to which the actual evidence about change can support very different interpretations? To what extent do the speaker's characteristics — especially change-relevant characteristics such as age — shape the audience's susceptibility to particular presentations of change facts or to particular change conclusions? In what ways are political change claims similar to fear appeals? If certain kinds of change claims can properly be termed fear appeals, is their effectiveness enhanced when combined with particular suggested courses of action? Are fear appeals that employ the rhetoric of change effective because of the ease with which people can be persuaded that change has occurred?

When looking at broader social contexts such as the persuasion context, another point about change judgments emerges that will be important for future consideration. People sometimes come to their initial change impressions not from the information itself but simply from hearing change conclusions made by others. In this book we have focused on those change claims that arise out of data use, but people's conclusions about change are sometimes secondhand in the sense of being based on the judgments of others rather than drawn from firsthand exposure to relevant data. The social construction of views on change has yet to be explored, and the use, if any, to which the perceiver puts information in such cases might well take a different course than the use that has been the focus of our investigations in these chapters.

In sum, a focus on context is likely to generate interesting questions that might otherwise remain unexamined. Whether it be the persuasion context or some other, such an expansion of focus may be useful in accounting for the rich variety of intuitive change judgments that occur in everyday life.

Considering Characteristics of the Judger

College students have served as subjects in the majority of the studies reported here; the use of this homogeneous population has considerably simplified the initial task of exploring change judgments by reducing concerns with individual differences. In future work it will be useful to consider the ways in which other populations may judge change differently and, more generally, it may be of value to consider the ways that change perception is influenced by particular perceiver characteristics. To illustrate the diversity of issues involving perceiver characteristics, three very different examples are introduced below: whether children see change differently than adults, whether those who are cognitively complex see change differently than those who are not, and whether those who are the objects of the change see change differently from those who are observers of the change.

When we think of change judgments, they often seem to be a particularly adult preoccupation. When do children first become interested in change? Do children perceive their friends, siblings, and parents as changing? Anecdotal evidence would seem to suggest that children sometimes worry about their parents changing and perhaps also about change in their friends or friendships (Rubin, 1980). If children do, in fact, form impressions of change, do these impressions typically show up as explicit change conclusions and are they based on the same kind of information use that is seen in adults? If, on the other hand, children do not see change, or are capable of seeing change but express no interest in this dimension, what transforms the issue of change into an interesting question in adulthood and what makes it uninteresting in youth?

The extent to which children of different ages make change judgments could be a function of any number of factors beyond the obvious one of cognitive development. For example, it is possible that a certain amount of experience is needed not only to see change but also to have change in others and in the social world seem important. A sense of objects and of people as stable at one point in time may be necessary for seeing change. It may even be the case that people must be perceived as having some stable set of traits before it is possible to imagine how those characteristics might undergo a change. Recent work has indicated that there is a developmental progression in children's tendencies to employ trait terms in thinking about others (Feldman & Ruble, 1981; Rotenberg, 1982); the progression of that tendency, paradoxically enough, may go hand-in-hand with the tendency to see true change as a possibility.

In addition to seeking to understand perceiver variables by way of a developmental focus, one might consider whether the tendency to see change occurs most readily in those who are cognitively complex or in those who view the world in simplified terms (Crockett, 1965). In other words, is change seen because of a tendency to view events in simplified terms—for example, as unidirectionally increasing or decreasing—rather than viewing events as occurring in unchanging cycles or patterns? Some of the work presented in the foregoing chapters would seem to support the thesis that the tendency to see change will be related to individual tendencies to view events in simplified terms. Additional work in this area may show, however, that the situation is not so straightforward. Indeed, seeing change would sometimes seem to be the simple interpretation, as in the case where change is seen because of a focus on frequency rather than rate. At other times, seeing change would seem to be the more complex interpretation, as might be the case when change is seen when frequencies have remained the same but the population itself has undergone a decline.

Individual differences among perceivers are likely to be relevant to understanding not only how readily people see social change but also how readily they make judgments of person change. There is evidence of individual differences in tendencies to draw various inferences from others' behaviors; some people, for example, seem to be especially willing to ascribe trait terms to others (Funder, 1980). Although such findings highlight the fact that individual differences are likely to be important to judging change in others, the relationships may be complex. For example, it should not be concluded that those who most readily apply trait terms will also be those who are most resistant to seeing others as having changed. The two tendencies may bear a complex relationship to one another, with perceivers needing to see a person as stable at one point in time (e.g., as consistent enough for a trait label to apply) in order to be ready to conclude at some later time that the person has indeed changed.

Two cases have thus far been suggested in which the consideration of perceiver variables might prove instructive; as a final example of how change judgments might be better understood by taking into account the perspective of the individual judger, let us consider the question of how individuals infer change in themselves and the ways in which such inferences may be different from or similar to analogous inferences made by others.

In this book, the judgments of person change we have examined have typically focused on the other rather than on the self, yet perceivers undoubtedly show a similar interest in judging self-change. As researchers have begun to explore this possibility (Conway & Ross, 1984; Kohli, 1986; Mortimer, Finch, & Kumba, 1982; Singer, 1977), it has become apparent that the motivational and informational factors influencing judgments of self-change cannot be assumed to be identical with those influencing change judgments made about others. To take one example, impressions of self-change may differ from judgments made about others in those cases where change impressions of others are brought on by not having been around the other in some time. In other words, change in another may often be noticeable because we have not been around that person recently. In contemporary life, it is not uncommon for there to be some hiatus in our interactions (e.g., we last saw the person a Christmas ago, or the previous summer, or at a convention several years ago). By the very nature of things, the self is different in this respect; in effect, one has limited opportunities to get away from the self. As a result, certain kinds of person change judgments may be less common for the self than for others, especially when the change in the self is gradual or is of a kind that is particularly difficult to see in the absence of a break. In such cases, whatever self-impressions of change people have may inevitably come from others' impressions; others may be important informants, with their reactions serving as the mirrors, however imperfect, that enable us to gauge change in ourselves.

The possibilities for examining judgments of self-change go well beyond the points made here, as evidenced by the rich and varied work on judgments of self that has been completed in recent years (Greenwald & Pratkanis, 1984). Some of that work suggests interesting directions for future exploration of impressions of self-change, particularly in regard to conclusions about change in the self that may differ from the judgments of change in others (Kohli, 1986).

As has been suggested throughout this section, the study of person variables represents an important direction for future research, albeit one that has its own share of difficulties and complexities. Person variables may turn out to be an important determinant of the extent to which change is perceived, as well as of the processes by which it is perceived. For various reasons — only some of which have been outlined here — individuals may come to hold very different views of change, a consequence that is likely to have considerable implications for social interactions where those changes, and the beliefs about them, are of central importance.

Final Reflections on the Perception of Change

Ultimately what remains so intriguing about perceivers' attempts to get an exact fix on whether things have changed is that those attempts take place in the ongoing flow of everyday experience. Events flow continuously in the life of both observer and observed, and in such a situation attempts to locate the change in absolute terms are almost certainly doomed to failure. Our ability as observers — either collectively or individually — to say definitively that something else has changed depends on our having observed events from a point that is itself not subject to change. Implicitly we seem to operate as if our observations were made from just such a constant vantage point, allowing us to gauge the amount of change that goes on around us as we stand still. But such points of constancy — points that are outside of change and are anchored against the flow of time — remain elusive in a world in which the observers are also a part of the change.

Can we say to what degree events around us have changed when we cannot independently know how much we as observers have changed? If the events of the 1960s happened now, would we interpret them in the same way they were inter-preted at the time, or has the accumulation of cultural experiences forever changed our very way of assigning meaning to those sorts of events? If holidays no longer feel the way they did when we were children, what has changed — the holidays or us? How are we to know whether the changes we see at age 70 in our interactions with spouses are changes in our partners, reflections of changes in ourselves, or perhaps a consequence of changes in prevailing cultural conceptions of aging? Paradoxical as it may seem, looking for change ultimately implies constancy at one level in order to judge change at another. But if, as has been suggested throughout this volume, the perception of change often has the properties of illusory perception, it is perhaps no less an illusion to believe that change can be judged against some fixed standard. In terms of our judging change, the issue is not so much that we are adrift in a sea of change as it is that we are limited by an irreducible inability to know when change has occurred except by the most relativistic and shifting of standards. In many cases, the choice of the period against which we elect to compare our current status may say more about our status than the inferences of change themselves.

References

Ager, S. (1983, August 5). For Dennis' creator, family life hasn't always been a comic strip. *Boston Globe*, pp. 47, 48.

Agostinelli, G., Sherman, S.J., Fazio, R.H., & Hearst, E. (1986). Detecting and identifying change: Additions versus deletions. *Journal of Experimental Psychology: Human Perception and Performance, 12,* 445–454.

American Humane Association (1970). *Child abuse legislation in the 1970's.* Denver: Author.

Anderson, C.A. (1983). Abstract and concrete data in the perseverance of social theories: When weak data lead to unshakable beliefs. *Journal of Experimental Social Psychology, 19,* 93–108.

Anderson, C.A., Lepper, M. R., & Ross, L. (1980). The perseverance of social theories: The role of explanation in the persistence of discredited information. *Journal of Personality and Social Psychology, 31,* 1037–1049.

Anderson, C.A., New, B.L., & Speer, J. R. (1985). Argument availability as a mediator of social theory perseverance. *Social Cognition, 3,* 235–249.

Archer, D., & Gartner, R. (1984). *Violence and crime in cross-national perspective.* New Haven: Yale University Press.

Aries, P. (1962). *Centuries of childhood: A social history of family life.* (R. Baldick, Trans.). New York: Knopf.

Asch, S.E. (1946). Forming impressions of personality. *Journal of Abnormal and Social Psychology, 41,* 258–290.

Asch, S.E. (1952). *Social psychology.* Englewood Cliffs, NJ: Prentice-Hall.

Azjen, I. (1977). Intuitive theories of events and the effects of base-rate information on prediction. *Journal of Personality and Social Psychology, 35,* 303–314.

Bacon, F.T. (1979). Credibility of repeated statements: Memory for trivia. *Journal of Experimental Psychology: Human Learning and Memory, 5,* 241–252.

Baer, D.M. (1970). An age-irrelevant concept of development. *Merrill-Palmer Quarterly, 16,* 238–245.

Ball, J. (1985, April 10). State suspends Dorchester day care home's license. *Boston Globe,* pp. 15–16.

Baltes, P.B. (1968). Longitudinal and cross-sectional sequences in the study of age and generation effects. *Human Development, 11,* 145–171.

Baltes, P.B. (1979). Life-span developmental psychology: Some converging observations on history and theory. In P.B. Baltes & O.G. Brim, Jr. (Eds.), *Life-span development and behavior* (Vol. 2, pp. 255–279). New York: Academic Press.

Baltes, P.B., Reese, H.W., & Lipsitt, L.P. (1980). Life-span developmental psychology. *Annual Review of Psychology, 31,* 65–110.

Baltes, P.B., Reese, H.W., & Nesselroade, J.R. (1977). *Life-span developmental psychology: Introduction to research methods.* Monterey, CA: Brooks/Cole.

Bargh, J.A. (1984). Automatic and conscious processing of social information. In R.S. Wyer, Jr. & T.K. Srull (Eds.), *Handbook of social cognition* (Vol. 3, pp. 1–44). Hillsdale, NJ: Erlbaum.

Baron, R.M. (1980). Social knowing from an ecological event perspective: A consideration of the relative domains of power for cognitive and perceptual modes of knowing. In J. Harvey (Ed.), *Cognition, social behavior, and the environment* (pp. 61–89). Hillsdale, NJ: Erlbaum.

Baruch, G., Barnett, R., & Rivers, C. (1983). *Life prints: New patterns of life and work for today's women.* New York: Plume.

Bauer, R. (1966). *Social indicators.* Cambridge, MA: MIT Press.

Baum, A., Fisher, J.D., & Singer, J.E. (1985). *Social psychology.* New York: Random House.

Baxter, A. (1985). *Techniques for dealing with child abuse.* Springfield, IL: Thomas.

Bell, L.G., Wicklund, R.A., Manko, G., & Larkin, C. (1976). When unexpected behavior is attributed to the environment. *Journal of Research in Personality, 10,* 316–327.

Bell, R.R., & Chaskes, J.B., (1970). Premarital sexual experience among coeds, 1958–1968. *Journal of Marriage and the Family, 32,* 81–84.

Bellak, L. (1975). *Overload: The new human condition.* New York: Human Sciences Press.

Bem, D.J., & McConnell, H.K. (1970). Testing the self-perception explanation of dissonance phenomena: On the salience of premanipulation attitudes. *Journal of Personality and Social Psychology, 14,* 23–31.

Bergin, A.E., & Lambert, M.J. (1978). The evaluation of therapeutic outcomes. In S.L. Garfield & A.E. Bergin (Eds.), *Handbook of psychotherapy and behavior change* (2nd ed., pp. 139–189). New York: Wiley.

Bernard, J. (1981). The good provider role: Its rise and fall. *American Psychologist, 36,* 1–12.

Bernard, J. (1984). Women's mental health in times of transition. In L.E. Walker (Ed.), *Women and mental health policy* (pp. 181–195). Beverly Hills, CA: Sage.

Block, C.R., & Block, R.L. (1984). Crime definition, crime measurement, and victim surveys. *Journal of Social Issues, 40,* 137–159.

Block, J. (1971). *Lives through time.* Berkeley, CA: Bancroft.

Block, J. (1977). Advancing the psychology of personality: Paradigmatic shift or improving the quality of research. In D. Magnussen & N.S. Endler (Eds.), *Personality at the crossroads: Current issues in interactional psychology* (pp. 37–63). Hillsdale, NJ: Erlbaum.

Blomqvist, N. (1977). On the relation between change and initial value. *Journal of the American Statistical Association, 72,* 746–749.

Bloom, B.S. (1974). *Stability and change in human characteristics.* New York: Wiley.

Boston Globe Magazine. (1982, May 30). Ask Beth: Familiar phases. p. 15.

Boston Globe Magazine. (1982, July 4). Ask Beth: Different drummers. p. 5.

Boston Quarterly Review. (1859). Cited in 'Death of the Family?' (1983, January 17). *Newsweek,* p. 26.

Boudan, R. (1983). Why theories of social change fail: Some methodological thoughts. *Public Opinion Quarterly, 47,* 143–160.

Bower, G.H., & Gilligan, S.G. (1979). Remembering information related to one's self. *Journal of Research in Personality, 13,* 420–432.

Bowker, L. H. (1978). *Women, crime, and the criminal justice system.* Lexington, MA: D.C. Heath.

Boyer, E.L. (1987). *College: The undergraduate experience in America.* New York: Harper & Row.

Brim, O.G., Jr., & Kagan, J. (Eds.). (1980). *Constancy and change in human development.* Cambridge, MA: Harvard University Press.

References

Brim, O.G., Jr., & Ryff, C.D. (1980). On the properties of life events. In P.B. Baltes & O. Brim, Jr. (Eds.), *Life-span developmental behavior* (Vol. 3, pp. 367–388). New York: Academic Press.

Brown, R., & Kulick, J. (1977). Flashbulb memories. *Cognition, 5,* 73–99.

Bryk, A.S., & Raudenbush, S.W. (1987). Application of hierarchical linear models to assessing change. *Psychological Bulletin, 101,* 147–158.

Bybee, R.W. (1979). Violence toward youth. *Journal of Social Issues, 35,* 1–14.

Callahan, E.J., & McCluskey, K.A. (Eds.). (1983). *Life-span developmental psychology: Nonnormative life events.* New York: Academic Press.

Campbell, A. (1980). *The sense of well-being in America: Recent patterns and trends.* New York: McGraw-Hill.

Campbell, A., & Converse, P.E. (Eds.). (1972). *The human meaning of social change.* New York: Russell Sage.

Campbell, D.T. (1969). Reforms as experiments. *American Psychologist, 24,* 409–429.

Campbell, D.T., & Ross, H.L. (1968). The Connecticut crackdown on speeding. *Law and Society Review, 3,* 33–53.

Cantor, N., & Mischel, W. (1979). Prototypes in person perception. In L. Berkowitz (Ed.), *Advances in experimental social psychology* (Vol. 12, pp. 3–52). New York: Academic Press.

Caplow, T., Bahr, H.M., Chadwick, B.A., Hill, R., & Williamson, M.H. (1983). *Middletown families: Fifty years of change and continuity.* Toronto: Bantam Books.

Carlston, D.E. (1980). The recall of and use of traits and events in social inference processes. *Journal of Experimental Social Psychology, 16,* 303–328.

Carroll, J.J. (1978). Causal attribution in expert parole decisions. *Journal of Personality and Social Psychology, 36,* 1501–1511.

Chappell, D. (1976). Forcible rape and the criminal justice system: Surveying present practices and projecting future trends. In M.J. Walker & S.L. Brosky (Eds.), *Sexual assault: The victim and the rapist.* Lexington, MA: D.C. Heath.

Chilman, C.S.(1979). *Adolescent sexuality in a changing American society: Social and psychological perspectives.* Washington, DC: U.S. Department of Health, Education, and Welfare.

Cialdini, R.B., Petty, R.E., & Cacioppo, J.T. (1981). Attitudes and attitude change. *Annual Review of Psychology, 32,* 357–404.

Clark, M.S., & Fiske, S.T. (Eds.). (1982). *Affect and cognition.* Hillsdale, NJ: Erlbaum.

Clark, T.B. (1982, December 12). The clout of the "new" Bob Dole. *New York Times Magazine,* pp. 65–82.

Colcord, J.C. (1919). *Broken homes.* New York: Russell Sage.

Colson, C.W. (1976). *Born again.* Toronto: Bantam Books.

Conway, F., & Siegelman, J. (1979). *Snapping: The epidemic of sudden personality change.* New York: Delta.

Conway, M., & Ross, M. (1984). Getting what you want by revising what you had. *Journal of Personality and Social Psychology, 47,* 738–748.

Conway, M., & Ross, M. (1985). Remembering one's own past: The construction of personal histories. In R. Sorrentino & E.T. Higgins (Eds.), *Handbook of motivation and cognition.* New York: Guilford.

Cook, T.D., & Campbell, D.T. (1979). *Quasi-experimentation: Design and analysis issues for field settings.* Chicago: Rand McNally.

Costa, P.T., Jr., & McCrae, R.R. (1980). Still stable after all these years: Personality as a key to some issues of aging. In P.B. Baltes & O.G. Brim, Jr. (Eds.), *Life-span development and behavior* (Vol. 3, pp. 66–102). New York: Academic Press.

"Cowboys don't shoot straight like they used to." (1981). Vogue Music and Tree Publishing Co, Inc. Copyright managed by Vogue Music, c/o The Welk Music Group, Santa Monica, CA 90401. Used by permission. International copyright reserved.

macy versus recency in retention of information and opinion change. *...ology, 101,* 87–96.

...D.B., & Weber, R. (1983). Person memory and causal attributions. *...ality and Social Psychology, 44,* 55–66.

...65). Cognitive complexity and impression formation. In B.A. Maher (Ed.), *...experimental personality research* (Vol. 2, pp. 47–90). New York: Academic

...ch, L.J., & Furby, L. (1970). How should we measure "change" – or should we? *Psychological Bulletin, 74,* 68–80.

...arley, J.M., & Batson, C.D. (1973). From Jerusalem to Jericho: A study of situational and dispositional variables in helping behavior. *Journal of Personality and Social Psychology, 27,* 100–108.

Davis, F. (1979). *Yearning for yesterday: A sociology of nostalgia.* New York: Free Press.

Davis, F. (1981). Contemporary nostalgia and the mass media. In E. Katz & T. Szecsko (Eds.), *Mass media and social change* (pp. 219–245). Beverly Hills, CA: Sage.

Deaux, K., & Wrightsman, L. (1984). *Social psychology in the '80s* (4th ed). Monterey, CA: Brooks/Cole.

Demos, J. (1979). Images of the family, then and now. In V. Tufte & B. Myerhoff (Eds.), *Changing images of the family* (pp. 43–60). New Haven: Yale University Press.

Demos, J. (1986). *Past, present, and personal: The family and life course in American history.* New York: Oxford University Press.

DeVos, G.A. (1976). *Responses to change: Society, culture, and personality.* New York: Van Nostrand.

Dielman, T.E. (1983). Pooled cross-sectional and time-series data: A survey of current statistical methodology. *Journal of the American Statistical Association, 78,* 111–122.

Dohrenwend, B.S., & Dohrenwend, B.P. (Eds.). (1974). *Stressful life events: Their nature and effect.* New York: Wiley.

Dohrenwend, B.S., & Dohrenwend, B.P. (Eds.). (1981). *Stressful life events and their contexts.* New York: Prodist.

Dreben, E.K., Fiske, S.T., & Hastie, R. (1979). The independence of evaluative and item information: Impression and recall order effects in behavior-based impression formation. *Journal of Personality and Social Psychology, 37,* 1758–1768.

Duck, S. (Ed.). (1982). *Personal relationships 4: Dissolving personal relationships.* London: Academic Press.

Duck, S. (Ed.). (1984). *Personal relationships 5: Repairing personal relationships.* London: Academic Press.

Eakins, P.S. (1983). *Mothers in transition: A study of the changing life course.* Cambridge, MA: Schenkman.

Editorials on File. (1982, April 16–30). Retarded infant dies after parents refuse surgery. *13,* p. 470.

Einhorn, H.J., & Hogarth, R.M. (1978). Confidence in judgment: Persistence of the illusion of validity. *Psychological Review, 85,* 395–416.

Einhorn, H.J., & Hogarth, R.M. (1981). Behavioral decision theory: Processes of judgment and choice. *Annual Review of Psychology, 32,* 53–88.

Elder, G.H., Jr. (1979). Historical change in life pattern and personality. In P.B. Baltes & O.G. Brim, Jr. (Eds.), *Life-span development and behavior* (Vol. 2, pp. 118–159). New York: Academic Press.

Epstein, S. (1977). Traits are alive and well. In D. Magnussen & N.S. Endler (Eds.), *Personality at the crossroads: Current issues in interactional psychology* (pp. 83–98). Hillsdale, NJ: Erlbaum.

Epstein, S., & O'Brien, E.J. (1985). The person-situation debate in historic and current perspective. *Psychological Bulletin, 98,* 513–537.

Eysenck, H.J. (1952). The effect of psychotherapy: An evaluation. *Journal of Consulting Psychology, 16,* 319–324.

Faunce, W.A. (1968). *Problems of an industrial society.* New York: McGraw-Hill.

Feiffer, J. (1982, December 5). *Boston Globe Magazine,* p. 91.

Feinsilber, M. (1987, March 5). Can Reagan change? He says yes, and so does Muskie. *Lowell Sun,* p. 60.

Feldman, N.S., & Ruble, D.N. (1981). The development of person perception: Cognitive and social factors. In S.S. Brehm, S.M. Kassin, & F.X. Gibbons (Eds.), *Developmental social psychology: Theory and research* (pp. 191–206). New York: Oxford University Press.

Feldman-Summers, S., & Ashworth, C.D. (1981). Factors related to intentions to report a rape. *Journal of Social Issues, 37,* 57–70.

Ferguson, T., & Rogers, J. (1986, May). The myth of America's turn to the right. *Atlantic,* pp. 43–53.

Ferriss, A.L. (1969). *Indicators of trends in American education.* New York: Russell Sage.

Finestone, H. (1976). *Victims of change: Juvenile delinquents in American society.* Westport, CT: Greenwood Press.

Fischhoff, B. (1975). Hindsight ≠ foresight: The effect of outcome knowledge on judgment under uncertainty. *Journal of Experimental Psychology: Human Perception and Performance, 1,* 288–299.

Fisher, J.E., & O'Donohue, W. (in press). Problems in (really) living: Behavioral approaches to the elderly's goals regarding dating, marriage, and sex. In P.A. Wisocki (Ed.), *Handbook of clinical behavior therapy for the elderly client.* New York: Plenum.

Fiske, S.T., & Taylor, S.E. (1984). *Social cognition.* Reading, MA: Addison-Wesley.

Florovsky, G. (1969). The study of the past. In R.H. Nash (Ed.), *Ideas of history* (Vol. 2, pp. 351–369). New York: Dutton.

Fong, G.T., Krantz, D.H., & Nisbett, R.E. (1986). The effects of statistical training on thinking about everyday problems. *Cognitive Psychology, 18,* 253–292.

Forehand, G. (Ed.). (1982). *New directions for program evaluation: Application of time series analysis to evaluation.* San Francisco: Jossey-Bass.

Freedman, J.L., Sears, D.O., & Carlsmith, J.M. (1981). *Social psychology* (4th ed.). Englewood Cliffs, NJ: Prentice-Hall.

Freund, T., Kruglanski, A.W., & Shpitzajen, A. (1985). The freezing and unfreezing of impressional primacy: Effects of the need for structure and the fear of invalidity. *Personality and Social Psychology Bulletin, 11,* 479–488.

Funder, D.C. (1980). The "trait" of ascribing traits: Individual differences in personality trait ascriptions. *Journal of Research in Personality, 14,* 376–385.

Funder, D.C. (1982). On the accuracy of dispositional versus situational attributions. *Social Cognition, 1,* 205–222.

Funder, D.C. (1987). Errors and mistakes: Evaluating the accuracy of social judgment. *Psychological Bulletin, 101,* 75–90.

Furby, L. (1973). Interpreting regression toward the mean in developmental research. *Developmental Psychology, 8,* 172–179.

Gager, N., & Schurr, C. (1976). *Sexual assault: Confronting rape in America.* New York: Grossett and Dunlap.

Geis, G., & Stotland, E. (Eds.). (1980). *White-collar crime: Theory and research.* Beverly Hills, CA: Sage.

Gelles, R.J. (1978). Violence toward children in the U.S. *American Journal of Orthopsychiatry, 48,* 580–592.

Gelles, R.J. (1987). What to learn from cross-cultural and historical research on child abuse and neglect: An overview. In R.J. Gelles & J.B. Lancaster (Eds.), *Child abuse and neglect: Biosocial dimensions* (pp. 15–30). New York: Aldine De Gruyter.

Gelles, R., & Straus, M. (1979). Violence in the American family. *Journal of Social Issues, 35*(2), 15–39.

Gerbner, G. (1972). Violence in televised drama: Trends and symbolic functions. In G.A. Comstock & E.A. Rubinstein (Eds.), *Television and social behavior: Vol. 1. Media content and control* (pp. 28–187). Washington, DC: Government Printing Office.

Gergen, K.J. (1977). Stability, change, and chance in understanding human development. In N. Datan & H.W. Reese (Eds.), *Life-span developmental psychology: Dialectical perspectives on experimental research* (pp. 135–157). New York: Academic Press.

Gergen, K.J. (1980). The emerging crisis in life-span developmental theory. In P.B.Baltes & O.G. Brim, Jr., (Eds.), *Life-span development and behavior* (Vol. 1, pp. 31–63). New York: Academic Press.

Gergen, K.J., & Gergen, M.M. (1984). Narratives of the self. In T. Sarbin & K. Scheibe (Eds.), *Studies in social identity* (pp. 254–273). New York: Praeger.

Gergen, K.J., Hepburn, A., & Fisher, D.C. (1986). Hermeneutics of personality description. *Journal of Personality and Social Psychology, 50,* 1261–1270.

Gifford, R.K. (1975). Information properties of descriptive words. *Journal of Personality and Social Psychology, 31,* 727–734.

Ginosar, Z., & Trope, Y. (1980). The effects of base rates and individuating information on judgments about another person. *Journal of Experimental Social Psychology, 16,* 228–242.

Glenn, N.D. (1970). Problems of comparability in trend studies with opinion poll data. *Public Opinion Quarterly, 34,* 82–91.

Glenn, N.D. (1976). Cohort analysts' futile quest: Statistical attempts to separate age, period, and cohort effects. *American Sociological Review, 41,* 900–904.

Glenn, N.D. (1980). Values, attitudes, and beliefs. In O.G. Brim, Jr. & J. Kagan (Eds.), *Constancy and change in human development* (pp. 596–640). Cambridge, MA: Harvard University Press.

Glenn, N.D., & Weaver, C.N. (1982). Enjoyment of work by full-time workers in the U.S., 1955 and 1980. *Public Opinion Quarterly, 46,* 459–470.

Goethals, G.R., & Reckman, R.F. (1973). The perception of consistency in attitudes. *Journal of Experimental Social Psychology, 9,* 491–501.

Goldberg, L.R. (1981). Unconfounding situational attributions from uncertain, neutral, and ambiguous ones: A psychometric analysis of descriptions of oneself and various others. *Journal of Personality and Social Psychology, 41,* 517–552.

Goldfried, M.R. (1980). Toward the delineation of therapeutic change principles. *American Psychologist, 35,* 991–999.

Goodman, E. (1979). *Turning points.* New York: Fawcett Columbine.

Goodman, E. (1982, April 29). There are strains, but family life today is still alive and well. *Boston Globe,* p. 15.

Greenwald, A.G. (1980). The totalitarian ego: Fabrication and revision of personal history. *American Psychologist, 35,* 603–618.

Greenwald, A.G., & Pratkanis, A.R. (1984). The self. In R.S. Wyer, Jr. & T.K. Srull (Eds.), *Handbook of social cognition* (Vol. 3, pp. 129–178). Hillsdale, NJ: Erlbaum.

Gurin, P. (1985). Women's gender consciousness. *Public Opinion Quarterly, 49,* 143–164.

Hamill, R., Wilson, T.D., & Nisbett, R.E. (1980). Insensitivity to sample bias: Generalizing from atypical cases. *Journal of Personality and Social Psychology, 39,* 578–589.

Hamilton, D.L. (1981). Cognitive representations of persons. In E.T. Higgins, C.P. Herman, & M.P. Zanna (Eds.), *Social cognition: The Ontario symposium* (pp. 135–160). Hillsdale, NJ: Erlbaum.

Hamilton, D.L., Katz, L.B., & Leirer, V.O. (1980). Organizational processes in impression formation. In R. Hastie, T.M. Ostrom, E.B. Ebbesen, R.S. Wyer, Jr., D.L. Hamilton, & D.E. Carlston (Eds.), *Person memory: The cognitive basis of social perception* (pp. 121–153). Hillsdale, NJ: Erlbaum.

Harris, C.W. (Ed.). (1963). *Problems in the measurement of change.* Madison: University of Wisconsin Press.

Harris, L. (1973). *The anguish of change.* New York: Norton.

Harris, P. (1982). Commentary. In D.M. Scott & B. Wishy (Eds.), *America's families: A documentary history* (p. 670). New York: Harper & Row.

Harvey, J.H., & Parks, M.M. (Eds.). (1982). *Psychotherapy research and behavior change.* Washington, DC: American Psychological Association.

Harvey, J.H., Town, J.P., & Yarkin, K.L. (1981). How fundamental is "The fundamental attribution error?" *Journal of Personality and Social Psychology, 40,* 346–349.

Harvey, J.H., & Weary, G. (1981). *Perspectives on attributional processes.* Dubuque, IA: Wm.C. Brown.

Hastie, R. (1980). Memory for behavioral information that confirms or contradicts a personality impression. In R. Hastie, T.M. Ostrom, E.B. Ebbesen, R.S. Wyer, Jr., D.L. Hamilton, & D.E. Carlston (Eds.), *Person memory: The cognitive basis of social perception* (pp. 155–177). Hillsdale, NJ: Erlbaum.

Hastie, R., Ostrom, T.M., Ebbesen, E.B., Wyer, R.S., Jr., Hamilton, D.L., & Carlston, D.E. (Eds.). (1980). *Person memory: The cognitive basis of social perception.* Hillsdale, NJ: Erlbaum.

Hastie, R., Park, B., & Weber, R. (1984). Social memory. In R.S. Wyer, Jr., & T.K. Srull (Eds.), *Handbook of social cognition* (Vol. 2, pp. 151–212). Hillsdale, NJ: Erlbaum.

Hayden, T., & Mischel, W. (1976). Maintaining trait consistency in the resolution of behavior inconsistency: The wolf in sheep's clothing? *Journal of Personality, 44,* 109–132.

Healy, R. (1985, September 18). Bush's image problem. *Boston Globe,* p. 19.

Heider, F. (1958). *The psychology of interpersonal relations.* New York: Wiley.

Helfer, R.E., & Kempe, R.S. (Eds.). (1987). *The battered child* (4th ed.). Chicago: University of Chicago Press.

Hero, A.O., Jr. (1973). *American religious groups view foreign policy: Trends in rank-and-file opinion, 1937–1969.* Durham, NC: Duke University Press.

Herzberger, S.D., & Clore, G.L. (1979). Actor-observer attributions in a multitrait-multimethod matrix. *Journal of Research in Personality, 13,* 1–15.

Higgins, E.T., & Bargh, J.A. (1987). Social cognition and social perception. *Annual Review of Psychology, 38,* 369–425.

Higgins, E.T., Herman, C.P., & Zanna, M.P. (Eds.). (1981). *Social cognition: The Ontario symposium.* Hillsdale, NJ: Erlbaum.

Higgins, E.T., Kuiper, N.A., & Olson, J.M. (1981). Social cognition: A need to get personal. In E.T. Higgins, C.P. Herman, & M.P. Zanna (Eds.), *Social cognition: The Ontario symposium* (pp. 395–420). Hillsdale, NJ: Erlbaum.

Higgins, E.T., & Parsons, J.E. (1983). Social cognition and the social life of the child: Stages as subcultures. In E.T. Higgins, D.N. Ruble, & W.H. Hartup (Eds.), *Social cognition and social development* (pp. 15–62). Cambridge, England: Cambridge University Press.

Hindelang, M.J. (1981). Variations in sex-race-age specific incidence rates of offending. *American Sociological Review, 46,* 461–474.

Hindelang, M.J., & Davis, B.L. (1977). Forcible rape in the U.S.: A statistical profile. In D. Chappell, R. Geis, & G. Geis (Eds.), *Forcible rape: The crime, the victim, and the offender* (pp. 87–114). New York: Columbia University Press.

Hintzman, D.L. (1974). Theoretical implications of the spacing effect. In R.L. Solso (Ed.), *Theories in cognitive psychology: The Loyola symposium* (pp. 77–99). Potomac, MD: Erlbaum.

Hobfall, S.E. (Ed.). (1986). *Stress, social support, and women.* New York: Hemisphere/Harper & Row.

Hogarth, R. (1987). *Judgment and choice* (2nd ed.). New York: Wiley.

Holmes, D.S. (1970). Differential change in affective intensity and the forgetting of unpleasant personal experience. *Journal of Personality and Social Psychology, 15,* 234–239.

Horn, J.L., & Donaldson, G. (1976). On the myth of intellectual decline in adulthood. *American Psychologist, 31,* 701–709.

Hostetler, A.J. (1987, May). Families under siege: Each hostage abroad leaves psychological captives at home. *APA Monitor,* p. 27.

House, J.S., & Wolf, S. (1978). Effects of urban residence on interpersonal trust and helping behavior. *Journal of Personality and Social Psychology, 36,* 1029–1043.

Innes De Neufville, J. (1975). *Social indicators and public policy: Interactive processes in design and application.* New York: Elsevier.

Jaffe, S.S., & Viertel, J. (1979). *Becoming parents: Preparing for the emotional changes of first-time parenthood.* New York: Athenium.

Jennings, D.L., Lepper, M.R., & Ross, L. (1981). Persistence of impressions of personal persuasiveness: Perseverance of erroneous self-assessments outside the debriefing paradigm. *Personality and Social Psychology Bulletin, 7,* 257-260.

Johnson, J. (1986, July). The children's wing: A mother, a son, a change. *Harper's,* pp. 66-69.

Johnson, M.K., Taylor, T.H., & Raye, R. (1977). Fact and fantasy: The effects of internally generated events on the apparent frequency of externally generated events. *Memory & Cognition, 5,* 116-122.

Jones, E.E. (1979). The rocky road from acts to dispositions. *American Psychologist, 34,* 107-117.

Jones, E.E., & Davis, K.E. (1965). From acts to dispositions: The attribution process in person perception. In L. Berkowitz (Ed.), *Advances in experimental social psychology* (Vol. 2, pp. 219-266). New York: Academic Press.

Jones, E.E., & Goethals, G.R. (1972). Order effects in impression formation: Attribution context and the nature of the entity. In E.E. Jones, D.E. Kanouse, H.H. Kelley, R.E. Nisbett, S. Valins, & B. Weiner (Eds.), *Attribution: Perceiving the causes of behavior* (pp. 27-46). Morristown, NJ: General Learning Corporation.

Jones, E.E., & Harris, V.A. (1967). The attribution of attitudes. *Journal of Experimental Social Psychology, 3,* 1-24.

Jones, E.E., & Nisbett, R.E. (1972). The actor and the observer: Divergent perceptions of the causes of behavior. In E.E. Jones, D.E. Kanouse, H.H. Kelley, R.E. Nisbett, S. Valins, & B. Weiner (Eds.), *Attribution: Perceiving the causes of behavior* (pp. 79-94). Morristown, NJ: General Learning Corporation.

Jones, E.E., Riggs, J.M., & Quattrone, G. (1979). Observer bias in the attitude attribution paradigm: Effect of time and information order. *Journal of Personality and Social Psychology, 37,* 1230-1238.

Kagan, J. (1980). Perspectives on continuity. In O.G. Brim, Jr. & J. Kagan (Eds.), *Constancy and change in human development* (pp. 26-74). Cambridge, MA: Harvard University Press.

Kagan, J. (1984). *The nature of the child.* New York: Basic Books.

Kahneman, D., Slovic, P., & Tversky, A. (Eds.). (1982). *Judgments under uncertainty: Heuristics and biases.* New York: Cambridge University Press.

Kahneman, D., & Tversky, A. (1973). On the psychology of prediction. *Psychological Review, 80,* 251-273.

Kanungo, R.N. (1982). *Work alienation.* New York: Praeger.

Kazdin, A.E. (1982). Methodology of psychotherapy outcome research: Recent developments and remaining limitations. In J.H. Harvey & M.M. Parks (Eds.), *Psychotherapy research and behavior change* (pp. 151-193). Washington, DC: American Psychological Association.

Kelley, H.H. (1967). Attribution theory in social psychology. In D. Levine (Ed.), *Nebraska symposium on motivation* (Vol. 15, pp. 192-240). Lincoln: University of Nebraska Press.

Kelley, H.H. (1972). Attributions in social interaction. In E.E. Jones, D.E. Kanouse, H.H. Kelley, R.E. Nisbett, S. Valins, & B. Weiner (Eds.), *Attribution: Perceiving the causes of behavior* (pp. 1-26). Morristown, NJ: General Learning Corporation.

Kelley, H.H., & Michela, J.L. (1980). Attribution theory and research. *Annual Review of Psychology, 31,* 457-501.

Keniston, K. (1965). *The uncommitted: Alienated youth in American society.* New York: Harcourt, Brace, & World.

Keniston, K. (1981, November 8). The mood of Americans today. *New York Times Book Review,* pp. 7, 42, 45.

Kessel, F., & Siegel, A.W. (Eds.). (1983). *The child and other cultural inventions.* New York: Praeger.

Kessler, R.C., & Greenberg, D.F. (1981). *Linear panel analysis: Models of quantitative change.* New York: Academic Press.

Kimmel, M.S. (Ed.). (1987). *Changing men: New directions in research on men and masculinity.* Newbury Park, CA: Sage.

Kinder, D.R., & Rhodebeck, L.A. (1982). Continuities in support for racial equality, 1972 to 1976. *Public Opinion Quarterly, 46,* 195–215.

Kluegel, J.R., & Smith, E.R. (1986). *Beliefs about inequality: Americans' views of what is and what ought to be.* Hawthorne, NY: Aldine de Gruyter.

Kohli, M. (1986). Social organization and subjective construction of the life course. In A.B. Sorensen, F.E. Weinert, & L.R. Sharrod (Eds.), *Human development and the life course: Multidisciplinary perspectives* (pp. 271–292). Hillsdale, NJ: Erlbaum.

Kruglanski, A.W., Friedland, N., & Farkash, E. (1984). Lay persons' sensitivity to statistical information: The case of high perceived applicability. *Journal of Personality and Social Psychology, 46,* 503–518.

Kubick, L. (1986, May 18). The word on Sylvester Stallone. *Boston Globe,* pp. All, A13.

Kulik, J.A. (1983). Confirmatory attribution and the perpetuation of social beliefs. *Journal of Personality and Social Psychology, 44,* 1171–1181.

Kunda, Z., & Nisbett, R.E. (1986). The psychometrics of everyday life. *Cognitive Psychology, 18,* 195–224.

Kundera, M. (1984). *The incredible lightness of being.* New York: Harper & Row.

Labouvie, E.W. (1982). The concept of change and regression toward the mean. *Psychological Bulletin, 92,* 251–257.

Lamb, D.H., & Reeder, G.D. (1986, June). Reliving golden days. *Psychology Today,* pp. 22–30.

Landers, A. (1982, February 2). (No title.) *Boston Globe,* p. 8.

Landers, A. (1982, May 20). Parents, time to do some soul searching. *Des Moines Register,* p. 22.

Landers, A. (1982, October 25). Shocked at the growth of indifference. *Boston Globe,* p. 38.

Landers, A. (1983, April 19). A husband's radical change. *Boston Globe,* p. 19.

LaRossa, R., & LaRossa, P. (1984). *Transition to parenthood: How infants change families.* New York: Pantheon.

Lasch, C. (1978). *The culture of narcissism: American life in an age of diminishing expectations.* New York: Norton.

Latane, B., & Darley, J.M. (1970). *The unresponsive bystander: Why doesn't he help?* New York: Appleton-Century-Crofts.

Lauer, R.H. (1974). Rate of change and stress: A test of the 'future shock' thesis. *Social Forces, 52,* 510–516.

Lauer, R.H. (1977). Social change:Meaning and myths. In R.H. Lauer (Ed.), *Perspectives on social change* (2nd ed., pp. 3–25). Boston: Allyn & Bacon.

Lauer, R.H., & Lauer, J.C. (1976). The experience of change: Tempo and stress. In G.K. Zollschan & W. Hirsch (Eds.), *Social change: Explorations, diagnoses, and conjectures* (pp. 520–545). New York: Wiley.

Lauer, R.H., & Thomas, R. (1976). A comparative analysis of the psychological consequences of change. *Human Relations, 29,* 239–248.

Layton, B.D., & Moehle, D. (1980). Attributional influence: The importance of observing change. *Journal of Experimental Social Psychology, 16,* 243–252.

Lenz, D. (1982). The Moonie life and how one left it. *U.S. News and World Report, 93,* p. 41.

Lewis, C., & O'Brien, M. (Eds.). (1987). *Reassessing fatherhood: New observations on fathers and the modern family.* London: Sage.

Linn, R.L., & Slinde, J.A. (1977). The determination of the significance of change between pre- and posttesting periods. *Review of Educational Research, 47,* 121–150.

Loftus, E.F. (1979). *Eyewitness testimony.* Cambridge, MA: Harvard University Press.

Longcope, K. (1982, October 31). ROTC's march back to college campuses. *Boston Globe,* pp. 79–83.

Lord, C.G., & Gilbert, D.T. (1983). The "same person" heuristic: An attributional procedure based on an assumption of person similarity. *Journal of Personality and Social Psychology, 45,* 751–762.

Luchins, A.S. (1957). Primacy-recency in impression formation. In C.I. Hovland (Ed.), *The order of presentation in persuasion* (pp. 33–61). New Haven, CT: Yale University Press.

Luchins, A.S. (1958). Definitiveness of impressions and primacy-recency effects in impression formation. *Journal of Social Psychology, 48,* 275–290.

Luchins, A.S., & Luchins, E.H. (1963). Effects of order of evidence on social influences on judgment. *Journal of Social Psychology, 61,* 345–363.

Luchins, A.S., & Luchins, E.H. (1986). Awareness of change in personality. *Journal of Psychology, 120,* 581–598.

Lupo, A. (1987, April 26). 'Ethics be damned' is business as usual. *Boston Globe,* p. 94.

Lynd, R.S., & Lynd, H.M. (1929). *Middletown: A study in American culture.* New York: Harcourt and Brace.

Lystad, M. (1986). *Violence in the home: Interdisciplinary perspectives.* New York: Brunner/ Mazel.

Mackie, D.M., & Allison, S.T. (1987). Group attribution errors and the illusion of group attitude change. *Journal of Experimental Social Psychology, 23,* 460–468.

MacMullan, J. (1987, June 24). Lewis' No. 1 priority: Stay the same person. *Boston Globe,* pp. 81–86.

Mahoney, M.J. (Ed.). (1980). *Psychotherapy process: Current issues and future directions.* New York: Plenum.

Mahoney, M.J. (1982). Psychotherapy and human change processes. In J.H. Harvey & M.M. Parks (Eds.), *Psychotherapy research and behavior change* (pp. 73–122). Washington, DC: American Psychological Association.

Malamuth, N.M., & Spinner, R.A. (1980). A longitudinal content analysis of sexual violence in the best-selling erotic magazines. *Journal of Sex Research, 16,* 226–237.

Markus, H., & Zajonc, R.B. (1985). The cognitive perspective in social psychology. In G. Lindzey & E. Aronson (Eds.), *Handbook of social psychology* (3rd ed., Vol. 2, pp. 137–230). New York: Random House.

Marris, P. (1974). *Loss and change.* New York: Pantheon Books.

Marris, P. (1986). *Loss and change.* London: Routledge & Kegan Paul.

Maugham, W.S. (1943). *The razor's edge.* New York: Penguin.

Mazur, A. (1977). Public confidence in science. *Social Studies of Science, 7,* 123–125.

McArthur, L.Z., & Baron, R.M. (1983). Toward an ecological theory of social perception. *Psychological Review, 90,* 215–238.

McCalls. (1978, July). Teenage pregnancy epidemic; special section. *105,* 45–52.

McCleary, R.B., Nienstedt, B.C., & Erven, J.M. (1982). Uniform crime reports as organizational outcomes: Three time series experiments. *Social Problems, 29,* 361–372.

McFarland, C., & Ross, M. (1987). The relation between current impressions and memories of self and dating partners. *Personality and Social Psychology Bulletin, 13,* 228–238.

McGrory, M. (1982, September 17). When stars were brighter. *Boston Globe,* p. 17.

McGuire, W.J. (1985). Attitudes and attitude change. In G. Lindzey & E. Aronson (Eds.), *Handbook of social psychology* (3rd ed., Vol. 2, pp. 233–346). New York: Random House.

McNeil, E.B. (1967). *The quiet furies.* Englewood Cliffs, NJ: Prentice-Hall.

Mednick, S.A., Harway, M., & Finello, K.M. (Eds.). (1984). *Handbook of longitudinal research. Vol. 1. Birth and childhood cohorts.* New York: Praeger.

Medved, M., & Wallechinsky, D. (1976). *What really happened to the class of '65?* New York: Ballentine.

Meyrowitz, J. (1985). *No sense of place.* New York: Oxford University Press.

Miller, A.G., Baer, R., & Schonberg, P. (1979). The bias phenomenon in attribution: Actor and observer perspectives. *Journal of Personality and Social Psychology, 37,* 1421–1431.

Miller, F.D., Smith, E.R., & Uleman, J. (1981). Measurement and interpretation of situational and dispositional attributions. *Journal of Experimental Social Psychology, 17,* 80–95.

Minz, J., Auerbach, A.H., Luborsky, L., & Johnson, M. (1973). Patients', therapists', and observers' views of psychotherapy: A "Rashomon" experience or a reasonable consensus? *British Journal of Medical Psychology, 46,* 83-89.

Mischel, W. (1968). *Personality and assessment.* New York: Wiley.

Mischel, W. (1973). Toward a cognitive social learning reconceptualization of personality. *Psychological Review, 80,* 252-283.

Monson, T.C., Keel, R., Stephens, D., & Genung, V. (1982). Trait attributions: Relative validity, covariation with behavior, and prospect of future interactions. *Journal of Personality and Social Psychology, 42,* 1014-1024.

Monson, T.C., & Snyder, M. (1977). Actors, observers, and the attribution process. *Journal of Experimental Social Psychology, 13,* 89-111.

Mortimer, J.T., Finch, M.D., & Kumba, D. (1982). Persistence and change in development: The multidimensional self-concept. In P.B. Baltes & O.G. Brim, Jr. (Eds.), *Life-span development and behavior* (Vol. 4, pp. 3-66). New York: Academic Press.

Moss, H.A., & Susman, E.J. (1980). Longitudinal study of personality development. In O.G. Brim, Jr. & J. Kagan (Eds.), *Constancy and change in human development* (pp. 530-595). Cambridge, MA: Harvard University Press.

Ms. Magazine. (1982, August). What's been happening to you in the last 10 years? pp. 16-42.

Mueller, C. (1983). In search of a constituency for the "new Religious Right." *Public Opinion Quarterly, 47,* 213-229.

Munnichs, J., & Munnichs, P. (Eds.). (1985). *Life-span and change in gerontological perspective.* New York: Academic Press.

Myers, D.G. (1983). *Social psychology.* New York: McGraw-Hill.

Myers, D.G. (1987). *Social psychology* (2nd ed.). New York: McGraw-Hill.

Nelson, B.J. (1984). *Making an issue of child abuse: Political agenda setting for social problems.* Chicago: University of Chicago Press.

Nesselroade, J.R. (1983). Temporal selection and factor invariance in the study of development and change. In P.B. Baltes & O.G. Brim, Jr. (Eds.), *Life-span development and behavior* (Vol. 5, pp. 59-87). New York: Academic Press.

Nesselroade, J.R., & Baltes, P.B. (1979). *Longitudinal research in the study of behavior and development.* New York: Academic Press.

Nesselroade, J.R., & Eye, A.V. (Eds.). (1984). *Individual development and social change: Explanatory analysis.* New York: Academic Press.

Nesselroade, J.R., & Reese, H.W. (1973). *Life-span developmental psychology: Methodological issues.* New York: Academic Press.

Nesselroade, J.R., Stigler, S.M., & Baltes, P.B. (1980). Regression toward the mean and the study of change. *Psychological Bulletin, 88,* 622-637.

Nisbett, R.E. (1980). The trait construct in lay and professional psychology. In L. Festinger (Ed.), *Retrospections in social psychology* (pp. 109-130). New York: Oxford University Press.

Nisbett, R.E., & Borgida, E. (1975). Attribution and the psychology of prediction. *Journal of Personality and Social Psychology, 32,* 932-943.

Nisbett, R.E., Borgida, E., Crandall, R., & Reed, H. (1976). Popular induction: Information is not necessarily informative. In J.S. Carroll & J.W. Payne (Eds.), *Cognition and social behavior* (pp. 113-133). Hillsdale, NJ: Erlbaum.

Nisbett, R.E., Caputo, C., Legant, P., & Marecek, J. (1973). Behavior as seen by the actor and as seen by the observer. *Journal of Personality and Social Psychology, 27,* 154-164.

Nisbett, R.E., Krantz, D.H., Jepson, C., & Kunda, Z. (1983). The use of statistical heuristics in everyday intuitive reasoning. *Psychological Review, 90,* 339-363.

Nisbett, R.E., & Kunda, Z. (1985). Perceptions of social distributions. *Journal of Personality and Social Psychology, 48,* 297-311.

Nisbett, R.E., & Ross, L. (1980). *Human inference: Strategies and shortcomings in social judgments.* Englewood Cliffs, NJ: Prentice-Hall.

Nisbett, R.E., & Wilson, T.D. (1977). Telling more than we can know: Verbal reports on mental processes. *Psychological Review, 84,* 231-259.

Nunnally, J.C. (1975). The study of change in evaluation: Principles concerning measurement, experimental design, and analysis. In E. Struening & M. Guttentag (Eds.), *Handbook of evaluation research* (Vol. 1, pp. 101–137). Beverly Hills, CA: Sage.

Nydegger, C.N. (1981). On being caught up in time. *Human Development, 24,* 1–12.

O'Brien, R.M. (1985). *Crime and victimization data.* Beverly Hills, CA: Sage.

Ohmer, M., Pollio, H.R., & Eison, J.A. (1986). *Making sense of college grades: Why the grading system does not work and what can be done about it.* San Francisco: Jossey-Bass.

Page, B.I., & Shapiro, R.Y. (1982). Changes in America's policy preferences, 1935–1979. *Public Opinion Quarterly, 46,* 24–42.

Pashdag, J. (1981). *Petersen's complete book of family and home protection.* Los Angeles: Petersen Publishing.

Peck, A. (1985). *Uncovering the sixties.* New York: Pantheon Books.

Pfoll, S.J. (1977). The "discovery" of child abuse. *Social Problems, 24,* 310–323.

Pillemer, K.A., & Wolf, R.S. (1986). *Elder abuse: Conflict in the family.* Dover, MA: Auburn House.

Pisarik, K. (1987, May 8). Trying to coach in an age of fallen diamond heros. *Lowell Sun,* pp. 19, 20.

Pleck, E. (1987). *Domestic tyranny: The making of social policy against family violence from colonial times to the present.* New York: Oxford University Press.

Plewis, I. (1985). *Analysing change: Measurement and explanation using longitudinal data.* New York: Wiley.

Pomper, M.M. (Ed.). (1981). *The election of 1980: Reports and interpretations.* Chatham, NJ: Chatham House.

Quattrone, G.A. (1982). Overattribution and unit formation: When behavior engulfs the person. *Journal of Personality and Social Psychology, 42,* 593–607.

Quattrone, G.A., & Jones, E.E. (1980). The perception of variability within in-groups and out-groups: Implications for the law of large numbers. *Journal of Personality and Social Psychology, 38,* 141–152.

Radbill, S.X. (1980). Children in a world of violence: A history of child abuse. In C.H. Kempe & R.E. Helfer (Eds.), *The battered child* (3rd ed., pp. 3–20). Chicago: University of Chicago Press.

Reich, C. (1971). *Greening of America.* New York: Bantam.

Reinke, B.J., Holmes, D.S., & Harris, R.L. (1985). The timing of psychosocial changes in women's lives: The years 25 to 45. *Journal of Personality and Social Psychology, 48,* 1353–1364.

Roberts, D.F., & Maccoby, N. (1985). Effects of mass communication. In G. Lindzey & E. Aronson (Eds.), *Handbook of social psychology* (3rd ed., Vol. 2, pp. 539–598). New York: Random House.

Robey, B. (1985). *The American people: A timely exploration of a changing America and the important new demographic trends around us.* New York: E.P. Dutton.

Robinson, M. (1985, October 13). Writers and the nostalgic fallacy. *New York Times Book Review,* pp. 1, 34, 35.

Rogosa, D.R., Brand, D., & Zimowski, M. (1982). A growth curve approach to the measurement of change. *Psychological Bulletin, 90,* 726–748.

Rosenthal, A.M. (1964, May 3). Study of the sickness called apathy: Concerning C. Genovese's murder. *New York Times Magazine,* pp. 24ff.

Ross. L. (1977). The intuitive psychologist and his shortcomings. In L. Berkowitz (Ed.), *Advances in experimental social psychology* (Vol. 10, pp. 173–220). New York: Academic Press.

Ross, L., Amabile, T.M., & Steinmetz, J. (1977). Social roles, social control, and biases in social perception processes. *Journal of Personality and Social Psychology, 35,* 485–494.

Ross, L., & Anderson, C.A. (1982). Shortcomings in the attribution process: On the origin and maintenance of erroneous social assessments. In D. Kahneman, P. Slovic, & A. Tversky (Eds.), *Judgments under uncertainty: Heuristics and biases* (pp. 129–152). Cambridge, England: Cambridge University Press.

Ross, L., Lepper, M.R., & Hubbard, M. (1975). Perseverance in self perception and social perception. *Journal of Personality and Social Psychology, 32,* 880–892.

Ross, L., Lepper, M.R., Strack, F., & Steinmetz, J.L. (1977). Social explanation and social expectation: The effects of real and hypothetical explanations upon subjective likelihood. *Journal of Personality and Social Psychology, 35,* 817–829.

Ross, M., & Fletcher, G.J.O. (1985). Attribution and social perception. In G. Lindzey & E. Aronson (Eds.), *Handbook of social psychology* (3rd ed., Vol. 2, pp. 73–122). New York: Random House.

Ross, M., McFarland, C., & Fletcher, G.J.O. (1981). The effect of attitude on recall of personal histories. *Journal of Personality and Social Psychology, 40,* 627–634.

Rossi, R.J., & Gilmartin, K.J. (1980). *The handbook of social indicators.* New York: Garland STMP Press.

Rotenberg, K.J. (1982). Development of character constancy in self and other. *Child Development, 53,* 505–511.

Rothbart, M., Evans, M., & Fulero, S. (1979). Recall of confirming events: Memory processes and the maintenance of social stereotypes. *Journal of Experimental Social Psychology, 15,* 343–355.

Rubin, Z. (1980). *Children's friendships.* Cambridge, MA: Harvard University Press.

Rubin, Z. (1981, May). Does personality really change after 20? *Psychology Today, 15,* 18–27.

Russell, D.E.H. (1984). *Sexual exploitation: Rape, child sexual abuse, and workplace harassment.* Beverly Hills, CA: Sage.

Russell, G. (1983). *The changing role of fathers.* Queensland, Australia: University of Queensland Press.

Ryan, B. (1987, June 21). Bird high scorer with press. *Boston Globe,* p. 90.

Ryff, C.D. (1982). Self-perceived personality change in adulthood and aging. *Journal of Personality and Social Psychology, 42,* 108–115.

Ryff, C.D. (1984). Personality development from the inside: The subjective experience of change in adulthood and aging. In P.B. Baltes & O.G. Brim, Jr. (Eds.), *Life-span development and behavior* (Vol. 6, 243–279). New York: Academic Press.

Sales, E., & Frieze, I.H. (1984). Women and work: Implications for mental health. In L.E. Walker (Ed.), *Women and mental health policy* (pp. 229–246). Beverly Hills, CA: Sage.

Schaie, K.W. (1965). A general model for the study of developmental problems. *Psychological Bulletin, 64,* 92–107.

Schaie, K.W. (Ed.). (1983). *Longitudinal studies of adult psychological development.* New York: Guilford.

Schneider, D.J. (1988). *Introduction to social psychology.* San Diego: Harcourt Brace Jovanovich.

Schneider, D.J., Hastorf, A.H., & Ellsworth, P.C. (1979). *Person perception* (2nd ed.). Reading, MA: Addison-Wesley.

Schneider, P. (1987, February). Lost innocents: The myth of missing children. *Harper's,* pp. 47–53.

Schwartz, T. (1981, August 30). It's prime time for veteran actors and women at work. *New York Times,* pp. 31, 32.

Scott, D.M., & Wishy, B. (Eds.). (1982). *America's families: A documentary history.* New York: Harper & Row.

Scott, N. (1984, July 10). Promotion strains co-workers' loyalties. *Bangor Daily News,* p. 5.

Seward, R.R. (1978). *The American family: A demographic history.* Beverly Hills, CA: Sage.

Shaw, R., & Pittenger, J. (1977). Perceiving the face of change in changing faces. In J.R. Shaw & J. Bransford (Eds.), *Perceiving, acting, and knowing: Toward an ecological psychology* (pp. 103–132). Hillsdale, NJ: Erlbaum.

Sheehy, G. (1977). *Passages.* New York: Bantam.

Sheley, J.F., & Ashkins, C.D. (1981). Crime, crime news, and crime views. *Public Opinion Quarterly, 45,* 492–506.

Sheridan, K. (1977). *Living with divorce.* Chicago: Thomas More Press.

Sifford, D. (1984, September 2). The freshman syndrome. *Boston Globe*, pp. 90, 92.

Silka, L. (1981). Effects of limited recall of variability on intuitive judgments of change. *Journal of Personality and Social Psychology, 40*, 1010–1016.

Silka, L. (1983). "You just can't count on things anymore": Perceptions of increased variability in the present. *Personality and Social Psychology Bulletin, 9*, 621–628.

Silka, L. (1984). Intuitive perception of change: An overlooked phenomenon in person perception. *Personality and Social Psychology Bulletin, 10*, 180–190.

Silka, L., & Albright, L. (1982). Assessing individual change in the absence of past information. Paper presented at the American Psychological Association meeting, Washington, DC.

Silka, L., & Albright, L. (1983). Intuitive judgments of rate change: The case of teenage pregnancies. *Basic and Applied Social Psychology, 4*, 337–352.

Singer, E. (1977). Subjective evaluations as indicators of change. *Journal of Health and Social Behavior, 18*, 84–90.

Skogan, W. (1986). Fear of crime and neighborhood change. In A.J. Reiss, Jr. & M. Tonry (Eds.), *Communities and crime* (pp. 203–230). Chicago: University of Chicago Press.

Slovic, P., Fischhoff, B., & Lichtenstein, S. (1982). Facts versus fears: Understanding perceived risk. In D. Kahneman, P. Slovic, & A. Tversky (Eds.), *Judgments under uncertainty: Heuristics and biases* (pp. 463–492). Cambridge: Cambridge University Press.

Slovic, P., & Lichtenstein, S. (1971). Comparison of Bayesian and regression approaches to the study of information processing in judgment. *Organizational Behavior and Human Performance, 6*, 649–744.

Smith, M.L., & Glass, G.V. (1977). Meta-analysis of psychotherapy outcome studies. *American Psychologist, 32*, 752–760.

Smith, T.W., & Dempsey, G.R. (1983). The polls: Ethnic social distance and prejudice. *Public Opinion Quarterly, 47*, 584–600.

Snyder, M. (1981). Seek and ye shall find: Testing hypotheses about other people. In E.T. Higgins, C.D. Herman, & M.P. Zanna (Eds.), *Social cognition: The Ontario symposium* (pp. 277–304). Hillsdale, NJ: Erlbaum.

Snyder, M. (1984). When belief creates reality. In L. Berkowitz (Ed.), *Advances in experimental social psychology* (Vol. 18, pp. 247–305). New York: Academic Press.

Snyder, M., & Cantor, N. (1979). Testing hypotheses about other people: The use of historical knowledge. *Journal of Experimental Social Psychology, 15*, 330–343.

Snyder, M., & Swann, W.B., Jr. (1978). Behavioral confirmation in social interaction: From social perception to social reality. *Journal of Experimental Social Psychology, 14*, 148–162.

Snyder, M., & Uranowitz, S.W. (1978). Reconstructing the past: Some cognitive consequences of person perception. *Journal of Personality and Social Psychology, 36*, 941–950.

Somerville, J. (1982). *The rise and fall of childhood*. Beverly Hills, CA: Sage.

Sorrentino, R., & Higgins, E.T. (Eds.). (1985). *Handbook of motivation and cognition*. New York: Guilford.

Srull, T.K. (1981). Person memory: Some tests of associative storage and retrieval models. *Journal of Experimental Psychology: Human Learning and Memory, 7*, 440–463.

Stern, L.D., Marrs, S., Millar, M.G., & Cole, E. (1984). Processing time and the recall of inconsistent and consistent behaviors of individuals and groups. *Journal of Personality and Social Psychology, 47*, 253–262.

Stiles, W.B., Shapiro, D.A., & Elliot, R. (1986). "Are all psychotherapies equivalent?" *American Psychologist, 41*, 165–180.

Storms, M.D. (1973). Videotape and the attribution process: Reversing actors' and observers' point of view. *Journal of Personality and Social Psychology, 27*, 165–175.

Straus, M.A., Gelles, R.J., & Steinmetz, A. (1980). *Behind closed doors: Violence in the American family*. Garden City, NY: Anchor Books.

Strupp, H.H. (1982). The outcome problem in psychotherapy: Contemporary perspectives. In J.H. Harvey & M.M. Parks (Eds.), *Psychotherapy research and behavior change* (pp. 73–122). Washington, DC: American Psychological Association.

Taylor, D.G. (1980). Procedures for evaluating trends in public opinion. *Public Opinion Quarterly, 44*, 86–100.

Taylor, S.E., & Crocker, J. (1981). Schematic basis of social information processing. In E.T. Higgins, C.P. Herman, & M.P. Zanna (Eds.), *Social cognition: The Ontario symposium* (pp. 89–134). Hillsdale, NJ: Erlbaum.

Taylor, S.E., & Fiske, S.T. (1978). Salience, attention, and attribution: Top of the head phenomena. In L. Berkowitz (Ed.), *Advances in experimental social psychology* (Vol. 11, pp. 250–288). New York: Academic Press.

The changing family. (1981, October 1). Channel 7 WNEV. Boston, MA.

Thomas, J. (1987, March 16). Solo 'adventure' at sea. *Boston Globe*, pp. 11, 12.

Thomas, J. (1987, April 22). 18 suicides from now. *Boston Globe*, p. 63.

Time. (1979). Hurry, my children, hurry. *113*, pp. 27–28.

Todd, J.T., Mark, L., Shaw, R., & Pittenger, J. (1980). The perception of growth. *Scientific American, 242*, 132–144.

Toffler, A. (1971). *Future shock.* New York: Bantam Books.

Toffler, A. (1980). *The third wave.* New York: Morrow.

Trope, Y., & Bassok, M. (1983). Information gathering strategies in hypothesis testing. *Journal of Experimental Social Psychology, 19*, 560–576.

Tuchfeld, B.S. (1979). Some approaches to assessing change. In L. Datta & R. Perloff (Eds.). *Improving evaluation* (pp. 103–109). Beverly Hills, CA: Sage.

Tufte, V., & Myerhoff, B. (1979). *Changing images of the family.* New Haven: Yale University Press.

Tversky, A., & Kahneman, D. (1973). Availability: A heuristic for judging frequency and probability. *Cognitive Psychology, 5*, 207–233.

Tversky, A., & Kahneman, D. (1982). Belief in the law of small numbers. In D. Kahneman, P. Slovic, & A. Tversky (Eds.), *Judgments under uncertainty: Heuristics and biases* (pp. 23–31). Cambridge: Cambridge University Press.

Tversky, A., & Kahneman, D. (1982). Causal schemas in judgments under uncertainty. In D. Kahneman, P. Slovic, & A. Tversky (Eds.), *Judgments under uncertainty: Heuristics and biases* (pp. 118–128). Cambridge: Cambridge University Press.

Tyler, T. (1984). Assessing the risk of crime victimization: The integration of personal victimization experience and socially transmitted information. *Journal of Social Issues, 40*, 27–38.

VandenBos, G.R. (Ed.). (1986). Psychotherapy research [Special issue]. *American Psychologist, 41*(2).

Van Niel, M.S. (1987, April 3). Too many young lives lost. *Boston Globe*, p. 11.

Veronen, L.J., & Kilpatrick, D.G. (1983). Rape: A precursor of change. In E.J. Callahan & K.A. McCluskey (Eds.), *Life-span developmental psychology: Nonnormative life events* (pp. 167–192). New York: Academic Press.

Wagenaar, W.A., & Timmers, H. (1979). The pond-and-duckweed problem: Three experiments on the misperception of exponential growth. *Acta Psychologica, 43*, 239–251.

Watson, D. (1982). The actor and the observer: How are their perceptions of causality divergent? *Psychological Bulletin, 92*, 682–700.

Watson, G. (1971). Resistance to change. *American Behavioral Scientist, 14*, 745–766.

Wegner, D.M., & Vallacher, R.R. (1977). *Implicit psychology.* New York: Oxford University Press.

Weiner, B. (1974). *Achievement motivation and attribution theory.* Morristown, NJ: General Learning Corporation.

Weiner, B. (1986). *An attributional theory of motivation and emotion.* New York: Springer-Verlag.

Weiner, B., Russell, D., & Lerman, D. (1978). Affective consequences of causal ascriptions. In J.H. Harvey, W.J. Ickes, & R.F. Kidd (Eds.), *New directions in attribution* (Vol. 2, pp. 59–90). Hillsdale, NJ: Erlbaum.

Wexler, H. (1979). Each year a million teenagers. *American Education, 15*, 6–14.

White, R.W. (1975). *Lives in progress: A study of the natural growth of personality*. New York: Holt, Rinehart, & Winston.

Wickman, P., & Dailey, T. (Eds.). (1982). *White-collar and economic crime: Multidisciplinary and cross-national perspectives*. Lexington, MA: Lexington Books.

Wilder, D.A. (1986). Social categorization: Implications for creation and reduction of intergroup bias. In L. Berkowitz (Ed.), *Advances in experimental social psychology* (Vol. 19, pp. 291–355). Orlando, FL: Academic Press.

Williamson, R.C., Swingle, P.G., & Sargent, S.S. (1982). *Social psychology*. Itasca, IL: F.E. Peacock.

Wilson, J.Q. (1978). *Varieties of police behavior: The management of law and order in eight communities*. Cambridge, MA: Harvard University Press.

Winn, M. (1983, May 8). The loss of childhood. *New York Times Magazine*, pp. 18–28.

Wirtz, W. (1977). *On further examination: Report of the advisory panel of Scholastic Aptitude Test score decline*. New York: College Entrance Examination Board.

Worchel, P., & Byrne, D. (Eds.). (1964). *Personality change*. New York: Wiley.

Worchel, S., & Cooper, J. (1979). *Understanding social psychology* (rev. ed.). Homewood, IL: Dorsey Press.

World almanac and book of facts. (1985). New York: Newspaper Enterprise Association.

Wrightsman, L., & Deaux, K. (1981). *Social psychology in the '80s* (3rd ed.). Monterey, CA: Brooks/Cole.

Wyer, R.S., Jr., & Srull, T.K. (1981). Category accessibility: Some theoretical and empirical issues concerning the processing of social stimulus information. In E.T. Higgins, C.P. Herman, & M.P. Zanna (Eds.), *Social cognition: The Ontario symposium* (pp. 161–197). Hillsdale, NJ: Erlbaum.

Wyer, R.S., Jr., & Srull, T.K. (Eds). (1984). *Handbook of social cognition* (Vols. 1, 2, 3). Hillsdale, NJ: Erlbaum.

Yankelovich, D. (1981). *New rules: Searching for self-fulfillment in a world turned upside down*. Toronto: Bantam Books.

Yarrow, M.R., Campbell, J.D., & Burton, R.V. (1970). Recollections of childhood: A study of the retrospective method. *Monographs of the Society for Research in Child Development, 35*, (Serial No. 138).

Zilbergeld, B. (1983). *The shrinking of America: Myths of psychological change*. Boston, MA: Little, Brown, and Co.

Zimbardo, P.G., Ebbesen, E.B., & Maslach, C. (1977). *Influencing attitudes and changing behaviors* (2nd ed.). Reading, MA: Addison-Wesley.

Zollschan, G.K., & Hirsch, W. (1976). *Social change: Explorations, diagnoses, and conjectures*. New York: Wiley.

Zurcher, L.A. (1972). The mutable self: An adaptation of accelerated sociological change. *Journal of Applied Behavioral Science, 3,* 3–15.

Zurcher, L.A. (1973). Alternative institutions and the mutable self: An overview. *Journal of Applied Behavioral Science, 9,* 369–380.

Author Index

Ager, S., 143
Agostinelli, G., 32
Albright, L., 80–84, 106–107
Allison, S.T., 33, 76, 94
Amabile, T.M., 65
American Humane Association, 21
Anderson, C.A., 65
Archer, D., 22
Aries, P., 9
Asch, S.E., 30, 59
Ashkins, C.D., 158
Ashworth, C.D., 22
Auerbach, A.H., 15
Azjen, I., 109, 162

Bacon, F.T., 47
Baer, D.M., 141
Baer, R., 70
Bahr, H.M., 19, 20
Ball, J., 87
Baltes, P.B., 19, 23, 24, 25, 26
Bargh, J.A., 37, 47, 77
Barnett, R., 19
Baron, R.M., 37
Baruch, G., 19
Bassok, M., 69
Batson, C.D., 154
Bauer, R., 26, 145, 147, 159, 161
Baum, A., 149

Baxter, A., 21
Bell, L.G., 31
Bell, R.R., 145
Bellak, L., 27, 28
Bem, D.J., 3
Bergin, A.E., 14, 19
Bernard, J., 27
Block, C.R., 19
Block, J., 23, 24, 26, 139, 141
Block, R.L., 19
Blomqvist, N., 25
Bloom, B.S., 23
Borgida, E., 87, 109
Boston Globe Magazine, 12
Boston Quarterly Review, 143
Boudan, R., 20
Bower, G.H., 47
Bowker, L.H., 22
Boyer, E.L., 19
Brand, D., 25
Brim, O.G., Jr., 25, 140
Brown, R., 47
Bryk, A.S., 25
Burton, R.V., 23
Bybee, R.W., 21, 145
Byrne, D., 130–131

Cacioppo, J.T., 180
Callahan, E.J., 131

Campbell, A., 28
Campbell, D.T., 13, 26, 109, 112
Campbell, J.D., 23
Cantor, N., 31, 48, 77
Caplow, T., 19, 20, 22, 143, 144–145, 146, 179
Caputo, C., 71
Carlsmith, J.M., 149
Carlston, D.E., 31, 37
Carroll, J.J., 70
Chadwick, B.A., 19, 20
Changing American Family, 6
Chappell, D., 22
Chaskes, J.B., 145
Chilman, C.S., 19, 27
Cialdini, R.B., 180
Clark, M.S., 179
Clark, T.B., 5
Clore, G.L., 70
Colcord, J.C., 156
Cole, E., 78
Colson, C.W., 3
Converse, P.E., 28
Conway, F., 12
Conway, M., 33, 108, 183
Cook, T.D., 26, 112
Cooper, J., 60, 70, 149
Costa, P.T., Jr., 9, 19, 23
Crandall, R., 87
Crano, W.D., 64
Crocker, J., 31, 32, 58, 70, 71, 78
Crockett, W., 182
Cronbach, L.J., 25

Dailey, T., 22, 144
Darley, J.M., 5, 144, 149, 154
Davis, B.L., 22
Davis, F., 49
Deaux, K., 60, 149
Demos, J., 21, 145, 146
Dempsey, G.R., 19
DeVos, G.A., 28
Dielman, T.E., 25
Dohrenwend, B.P., 28

Dohrenwend, B.S., 28
Donaldson, G., 23
Dreben, E.K., 64
Duck, S., 136

Eakins, P.S., 28
Ebbesen, E.B., 37, 128
Editorials on File, 5
Einhorn, H.J., 37, 47
Eison, J.A., 22
Elder, G.H., Jr., 141
Elliot, R., 15
Epstein, S., 32
Erven, J.M., 22
Evans, M., 31
Eye, A.V., 20
Eysenck, H.J., 14

Farkash, E., 109
Faunce, W.A, 28
Fazio, R.H., 32
Feiffer, J., 121
Feinsilber, M., 11
Feldman, N.S., 182
Feldman-Summers, S., 22
Ferguson, T., 145
Ferriss, A.L., 19
Finch, M.D., 183
Finello, K.M., 23
Finestone, H., 28
Fischhoff, B., 87, 168
Fisher, D.C., 127
Fisher, J.D., 149
Fisher, J.E., 141
Fiske, S.T., 64, 65, 75, 77, 179
Fletcher, G.J.O., 3, 70
Florovsky, G., 168
Fong, G.T., 47, 90
Forehand, G., 26
Freedman, J.L., 149
Freund, T., 64
Friedland, N., 109
Frieze, I.H., 27

Fulero, S., 31
Funder, D.C., 70, 182
Furby, L., 25

Gager, N., 22
Gartner, R., 22
Geis, G., 22
Gelles, R.J., 19, 21
Genung, V., 31
Gerbner, G., 19
Gergen, K.J., 9, 24, 25, 124, 127,
    137–138
Gergen, M.M., 137–138
Gifford, R.K., 76
Gilbert, D.T., 76
Gilligan, S.G., 47
Gilmartin, K.J., 26
Ginosar, Z., 162
Glass, G.V., 19
Glenn, N.D., 26, 27
Goethals, G.R., 3, 60, 61
Goldberg, L.R., 71
Goldfried, M.R., 14
Goodman, E., 10, 12, 13, 134, 146
Greenberg, D.F., 26
Greenwald, A.G., 31, 183
Gurin, P., 19

Hamill, R., 154
Hamilton, D.L., 31, 37, 61, 77
Hannah, D.B., 31, 78
Harris, C.W., 20, 25
Harris, L., 28
Harris, P., 144
Harris, R.L., 33
Harris, V.A., 71
Harvey, J.H., 14, 70, 179
Harway, M., 23
Hastie, R., 37, 46, 64, 77
Hayden, T., 31, 32
Healy, R., 5
Hearst, E., 32
Heider, F., 30, 69–70

Helfer, R.E., 21
Hepburn, A., 127
Herman, C.P., 37, 77
Hero, A.O., Jr., 19
Herzberger, S.D., 70
Higgins, E.T., 37, 46, 77, 140–141,
    179
Hill, R., 19, 20
Hindelang, M.J., 22, 162
Hintzman, D.L., 77
Hirsch, W., 20, 30
Hobfall, S.E., 27
Hogarth, R.M., 37, 47, 109
Holmes, D.S., 33, 47
Horn, J.L., 23
Hostetler, A.J., 69, 131
House, J.S., 23, 145
Hubbard, M., 65

Innes De Neufville, J., 22, 23, 26

Jaffe, S.S., 10
Jennings, D.L., 65
Jepson, C., 47
Johnson, J., 68
Johnson, M., 15
Johnson, M.K., 47, 89
Jones, E.E., 47, 60, 61, 70, 71

Kagan, J., 9, 24, 25, 124, 125, 126
Kahneman, D., 37, 47, 68, 90, 109,
    127
Kanungo, R.N., 27
Katz, L.B., 31
Kazdin, A.E., 14, 19
Keel, R., 31
Kelley, H.H., 70, 75, 76
Kempe, R.S., 21
Keniston, K., 5, 27, 28
Kessel, F., 9
Kessler, R.C., 26
Kilpatrick, D.G., 131

Kimmel, M.S., 19, 27
Kinder, D.R., 19
Kluegel, J.R., 19
Kohli, M., 183
Krantz, D.H., 47
Kruglanski, A.W., 64, 109
Kubick, L., 105
Kuiper, N.A., 77
Kulick, J., 47
Kulik, J.A., 58
Kumba, D., 183
Kunda, Z., 47, 95, 118
Kundera, M., 168

Labouvie, E.W., 25
Lamb, D.H., 10
Lambert, M.J., 14, 19
Landers, A., 6, 12, 144
Larkin, C., 31
LaRossa, P., 103
LaRossa, R., 103
Lasch, C., 4
Latane, B., 5, 144, 149
Lauer, J.C., 27
Lauer, R.H., 27, 30
Layton, B.D., 76
Legant, P., 71
Leirer, V.O., 31
Lenz, D., 103
Lepper, M.R., 65
Lerman, D., 76
Lewis, C., 28
Lichtenstein, S., 87, 109
Linn, R.L., 25
Lipsitt, L.P., 25
Loftus, E.F., 47
Longcope, K., 4
Lord, C.G., 76
Luborsky, L., 15
Luchins, A.S., 61–63, 64
Luchins, E.H., 62, 64
Lupo, A., 144
Lynd, H.M., 143, 144, 156
Lynd, R.S., 143, 144, 156
Lystad, M., 29

Maccoby, N., 180
Mackie, D.M., 33, 76, 94
MacMullan, J., 11
Mahoney, M.J., 19, 20
Malamuth, N.M., 19
Manko, G., 31
Marecek, J., 71
Mark, L., 32
Markus, H., 48, 77
Marris, P., 28, 178
Marrs, S., 78
Maslach, C., 128
Maugham, W.S., 11–12
Mazur, A., 3
McArthur, L.Z., 37
McCalls, 83
McCleary, R.B., 22
McCluskey, K.A., 131
McConnell, H.K., 3
McCrae, R.R., 9, 19, 23
McFarland, C., 3, 58, 136
McGrory, M., 6
McGuire, W.J., 180
McNeil, E.B., 124
Mednick, S.A., 23
Medved, M., 67, 68, 124
Meyrowitz, J., 28
Michela, J.L., 70, 75
Millar, M.G., 78
Miller, A.G., 70
Miller, F.D., 71, 76
Minz, J., 15
Mischel, W., 31, 32, 48
Moehle, D., 76
Monson, T.C., 31, 71
Mortimer, J.T., 183
Moss, H.A., 19, 24–25
Ms. Magazine, 12
Mueller, C., 19
Munnichs, J., 20
Munnichs, P., 20
Myerhoff, B., 143
Myers, D.G., 60, 70, 128

Nelson, B.J., 21

Nesselroade, J.R., 19, 20, 24, 25, 26
New, B.L., 65
Nienstedt, B.C., 22
Nisbett, R.E., 31, 47, 59–60, 61, 64,
   65, 68, 69, 70, 71, 87, 89, 95,
   109, 117, 118, 154, 162
Nunnally, J.C., 26
Nydegger, C.N., 23

O'Brien, E.J., 21–22, 32
O'Brien, M., 28
O'Brien, R.M., 162
O'Donohue, W., 141
Ohmer, M., 22
Olson, J.M., 77
Ostrom, T.M., 37

Page, B.I., 19
Park, B., 77
Parks, M.M., 14
Parsons, J.E., 140–141
Pashdag, J., 5
Peck, A., 44
Petty, R.E., 180
Pfoll, S.J., 21
Pillemer, K.A., 29
Pisarik, K., 6
Pittenger, J., 32
Pleck, E., 21, 145
Plewis, I., 25
Pollio, H.R., 22
Pomper, M.M., 145
Pratkanis, A.R., 183

Quattrone, G.A., 47, 70, 73

Radbill, S.X., 21, 145
Raudenbush, S.W., 25
Raye, R., 47
Reckman, R.F., 3
Reed, H., 87
Reeder, G.D., 10

Reese, H.W., 19, 20, 25
Reich, C., 4
Reinke, B.J., 33, 140
Rhodebeck, L.A., 19
Riggs, J.M., 70
Rivers, C., 19
Roberts, D.F., 180
Robey, B., 162
Robinson, M., 49
Rogers, J., 145
Rogosa, D.R., 25
Rosenthal, A.M., 149
Ross, H.L., 109
Ross, L., 31, 32, 59–60, 61, 64, 65,
   66–67, 68, 69, 70
Ross, M., 3, 33, 58, 70, 108, 136, 183
Rossi, R.J., 26
Rotenberg, K.J., 182
Rothbart, M., 31
Rubin, Z., 24, 123, 182
Ruble, D.N., 182
Russell, D., 76
Russell, D.E.H., 27, 28
Russell, G., 28
Ryan, B., 10
Ryff, C.D., 29, 33, 137, 140

Sales, E., 27
Sargent, S.S., 150
Schaie, K.W., 23, 26
Schneider, D.J., 31, 60, 70, 149
Schneider, P., 22
Schonberg, P., 70
Schurr, C., 22
Schwartz, T., 5
Scott, D.M., 143, 144, 145
Scott, N., 10
Sears, D.O., 149
Seward, R.R., 27, 143, 145
Shapiro, D.A., 15
Shapiro, R.Y., 19
Shaw, R., 32
Sheehy, G., 103
Sheley, J.F., 158
Sheridan, K., 103

Sherman, S.J., 32
Shpitzajen, A., 64
Siegel, A.W., 9
Siegelman, J., 12
Sifford, D., 3
Silka, L., 62–63, 80–84, 92–94, 95–97, 106–107
Singer, E., 183
Singer, J.E., 149
Skogan, W., 158
Slinde, J.A., 25
Slovic, P., 37, 87, 109
Smith, E.R., 19, 71
Smith, M.L., 19
Smith, T.W., 19
Snyder, M., 31, 69, 71, 77
Somerville, J., 27
Sorrentino, R., 179
Speer, J.R., 65
Spinner, R.A., 19
Srull, T.K., 31, 37, 38, 46, 47, 77
Steinmetz, A., 19
Steinmetz, J.L., 65
Stephens, D., 31
Stern, L.D., 78
Stigler, S.M., 26
Stiles, W.B., 15
Storms, M.D., 71
Stotland, E., 22
Strack, F., 65
Straus, M.A., 19, 21, 22, 156
Strupp, H.H., 14, 19
Susman, E.J., 19, 24–25
Swann, W.B., Jr., 69
Swingle, P.G., 150

Taylor, S.E., 26, 31, 32, 47, 65, 70, 75, 77
Thomas, J., 5, 8
Thomas, R., 27
Time, 103
Timmers, H., 32
Todd, J.T., 32
Toffler, A., 4, 27, 28

Town, J.P., 70
Trope, Y., 69, 162
Tuchfeld, B.S., 26
Tufte, V., 143
Tversky, A., 37, 68, 90, 109, 127
Tyler, T., 158–159

Uleman, J., 71
Uranowitz, S.W., 31, 77

Vallacher, R.R., 179
VandenBos, G.R., 14
Van Niel, M.S., 5
Veronen, L.J., 131
Viertel, J., 10

Wagenaar, W.A., 32
Wallechinsky, D., 67, 68, 124
Watson, D., 70, 71
Watson, G., 27
Weary, G., 70, 179
Weaver, C.N., 27
Weber, R., 31, 77, 78
Wegner, D.M., 179
Weiner, B., 76, 179
Wexler, H., 82
White, R.W., 124
Wicklund, R.A., 31
Wickman, P., 22, 144
Wilder, D.A., 119
Williamson, M.H., 19, 20
Williamson, R.C., 150
Wilson, J.Q., 22
Wilson, T.D., 47, 154
Winn, M., 9
Wirtz, W., 19, 22, 162
Wishy, B., 143, 144, 145
Wolf, R.S., 29

Wolf, S., 23, 145
Worchel, P., 130–131
Worchel, S., 60, 70, 149
World Almanac & Book of Facts, 159,
    163
Wrightsman, L., 60, 149
Wyer, R.S., Jr., 31, 37, 38, 46, 47,
    77

Yankelovich, D., 4

Yarkin, K.L., 70
Yarrow, M.R., 23

Zajonc, R.B., 48, 77
Zanna, M.P., 37
Zilbergeld, B., 14, 103
Zimbardo, P.G., 128, 130
Zimowski, M., 25
Zollschan, G.K., 20, 30
Zurcher, L.A., 141